Roger Ballen
ASYLUM OF THE BIRDS

with 100 illustrations

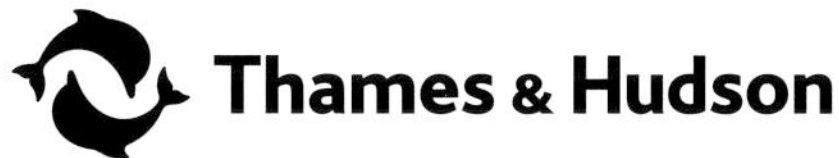

Thames & Hudson

This book is dedicated to the spirit of the birds who inhabit our planet,
who fly above us, who mysteriously link the heavens with the earth.

page 1
Nostalgia 2010

page 2
Scream 2012

First published in the United Kingdom in 2014 by Thames & Hudson Ltd,
181A High Holborn, London WC1V 7QX

First paperback edition published in 2019

Asylum of the Birds © 2014 and 2019 Roger Ballen
Photographs © 2014 Roger Ballen

Designed by Sarah Praill

All Rights Reserved. No part of this publication may be reproduced or
transmitted in any form or by any means, electronic or mechanical, including
photocopy, recording or any other information storage and retrieval system,
without prior permission in writing from the publisher.

British Library Cataloguing-in-Publication Data
A catalogue record for this book is available from the British Library

ISBN 978-0-500-29486-4

Printed and bound in China by Toppan Leefung Printing Limited

To find out about all our publications, please visit **www.thamesandhudson.com**.
There you can subscribe to our e-newsletter, browse or download our current
catalogue, and buy any titles that are in print.

Acknowledgments

Above all, I would like to thank Marguerite Rossouw for her dedication,
hard work, artistic vision, and technical skill. Her insightful input was
paramount and irreplaceable.

To Gerard Rossouw for his ability to translate film into fine prints and to
Simone Stiglingh and Tatiana Goodchild for their administration skills.

To Andrew Sanigar whose faith in the project was instrumental in
its fruition and whose discerning sensibility was crucial to the project.
His faith in the inherent value of my imagery led to the creation of
this book.

To Sarah Praill for her aesthetic input and design and to Ginny Liggitt
for her valuable technical input. And to Ilona de Nemethy Sanigar for
her valuable comments on the text.

I am indebted to Didi Bozzini for his poetic and philosophical
interpretation of my imagery.

To the many animals, friends, comrades, who have contributed in some
way or another to the imagery of this book. In some way or another your
being is interwoven into each one of these photographs.

Contents

INTRODUCTION

The work of Roger Ballen is a web of images nestled in the depths. His photographs are complex visual and mental concretions. Clustered within a cloistral universe that is perfectly square, they rise to the surface like crystals, glimmering with infinite reflections of grey. They travel through the full spectrum, between the dullness of slate and the shine of silica, from the translucent white of calcite to the impenetrable black of onyx.

His world is a buried gallery, both psychological and geological, housing an accumulation of graffiti, cables, shadows, stains, rubble, bones, masks, dolls, animals, human faces, and bodies fragmented and jumbled in the magma.

His rooms are inner landscapes, incongruous yet skilfully constructed, illogical as dreams and pure like gems. It is as if the silver gelatin process turned the artist's practice into a branch of geology that delves into his psyche like a mine, searching for meaning by taking core samples of its successive layers, deeper and deeper, turning up unexpected materials, sediments and fossils. Reaching down into the twilight of consciousness where memories amass and dreams are born – the murky place that lies at the centre of the earth, of life, of the human being.

Ballen's camera works like a drill: his pictures dig into time. They move in a spiral, from the surface of the moment into the nether regions of the most distant past. From his earliest photos, which depicted the actual presence of a place or face, to his most recent works, which form the dreamlike image of an ancestral era, before time even began to pass. In an inverse chronology that unwinds from a now towards a then so remote that it is lost in the dusk of memory.

His pictures dig into space. They advance in concentric circles, their gaze burrowing from the level of the immediate surroundings into the submerged inner workings of the individual. From the rural villages of his earliest career to the cerebral chambers of his most recent works, tracing a reverse topography, from outside in, from world to self.

They are photographs that come to light like the findings of a probe.

They carry with them traces of a lost time and a secret space, cast in black and white, which is not the absence of colour, but rather the colour of thought.

White like paper and black like ink.

White like a dove, or a mouse, or their carcasses stripped clean by the passage of years.

Black like coal, or the traces of drawings left on a cave wall.

Grey, like the result of their mingling. Like stones, like dust, like shadows, like the brain.

These are the colours that the mind projects on reality, certainly not the ones the eye sees in it.

The colours of fantasies, memories, nightmares, dreams, conjectures. Notes, sketches, drawings: all the processes that in a word are called art.

The art of Ballen is a journey to the centre of consciousness.
His journey is driven by passion and fuelled by memory.
'Hope and Memory have one daughter and her name is Art',
as W. B. Yeats wrote.

These photographs show the objects of memory-like traces of
a personal itinerary inscribed in a universal landscape. One man's
path on the earth trodden by all. Childhood games among the
debris piled up in a mysterious, fascinating storehouse, hours
spent climbing trees to catch a glimpse of birds up close, dreams
at night and reveries by day, portraits hung on the walls at home,
faces and the stories that their wrinkles tell. And then the season
of maturity, the clear sense of being part of a whole that precedes
and survives those experiences, shapes and summates them,
forever and ever.

These photographs render visible the yearned goal that is simply
the definition of a man's identity. A journey between self and
self, passing through the world. With a camera around his neck to
see what eyes cannot make out, to understand what ideas cannot
explain. A device that captures and projects images, limits the
view and increases vision. A telescope, a microscope, and a mirror,
all at the same time.

Meaning

The imagination finds more reality in what hides itself than in what
shows itself.
GASTON BACHELARD

Asylum of the Birds is the title under which Ballen has chosen to
collect his recent work. Words with different meanings lodged
beneath their surface.

On the one hand, a house on the outskirts of Johannesburg,
which, mingling truth and fiction, harbours a motley assortment
of inhabitants and a remarkable number of birds, flying free.
On the other hand, a symbolic place at the meeting point of earth
and sky, life and death, freedom and constraint, hell and heaven.
Asylum, both refuge and prison, nest and cage.

Birds, white dove or black raven, a Biblical apparition that is the
harbinger of the future or the delirious dream of an end without
end, as in the verses by Poe.

In the ambiguity of symbols and metaphors, this group of
photographs delineates a universe reminiscent of the one in
Goya's *Caprichos*. It is a *sueño de la razón*, a sleep or a dream
– in Spanish the word is ambivalent – of reason that '*produce
monstruos*', generates monsters, in the original sense of the
word: extraordinary beings, prodigious events. A plunge into
the winding tunnels of the subconscious all the way to the
underworld, until the souls of the dead appear to say, '*Ya es
hora*' – the time has come.

Indeed, Ballen leaves his thoughts free to slip back beyond reason
and logic. He ventures into the mazes of the mind that precede

ideas, where images reign supreme, where they first come into being, flowing down the current of analogy and following fast upon each other, driven by uncontrollable forces. They cannot be explained through the rational construction of a scale of values. *Asylum of the Birds* is a visionary, alogical and amoral universe where good and evil exist side by side without excluding each other. Beauty does not correspond to the former, nor ugliness necessarily to the latter. It is a place where even beauty and ugliness are still – or are now – blurred together. An aesthetic universe founded on wonder, not on harmony. A world where appearances have no importance in and of themselves, because everything, whether animal or human, is much more than can be seen, is an apparition. It manifests itself as a husk of matter, but at the same time, it is a reliquary from which the invisible can be conjured forth.

The artist's work thus becomes a sort of shamanic ritual, aimed at revealing what every photograph conceals under the guise of an objective depiction of reality.

This desire to reach a parallel world – a life beyond which is life's hidden double, which precedes and follows it – becomes absolutely clear in the last photos of this collection, from *Deathbed* to *You Can't Come Back*, and those that follow. The images, becoming ever sparer and starker, take on the semblance of jujus and amulets. Talismans. They are the implements of a funeral rite, at first, and then of a magical celebration of rebirth. Symbols of falling and of flight. Visions of the underworld and of heaven, which coexist within the same mind.

The mind dark as a well at the bottom of which everything comes to an end. The mind shining like a spark from which light springs. *Asylum of the Birds* is a world where madness and wisdom blend together.

The images travel the thin line along which fact encounters fiction, perception becomes a mirage, and illusion, revelation. It is a book of changes, of material and symbolic metamorphoses. The place where identity wavers between self and its representation, its shadows and its reflections. These mutations of selfhood come thick and fast: they multiply. The subject becomes something separate from itself, both different and paradoxically identical. As in the photographs titled *Demented*, *Headless* and *Liberation*, where the human heads are plucked from their bodies and the faces disappear, masked or replaced by those of mannequins. Or *Mirrored*, *Omen* and *Consolation*, where they are reduced to flat clichés and old newspaper cuttings. Images of images. And it is not the head alone, as the seat of thought, which symbolizes the ongoing process of transformation that is a path to knowledge. The body, too, the vessel of the senses and emotions, incarnates its manifestations.

And so, *Transformation*, *Inflated* and *Deflated*, *Mourning*, *Seduction*, *Serpent Lady* and *Offering* show silhouettes, effigies, carcasses, drawings, dolls and statues like steps in a journey through realms of flesh which imperceptibly blur into each other, from sexuality to disease, from bloom to withering, from pleasure to pain.

It is a gallery of magic mirrors, which reveal to the photographer – and with him, the viewer – the images of self that the trappings of reality conceal.

The birds are witnesses to this inward exploration. Omnipresent, sometimes as accomplices and sometimes as victims, they are both enigmatic figures and augural omens, real presences and dream apparitions. Mental projections and travelling companions of the artist.

Just like plate 43 of the *Caprichos*, where Goya has etched his own portrait surrounded by a flock of birds, his eyes closed and his head cradled in his hands, Ballen likewise takes a snapshot of himself through this book. As, gaze turned inward, he searches for self amid shadow and reflection. To find the person he is, that every person is.

Matter and manner

We photograph things in order to drive them out of our minds.
FRANZ KAFKA

If Ballen's poetic sense harbours the urgency of an existential query, his aesthetic sense is marked by the formal rigour that frames its spasms. A distinctive and incessant discipline, moulded after the order of nature, which organizes the chaotic proliferation of simple organisms into complex, coherent groups. Not a style, but a canon. Motivated by concrete reasons, meant to reveal rather than deceive. The square space of his photographs demands that our eyes range through the image without favouring any one dimension, allotting equal presence to the elements that make it up. And this absence of a geometric hierarchy is the visible aspect of the free flow of apparitions in the mind.

It is a stream of consciousness in which a stain on the wall could be mistaken for a drawing by Jean Dubuffet, a tangle of wire could be the echo of a pastel by Wols, and a doll's head might be a piece of an old toy or else a page out of a book by Hans Bellmer. The lighting, which is never natural, makes the shadows of bodies and things turn into ever-different bodies and ever-different things. The black and white tinges truth with hues of doubt and transforms reality into hypothesis.

Nevertheless, each of these photos conveys to the viewer a sense of absolute authenticity. One sees a room, not a studio; things, not props; people, not models; in action, not posed.

This is because Ballen's photographic drama combines artifice and reality as the inseparable elements and mirror images of a poetic universe, which is in turn the mental double of the real world. It is a stagecraft akin to the luminous insights of Artaud, the deep humanity and stark minimalism of Samuel Beckett's theatre, the lucid acuity in exploring existential labyrinths of James Joyce's fiction. A canon that is a substance, because his art evolves like a waking dream, in which form and content constitute a whole, a mixture of infinite signifying relations between what appears and how it appears. This is the dream of an artist who creates a unique, singular universe, but a dream any one of us has experienced.

Didi Bozzini

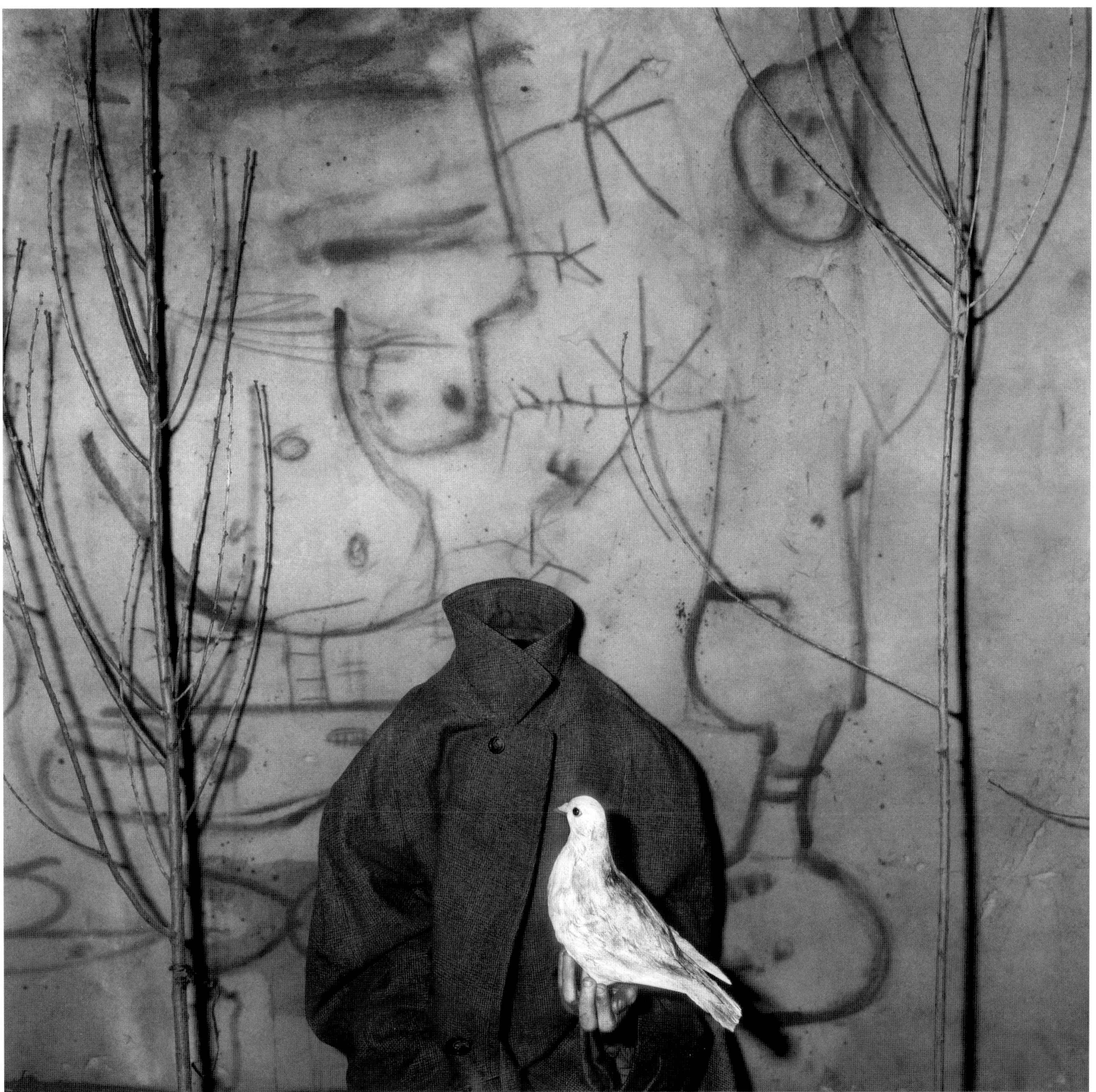

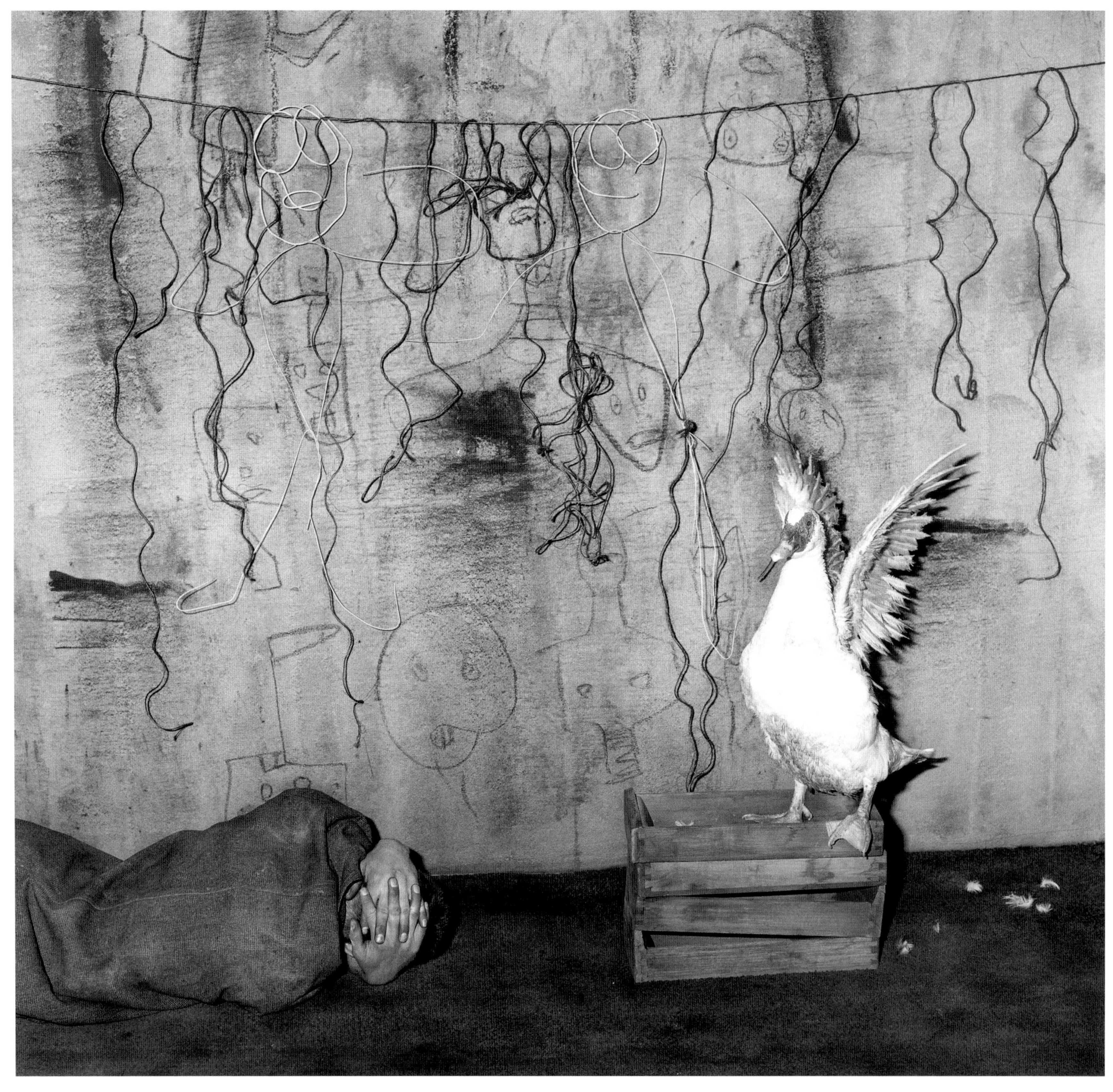

Defeated 2005

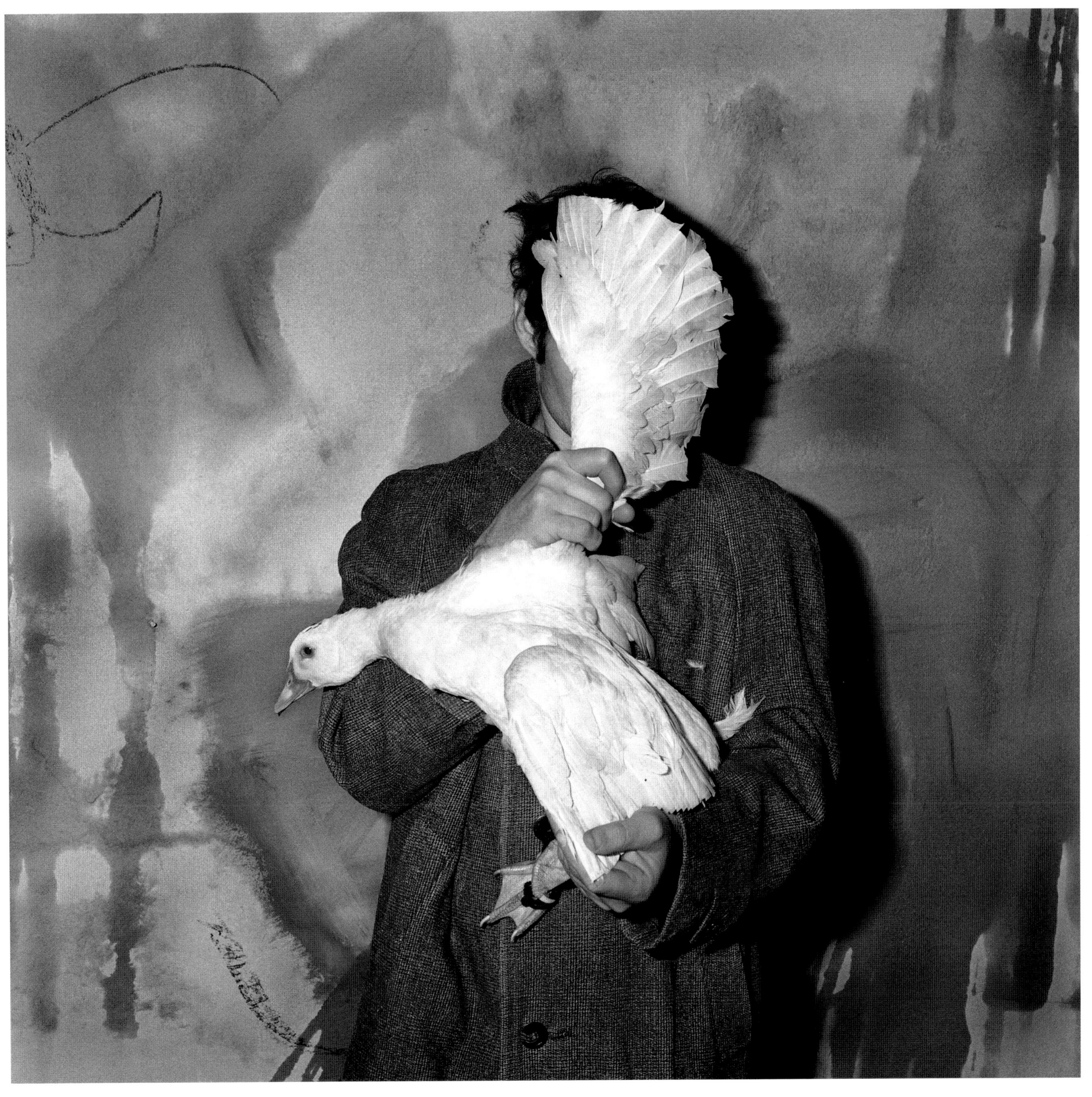

Blinded 2005

Smirk 2009

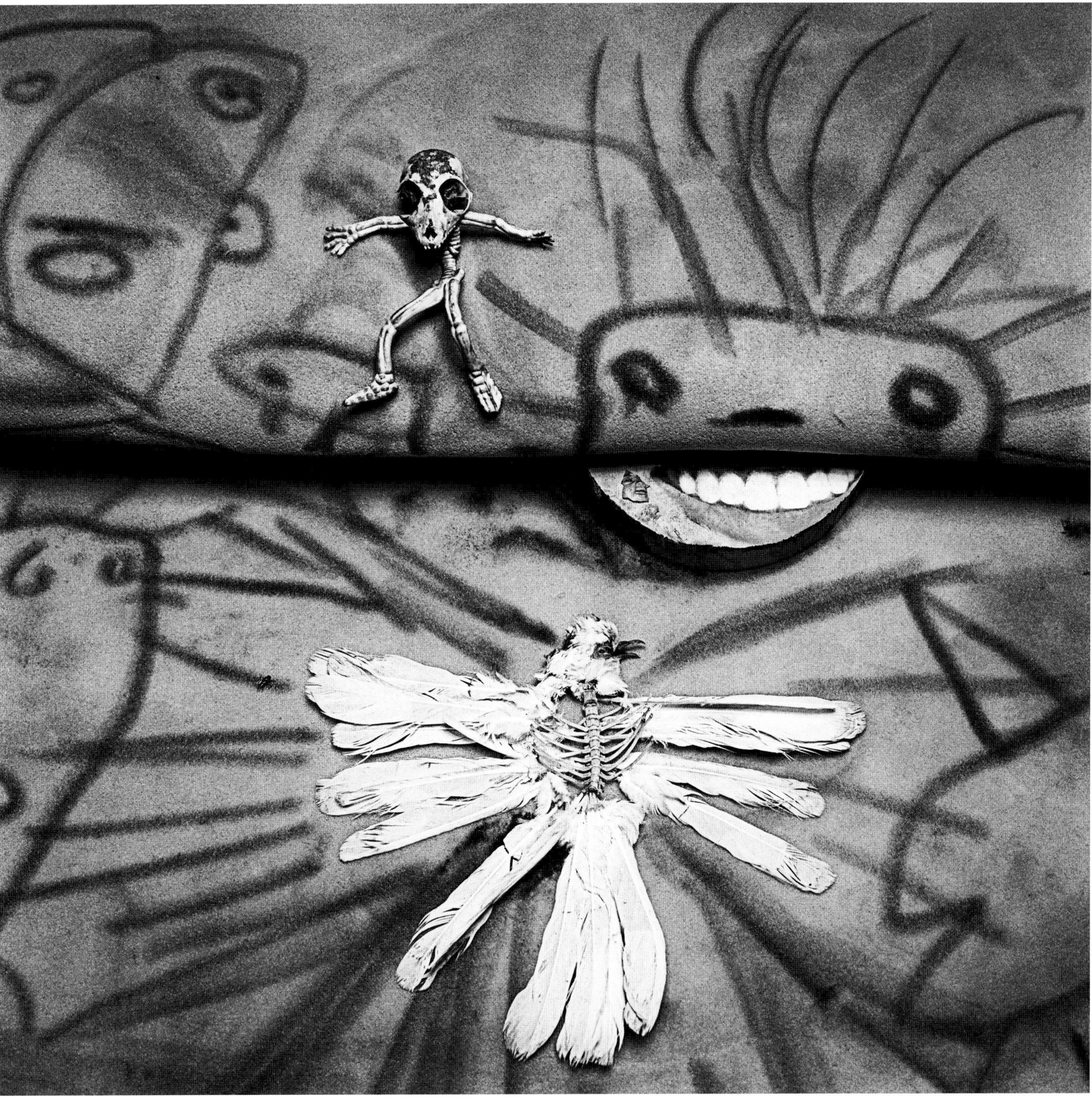

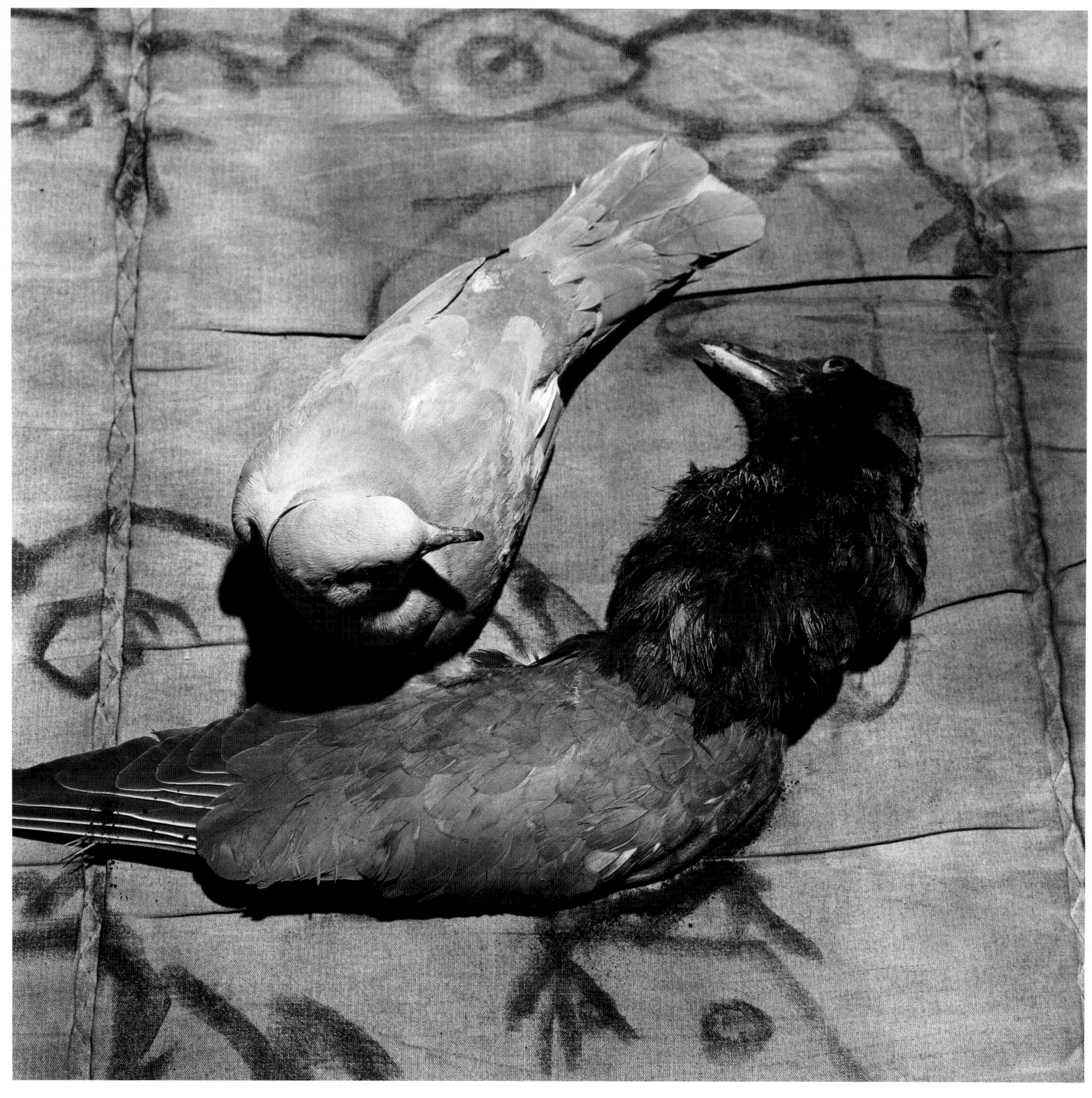

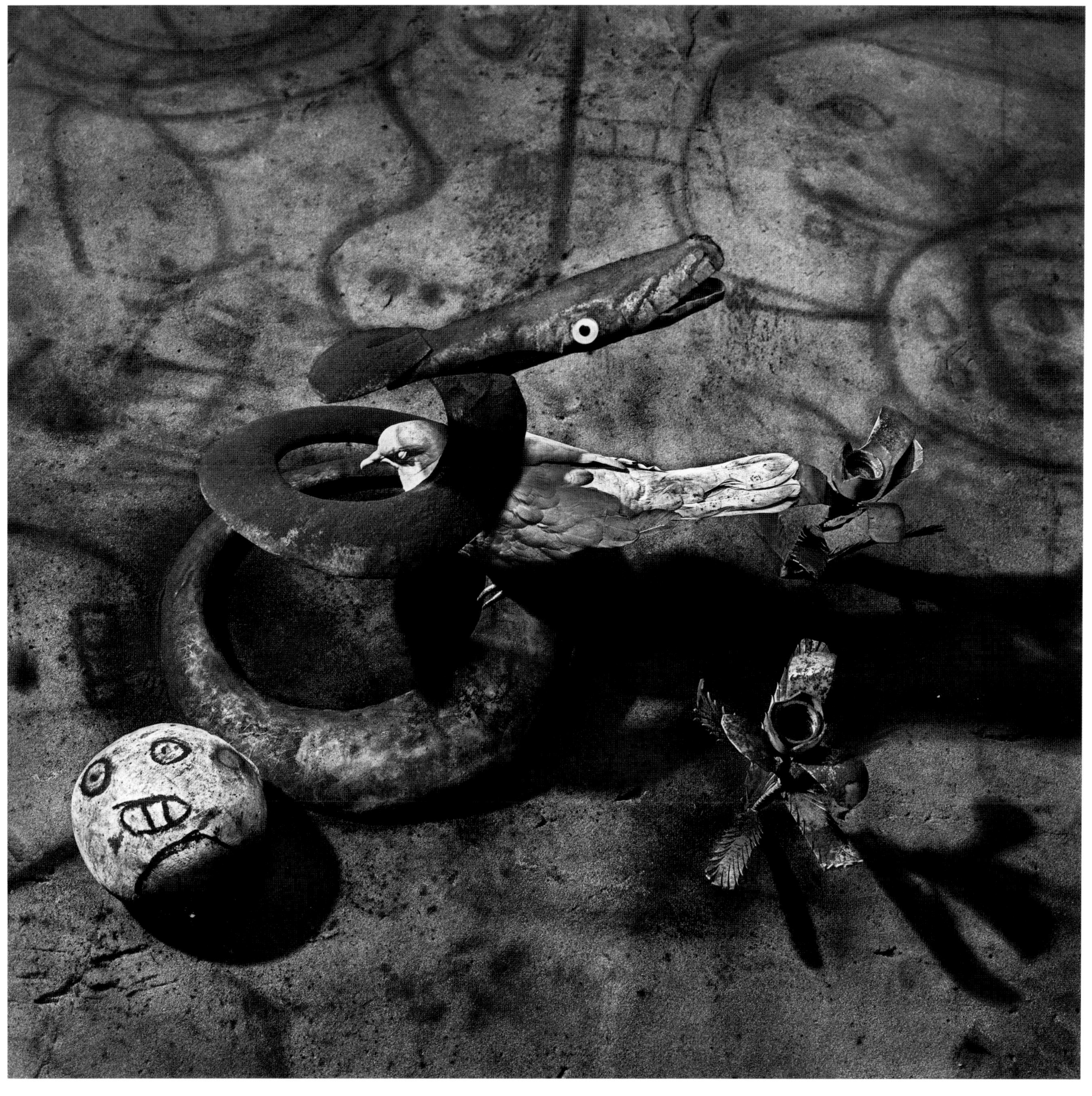

Mesmerised 2009

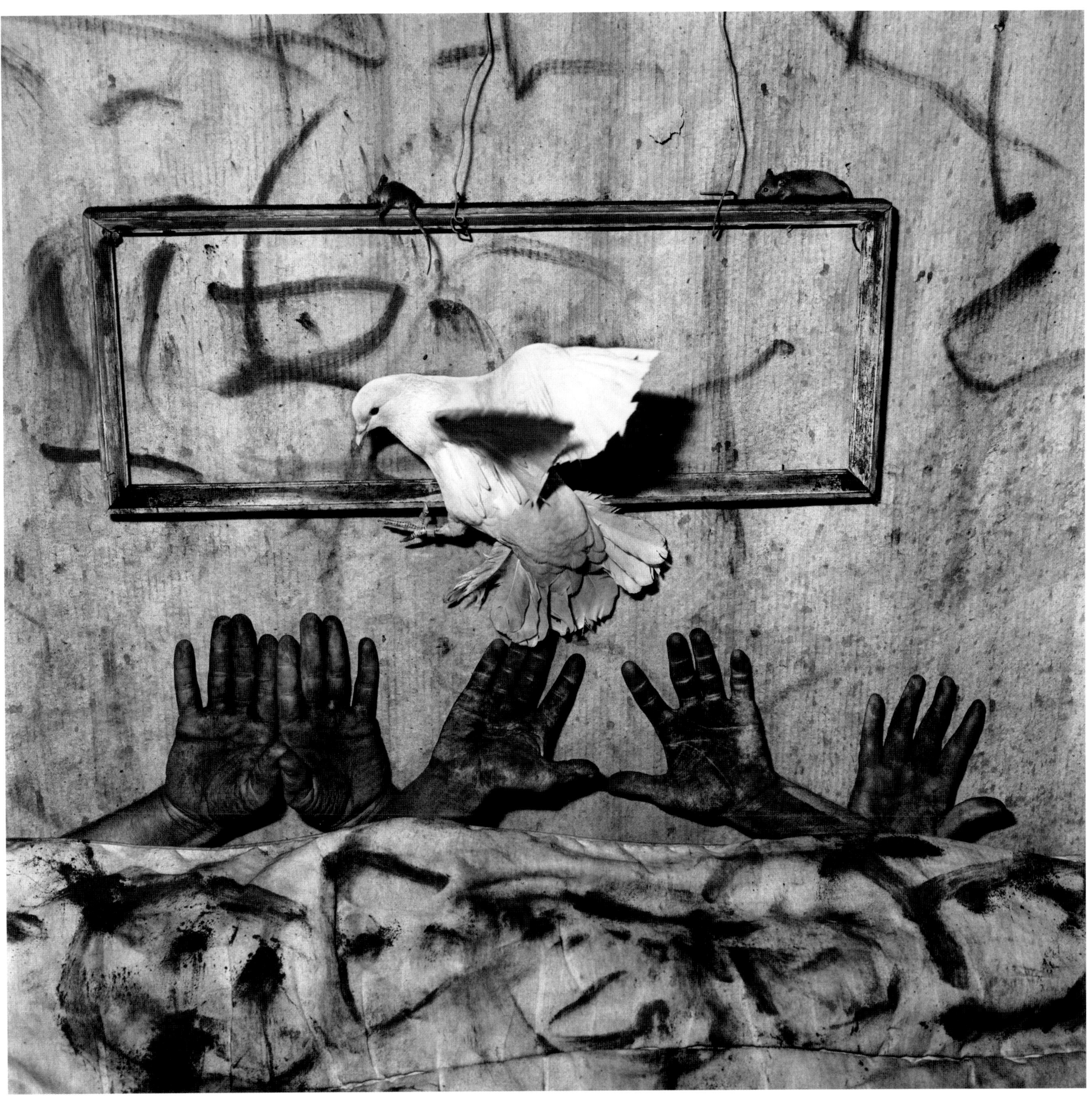

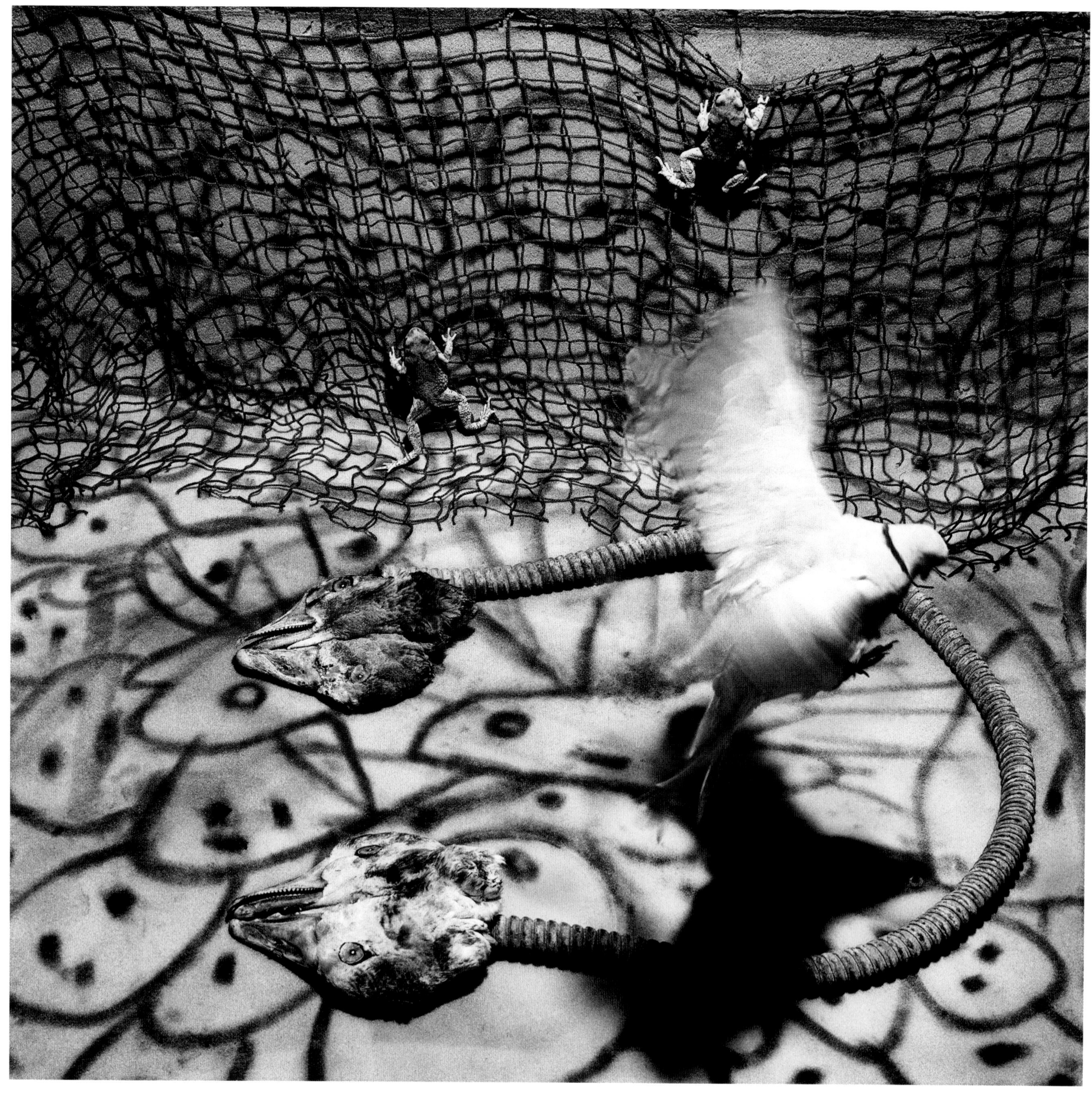

Lift Off 2009

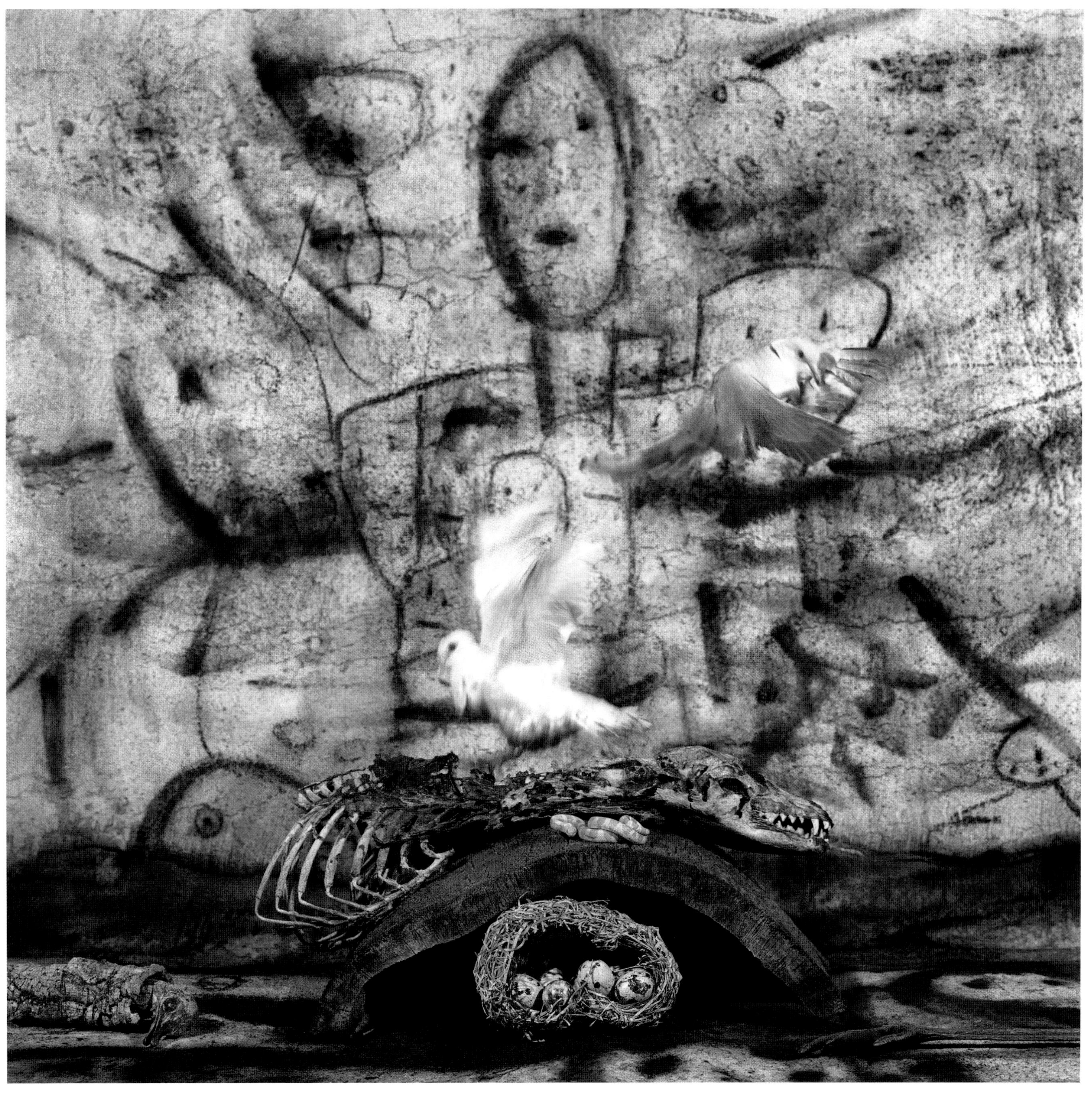

Gaping 2010

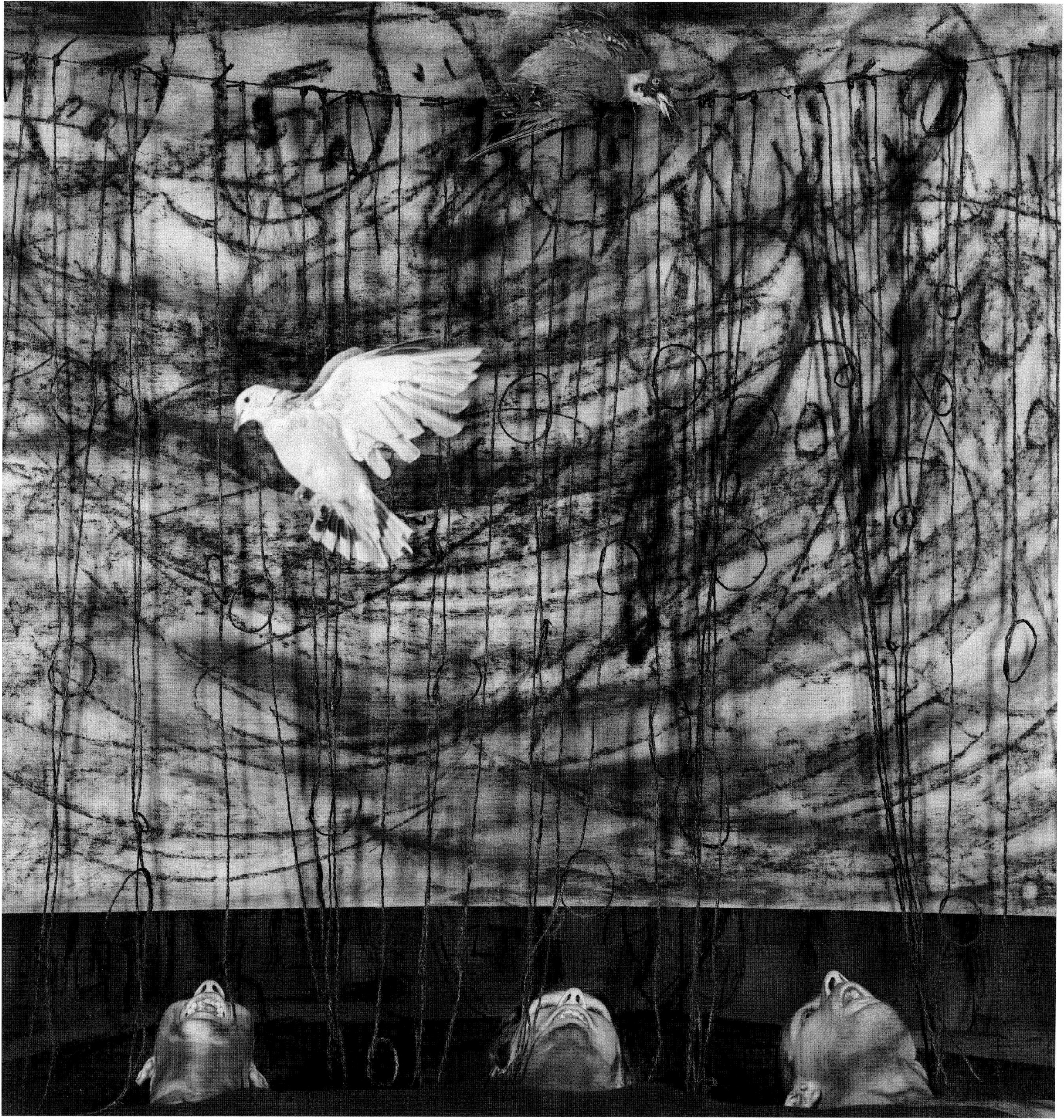

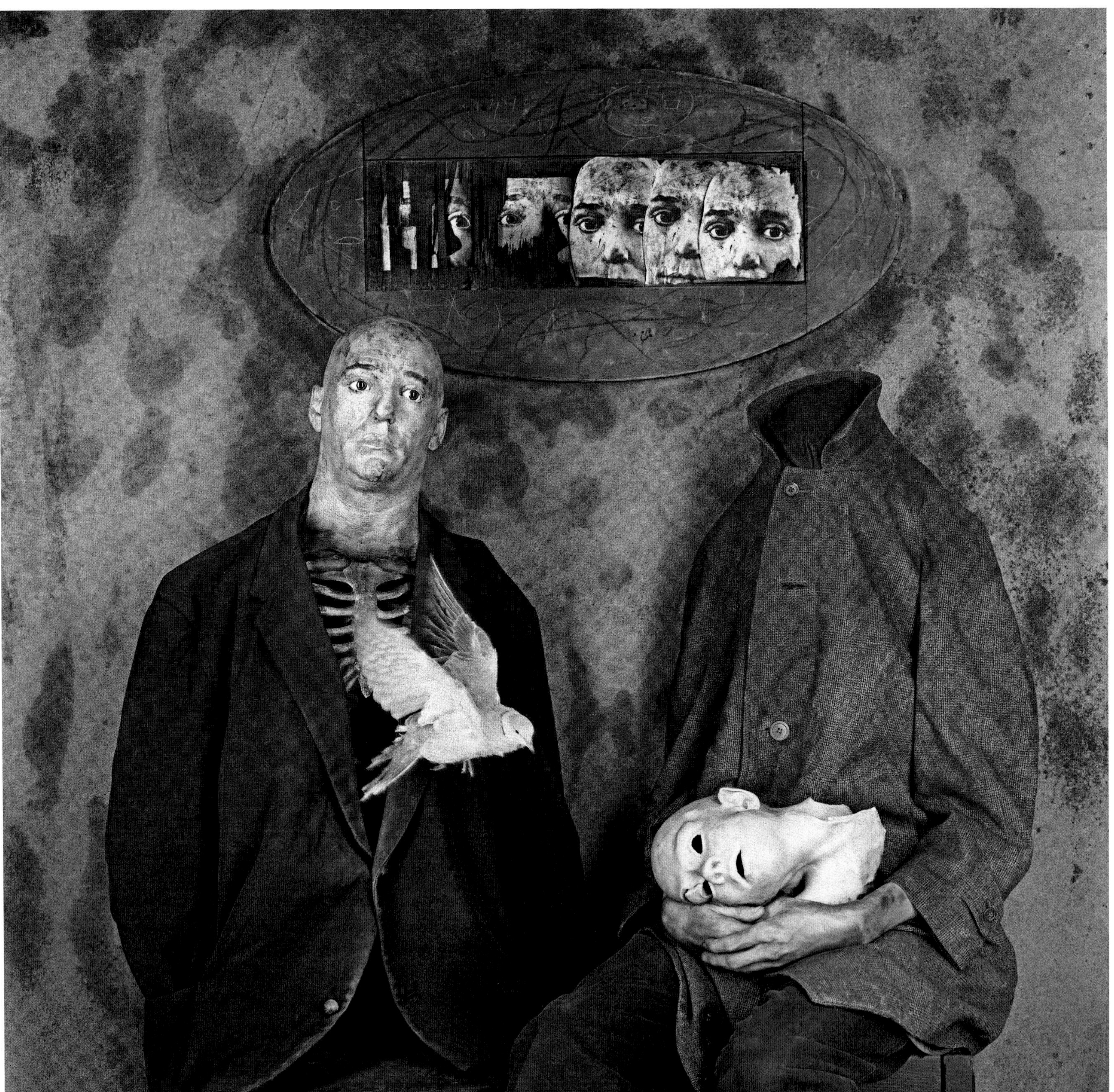

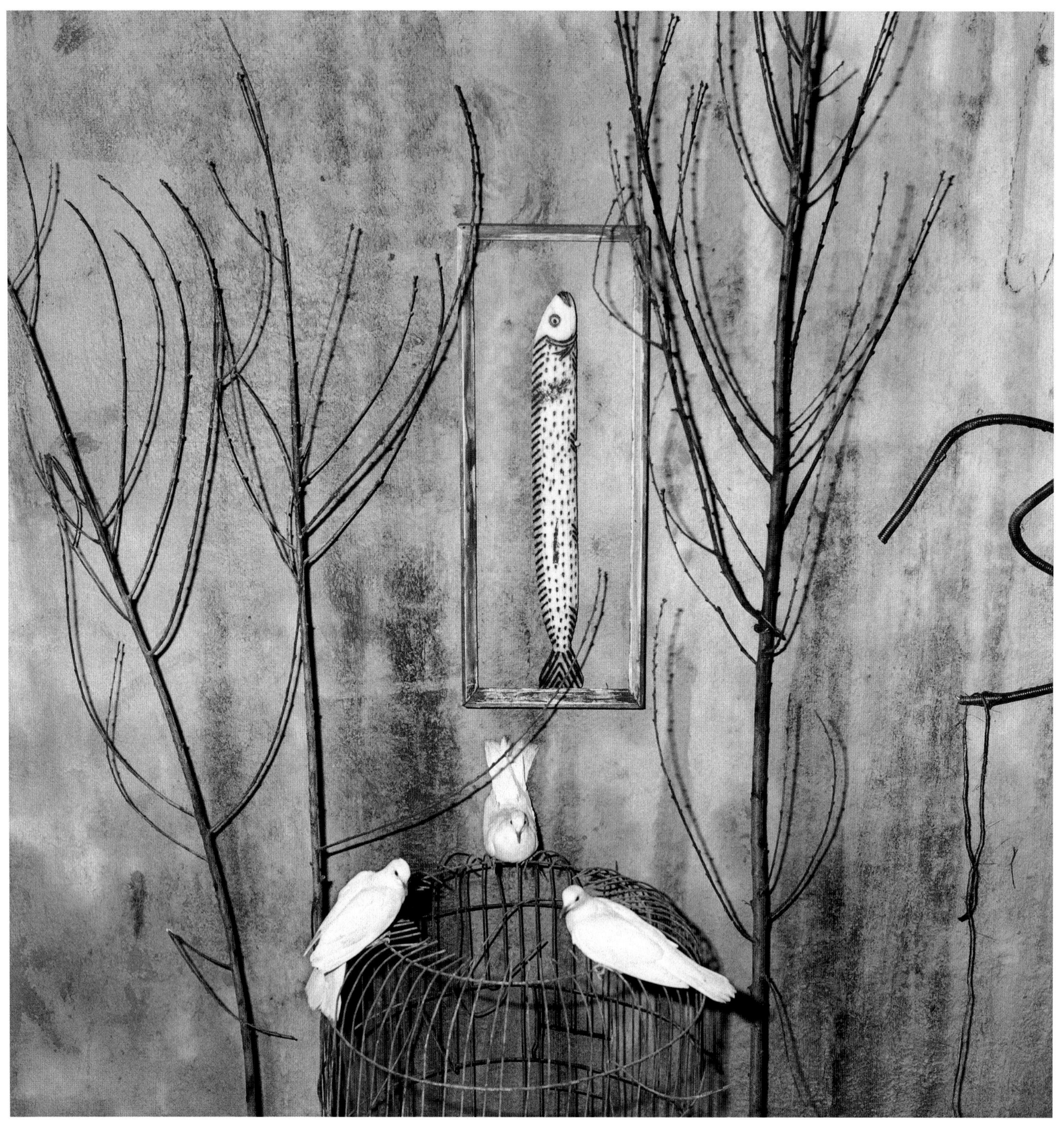

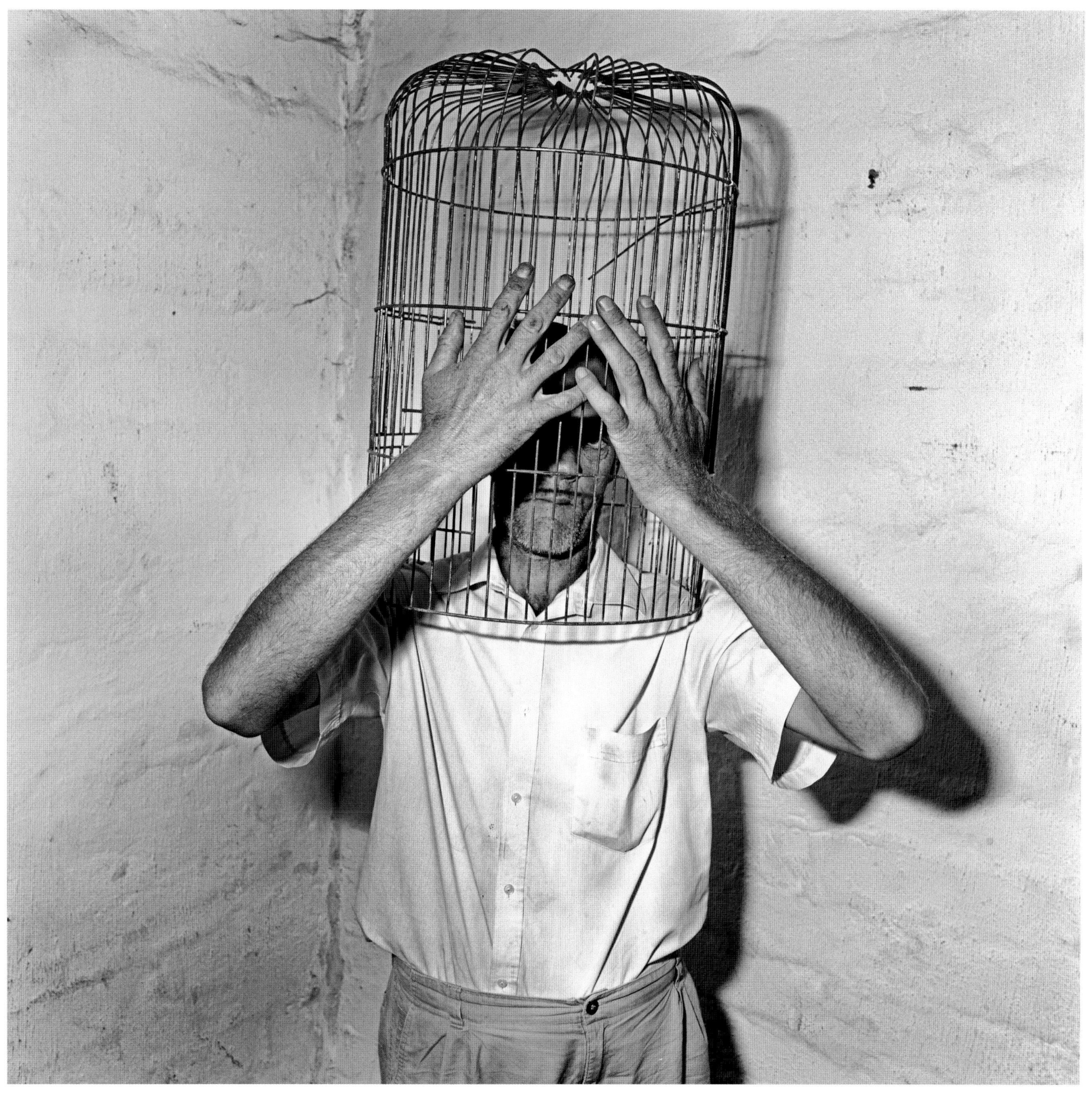

Encaged 1996

27

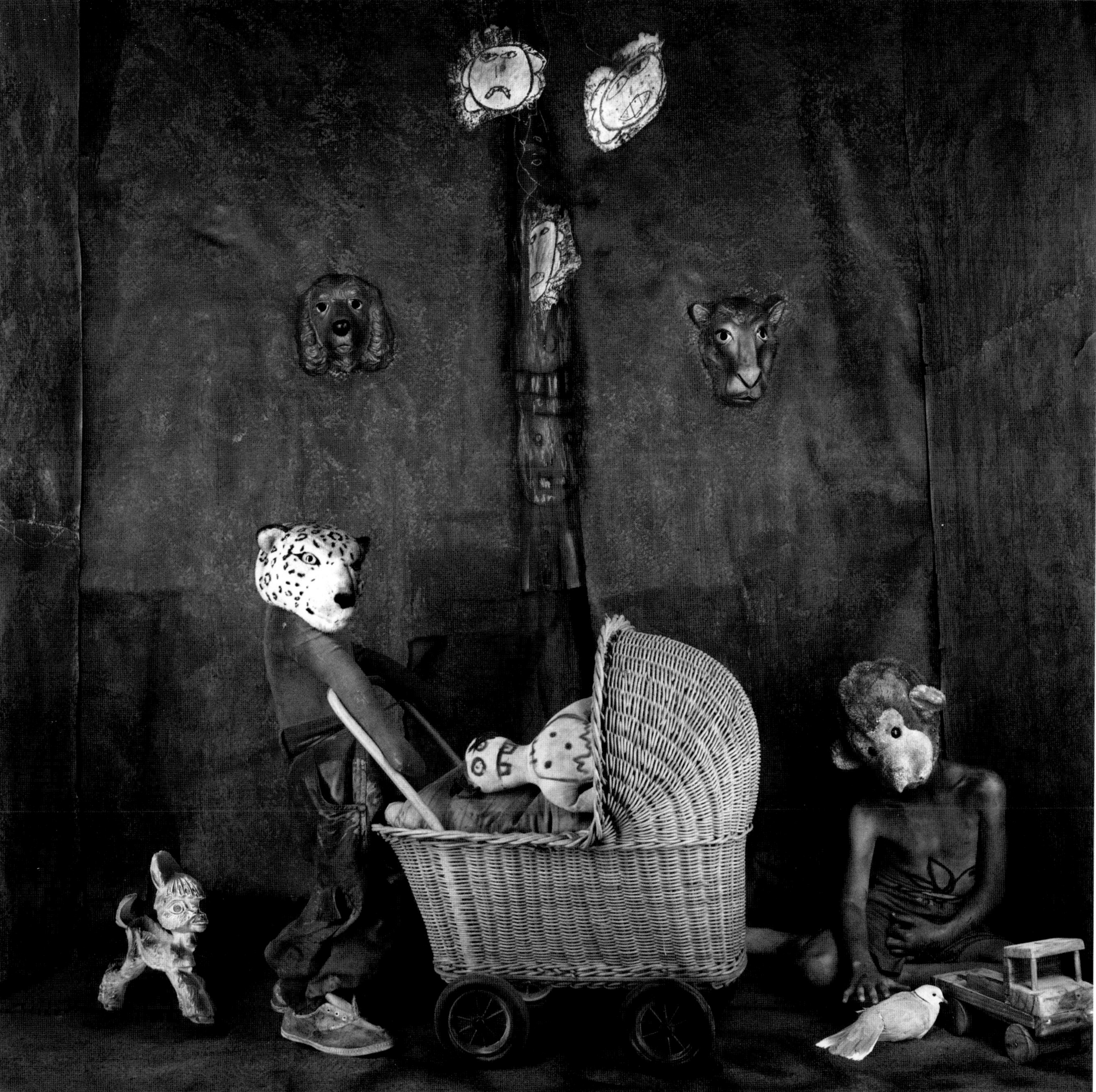

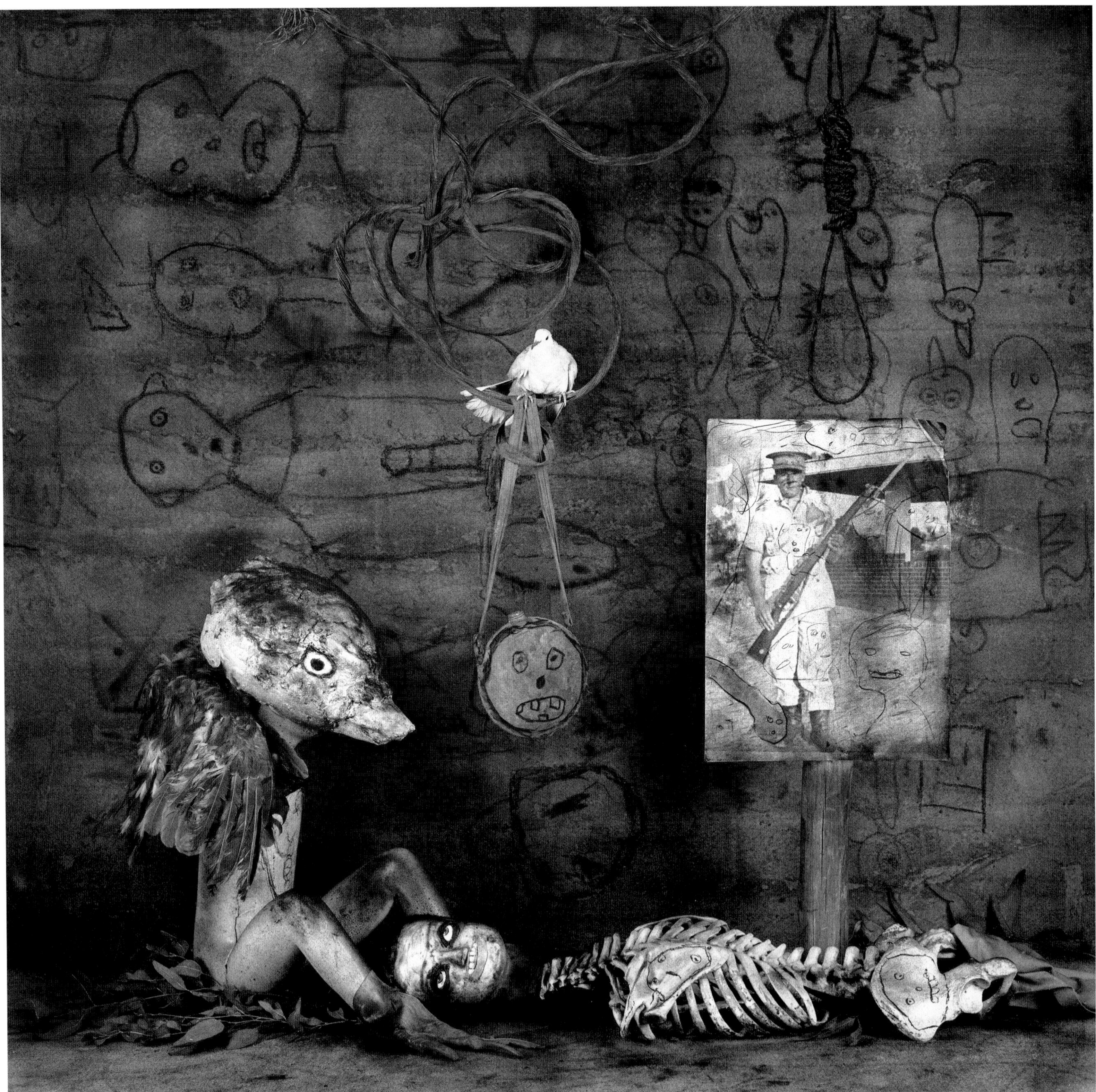

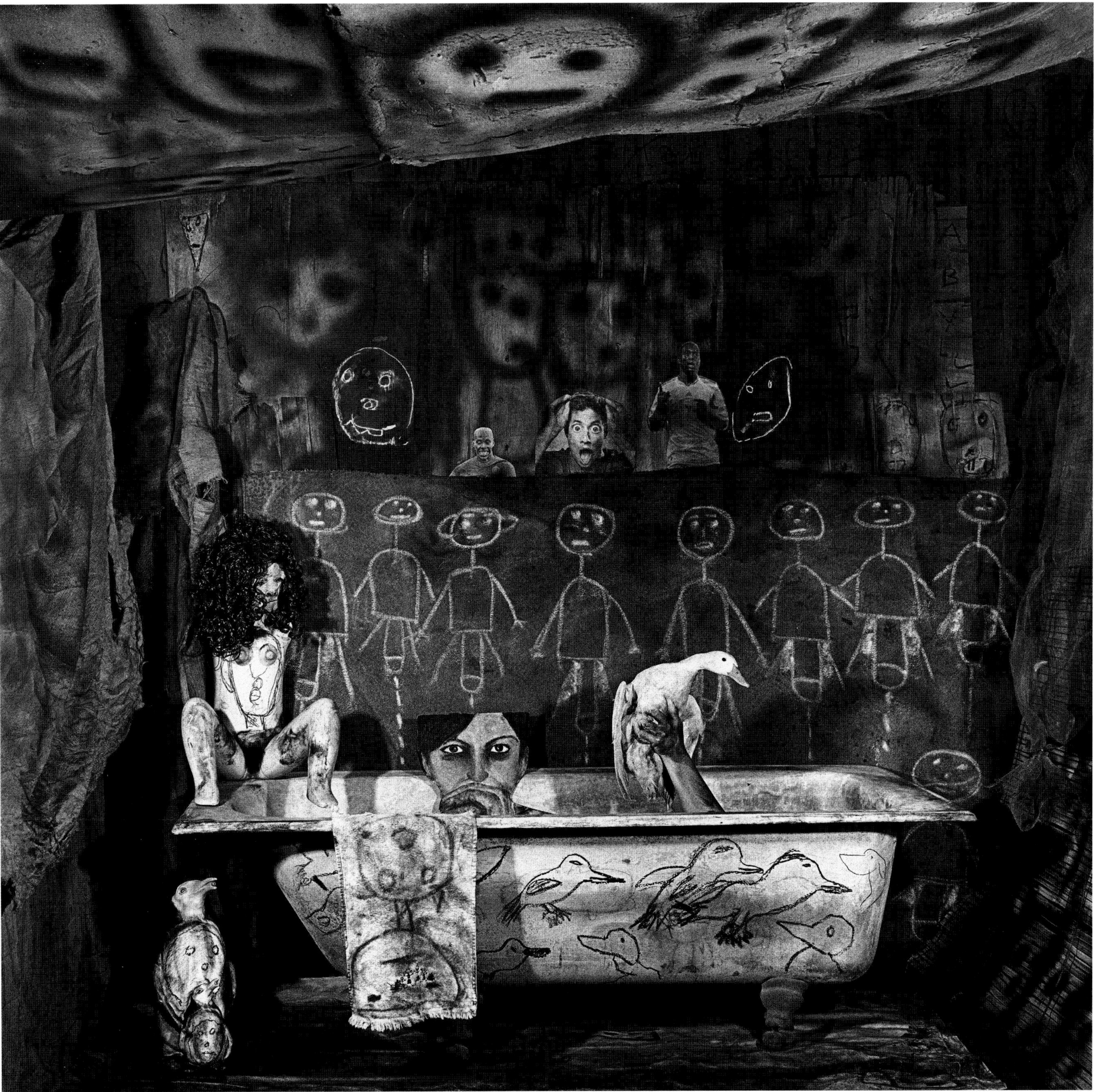

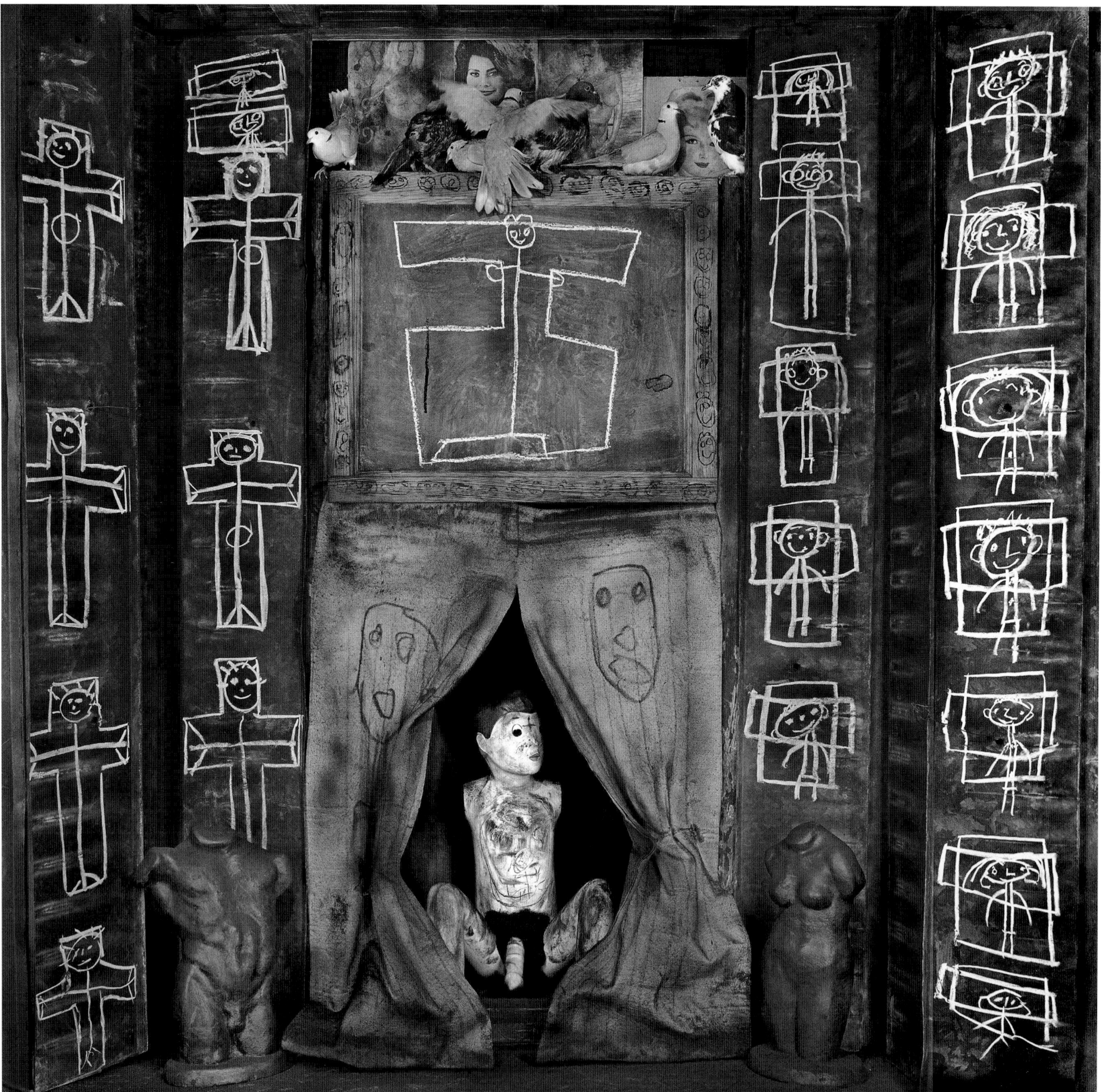

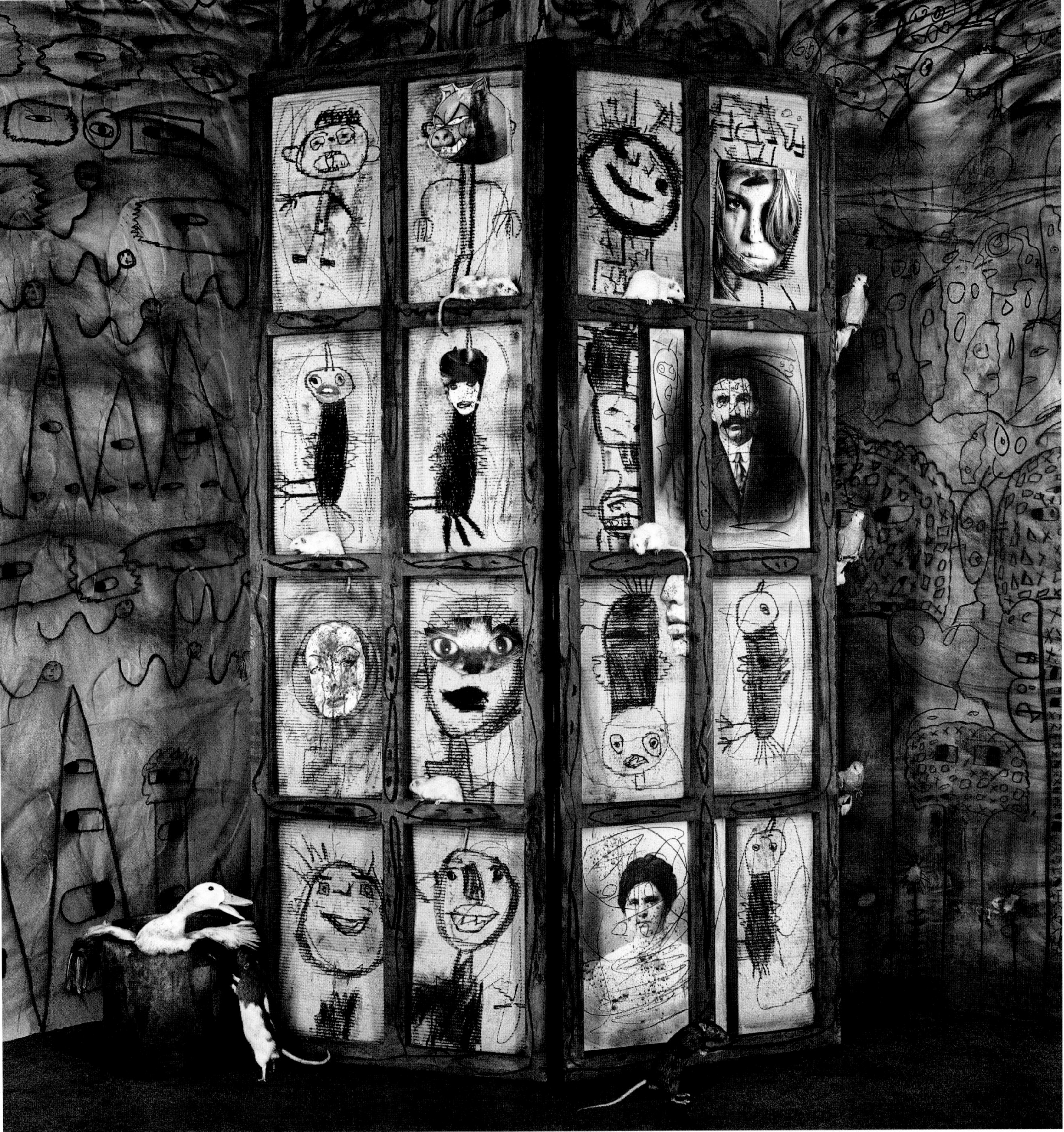

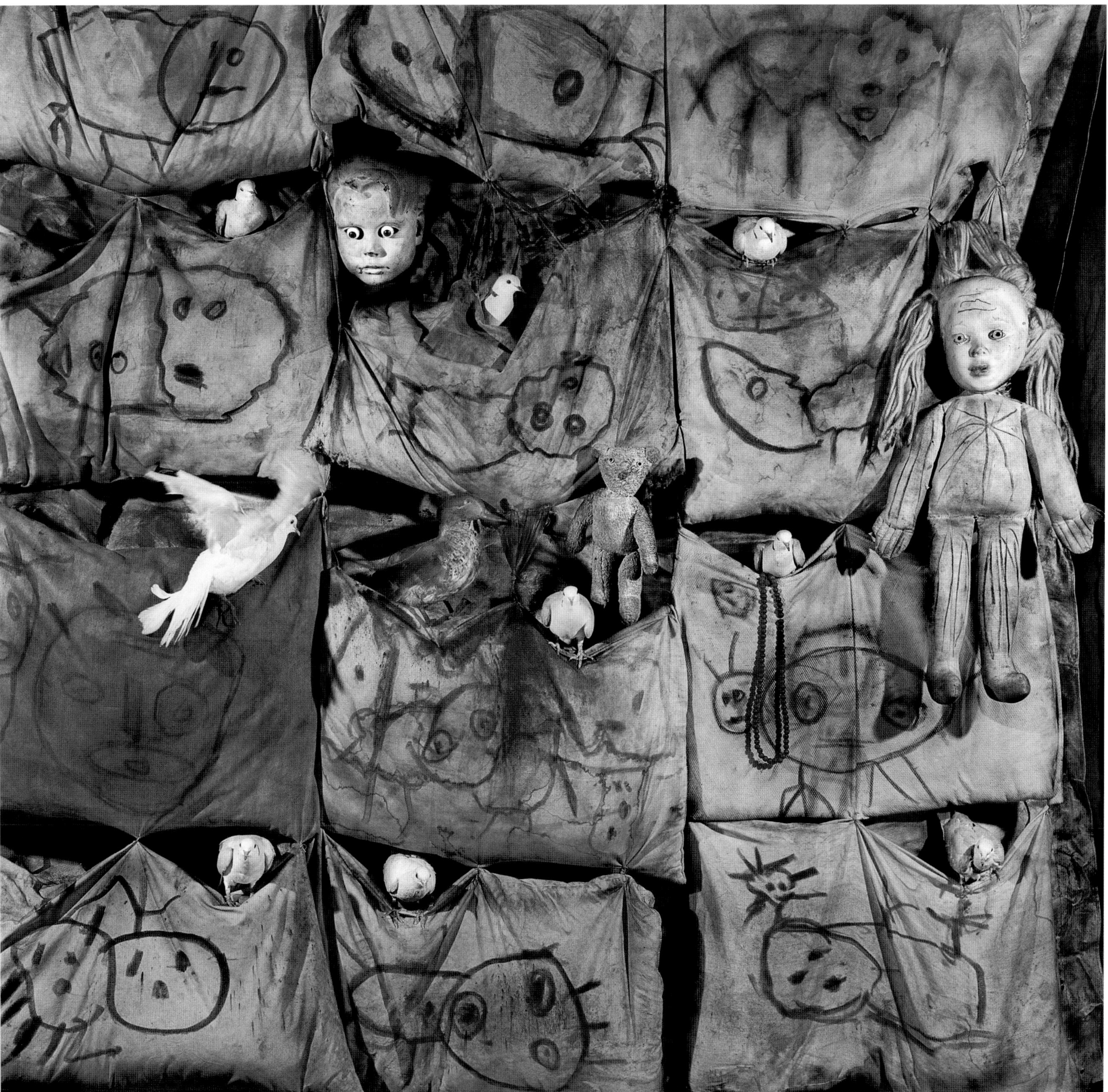

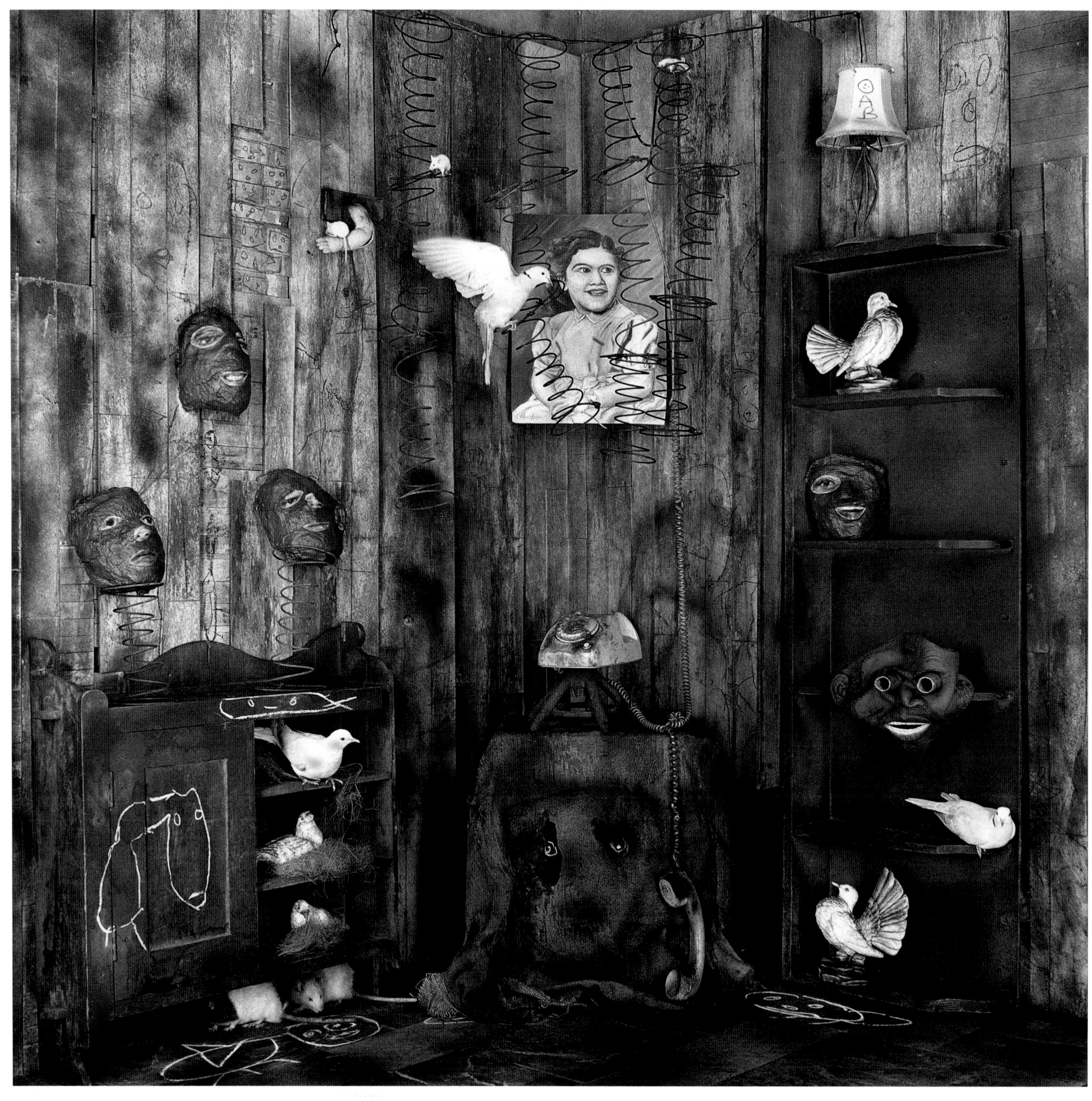

Room of the Birds 2010

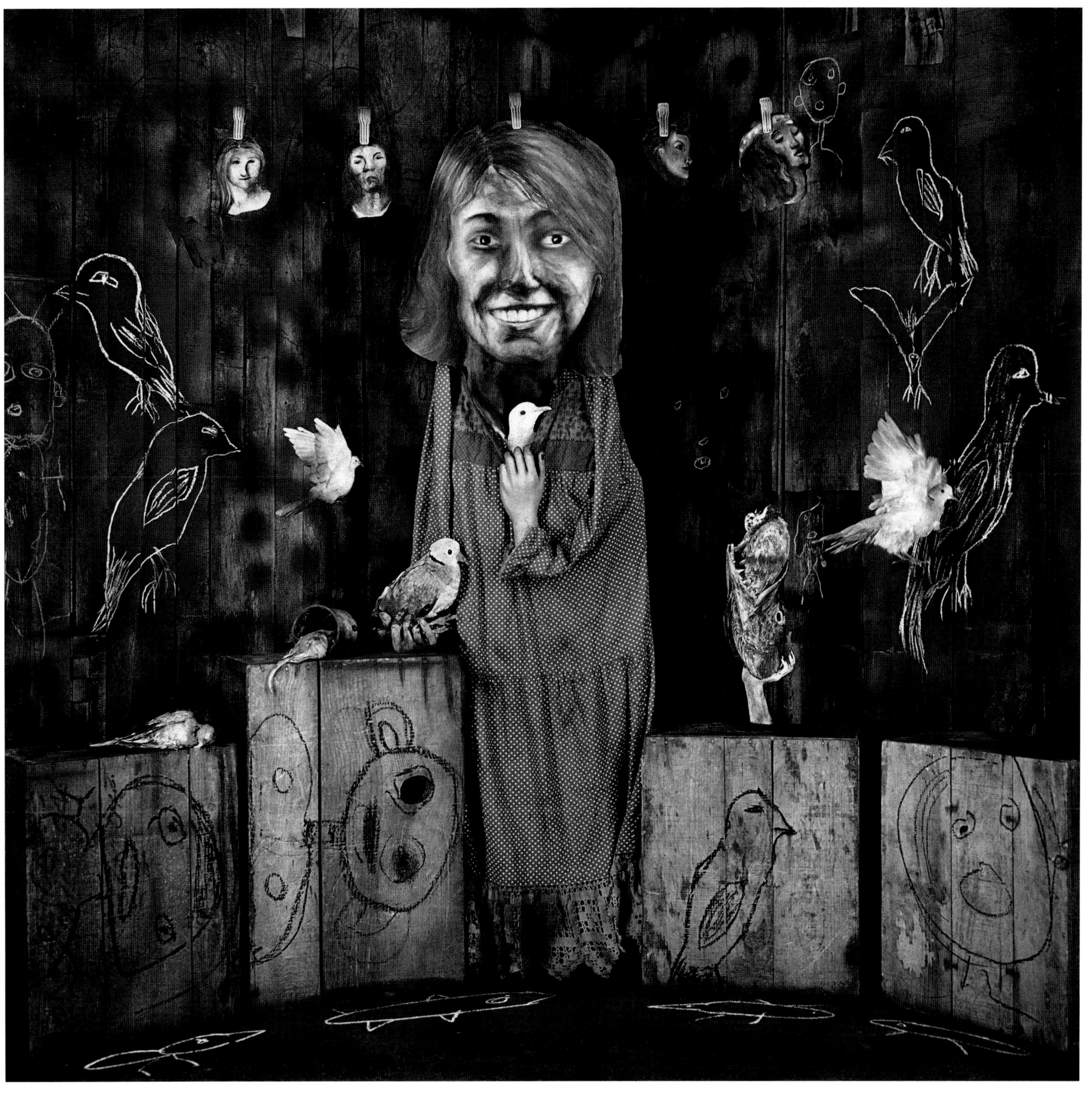

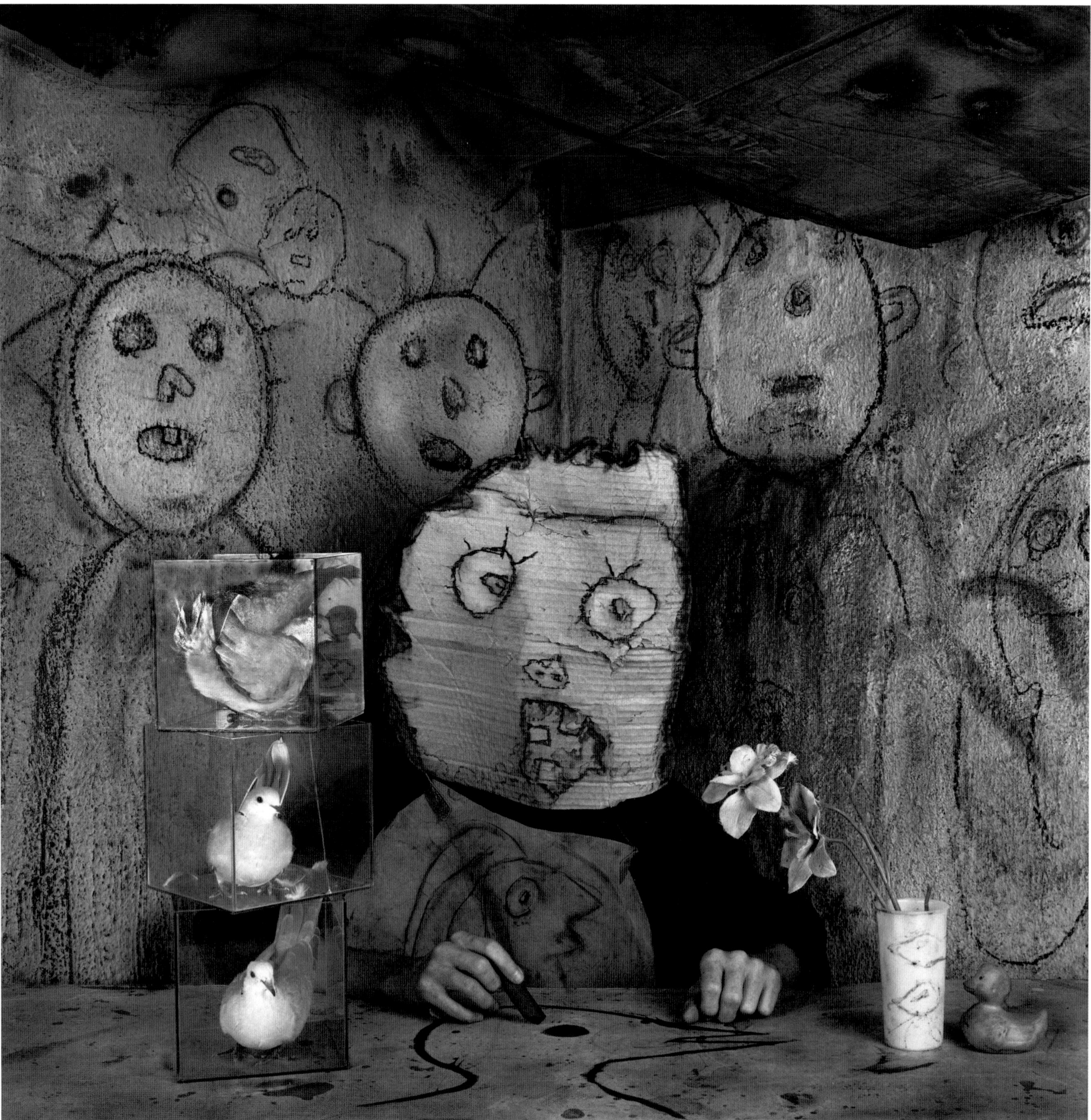

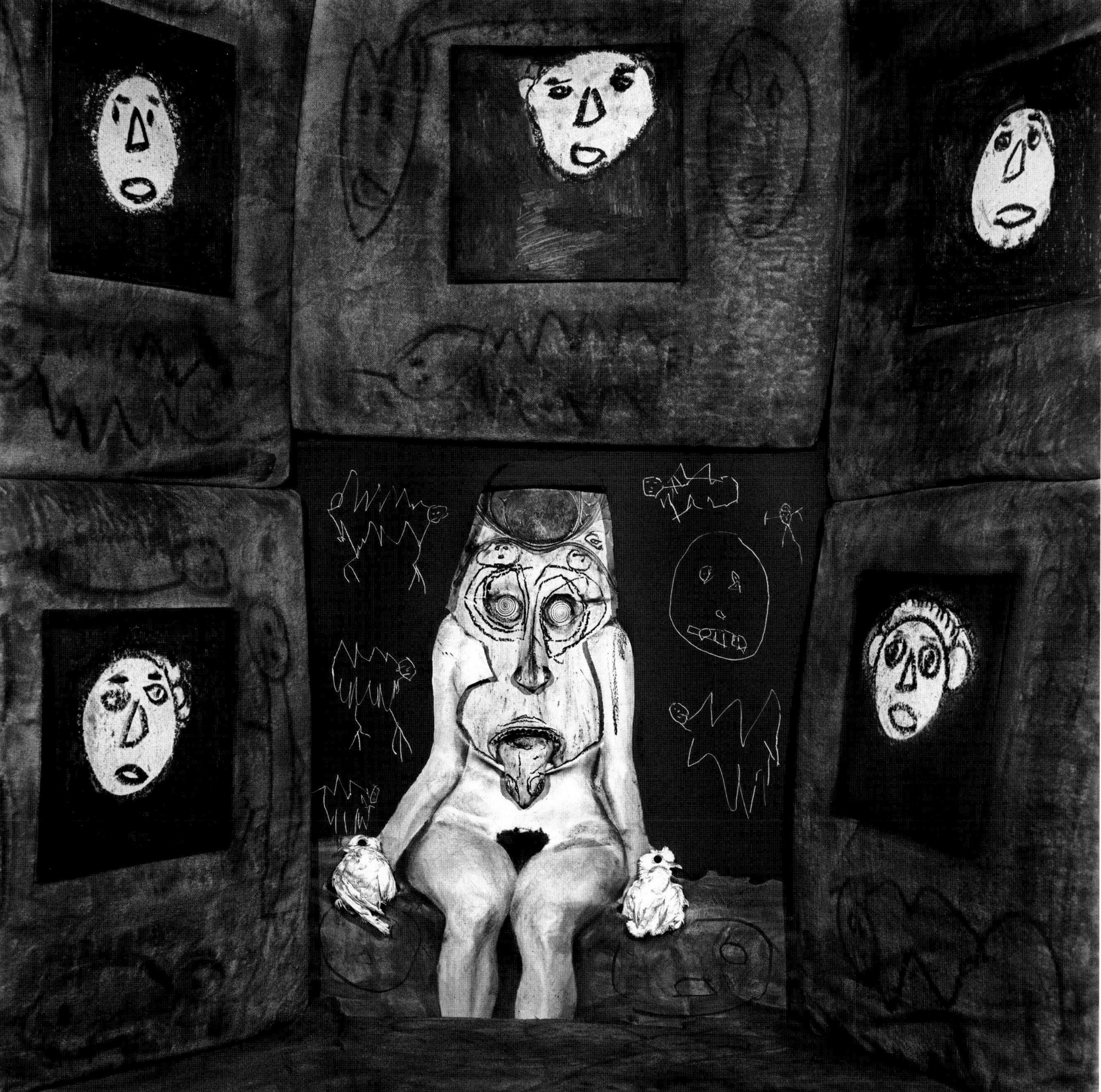

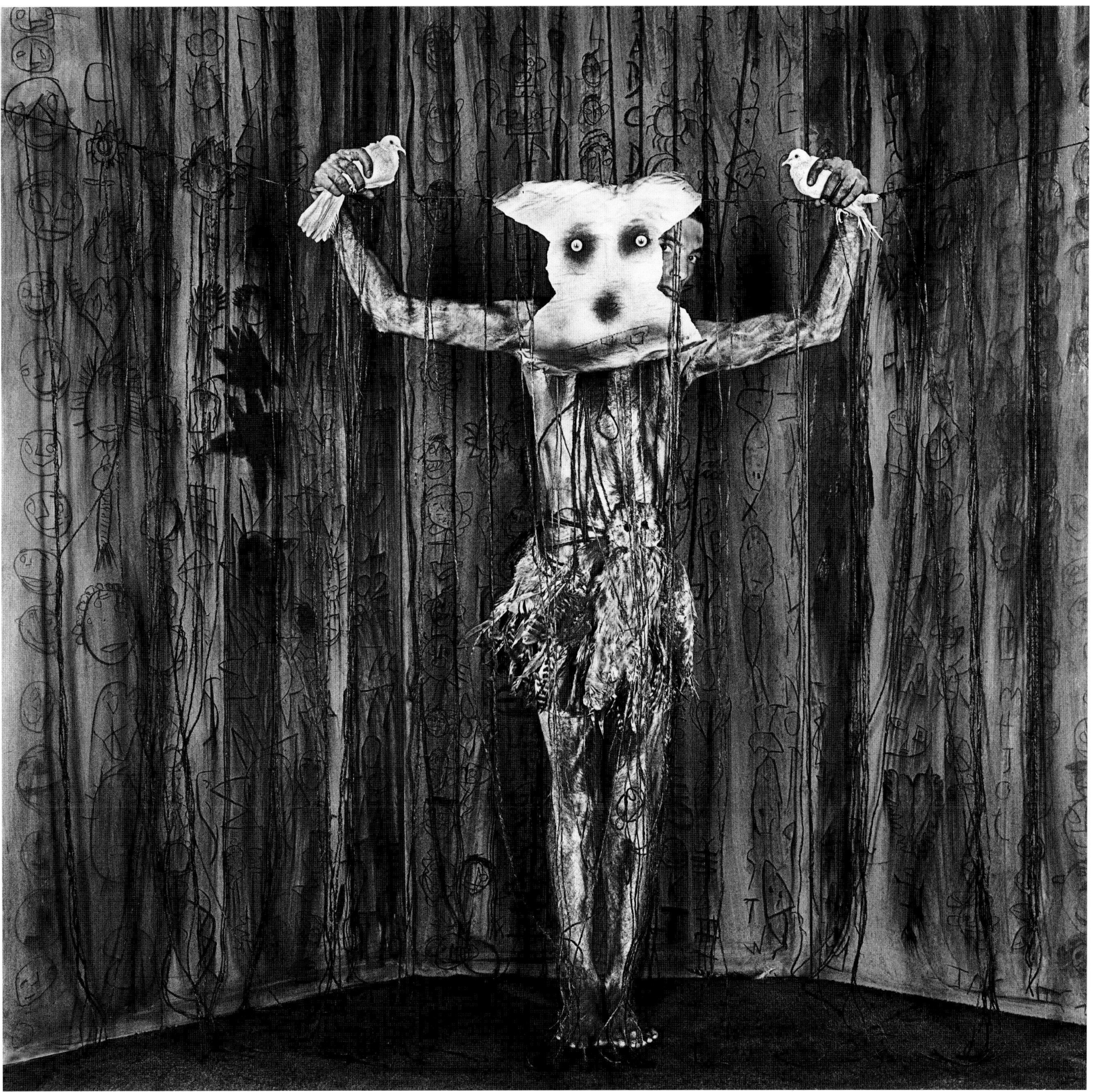

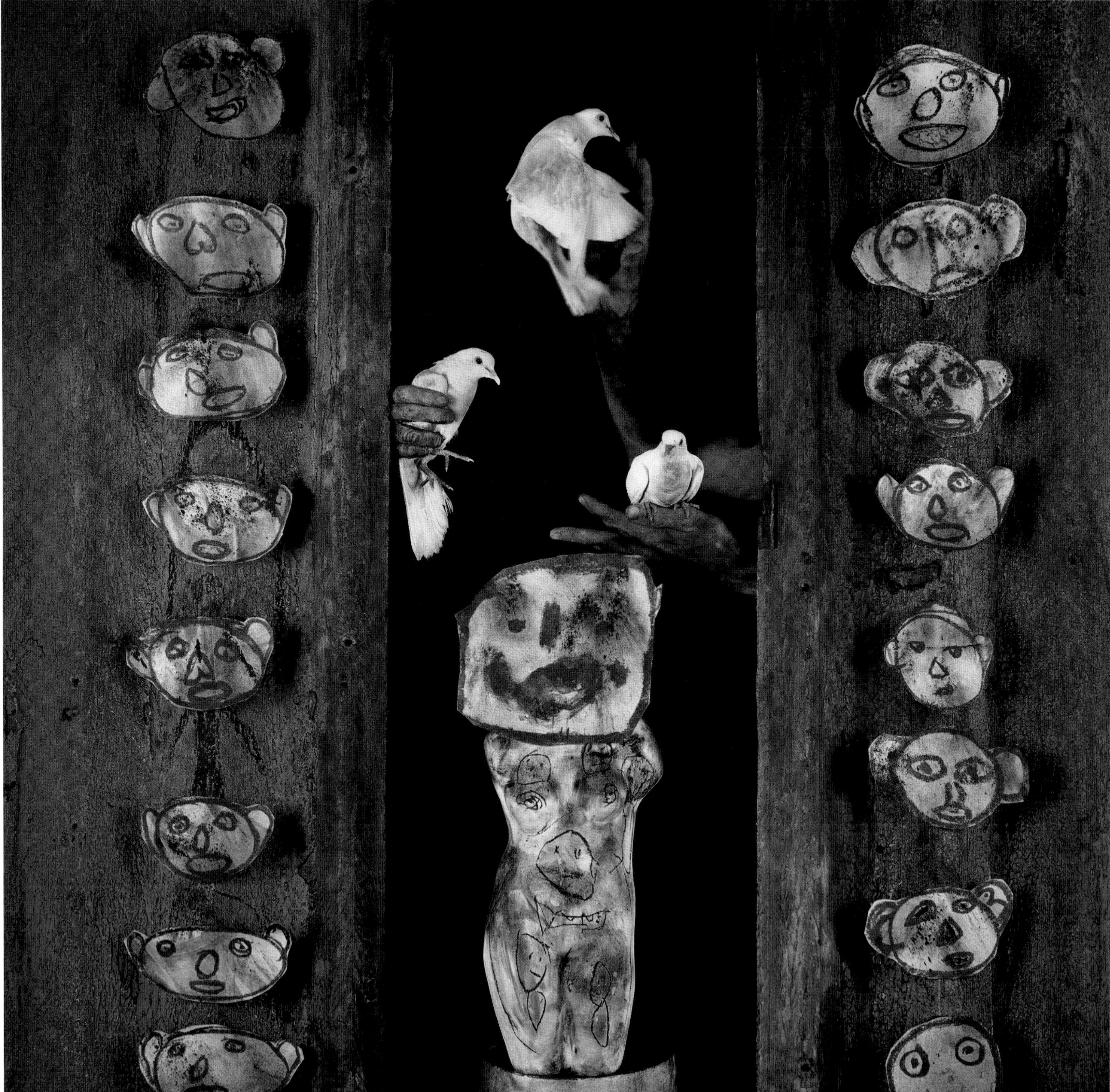

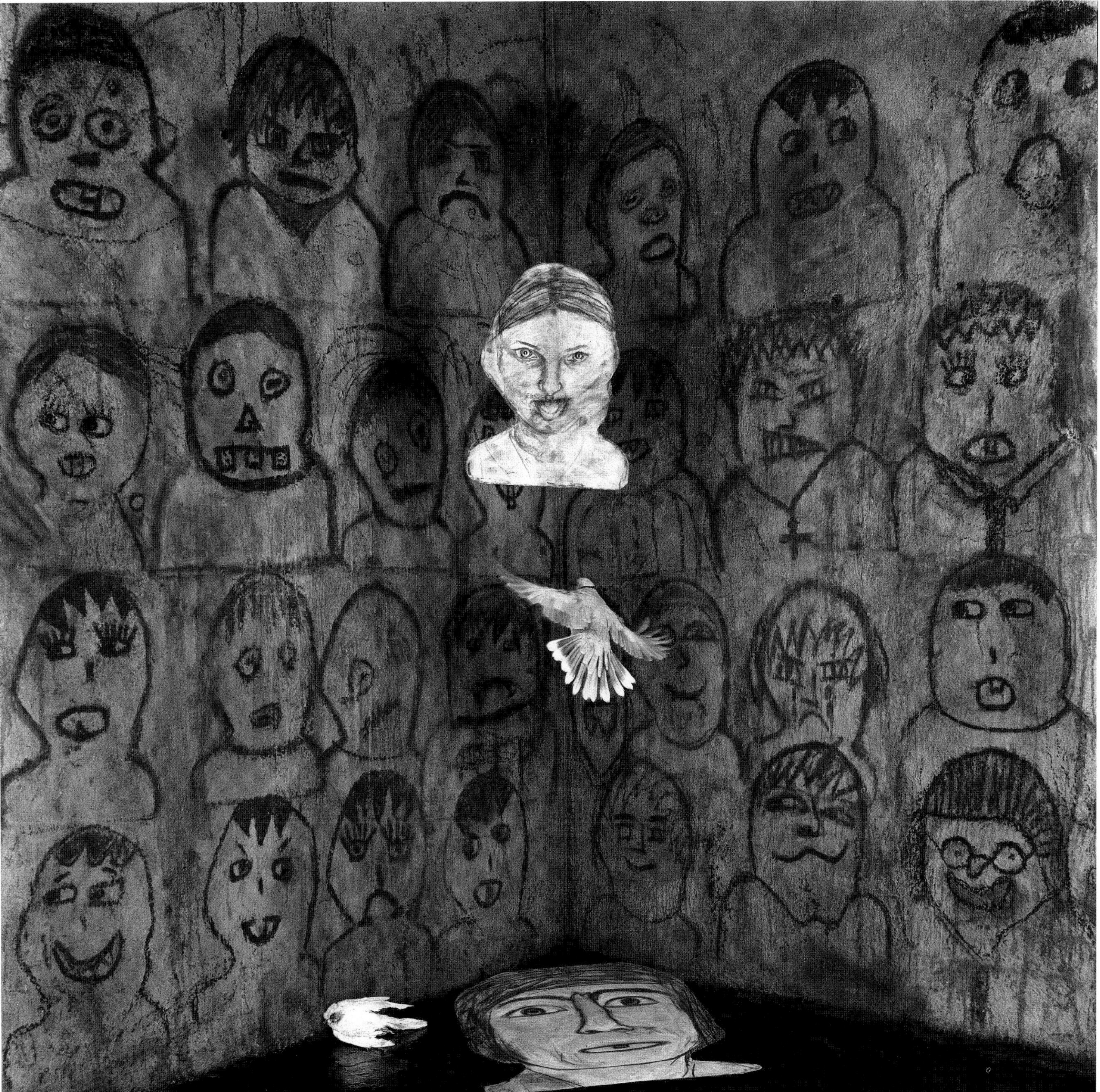

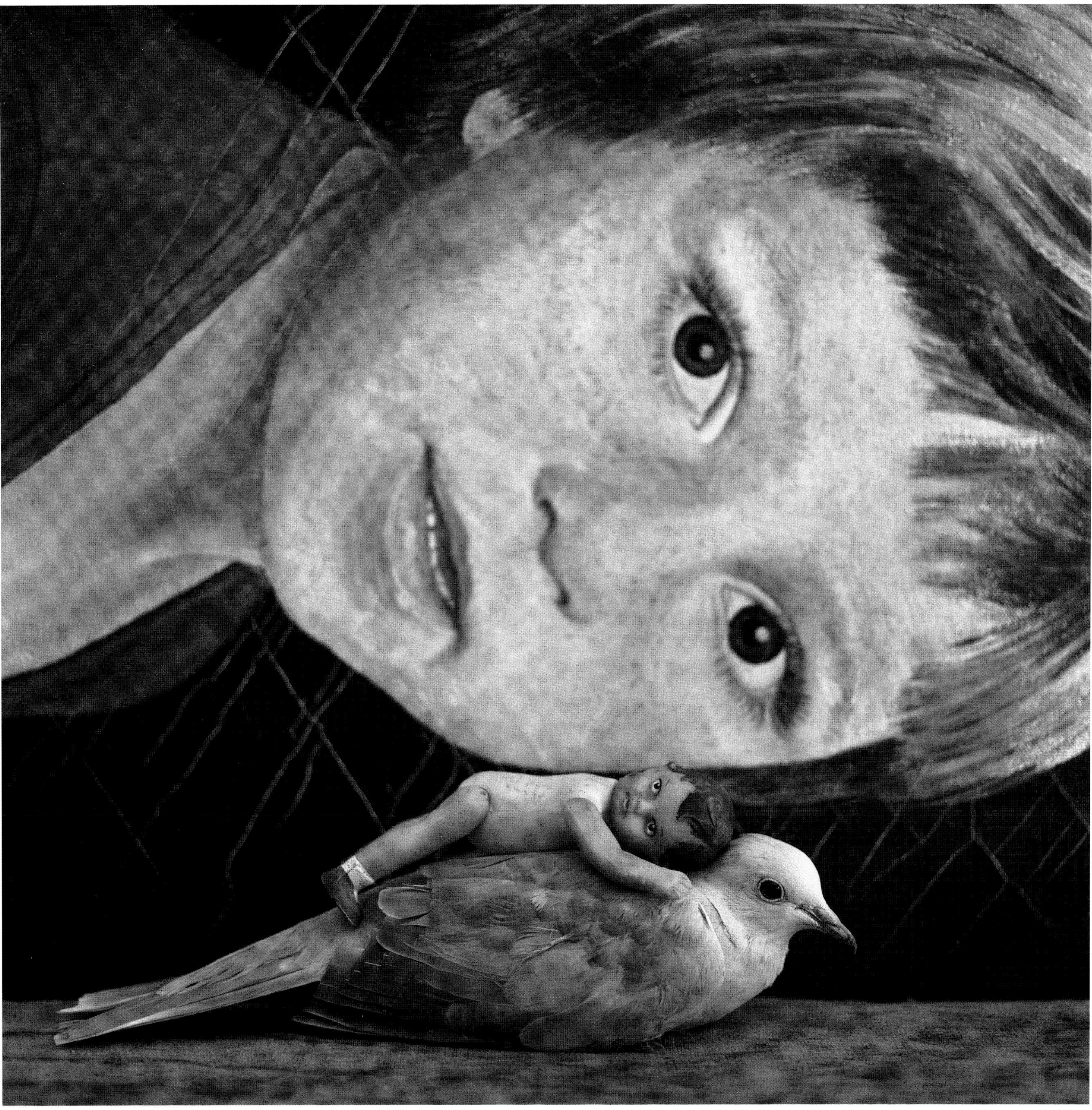

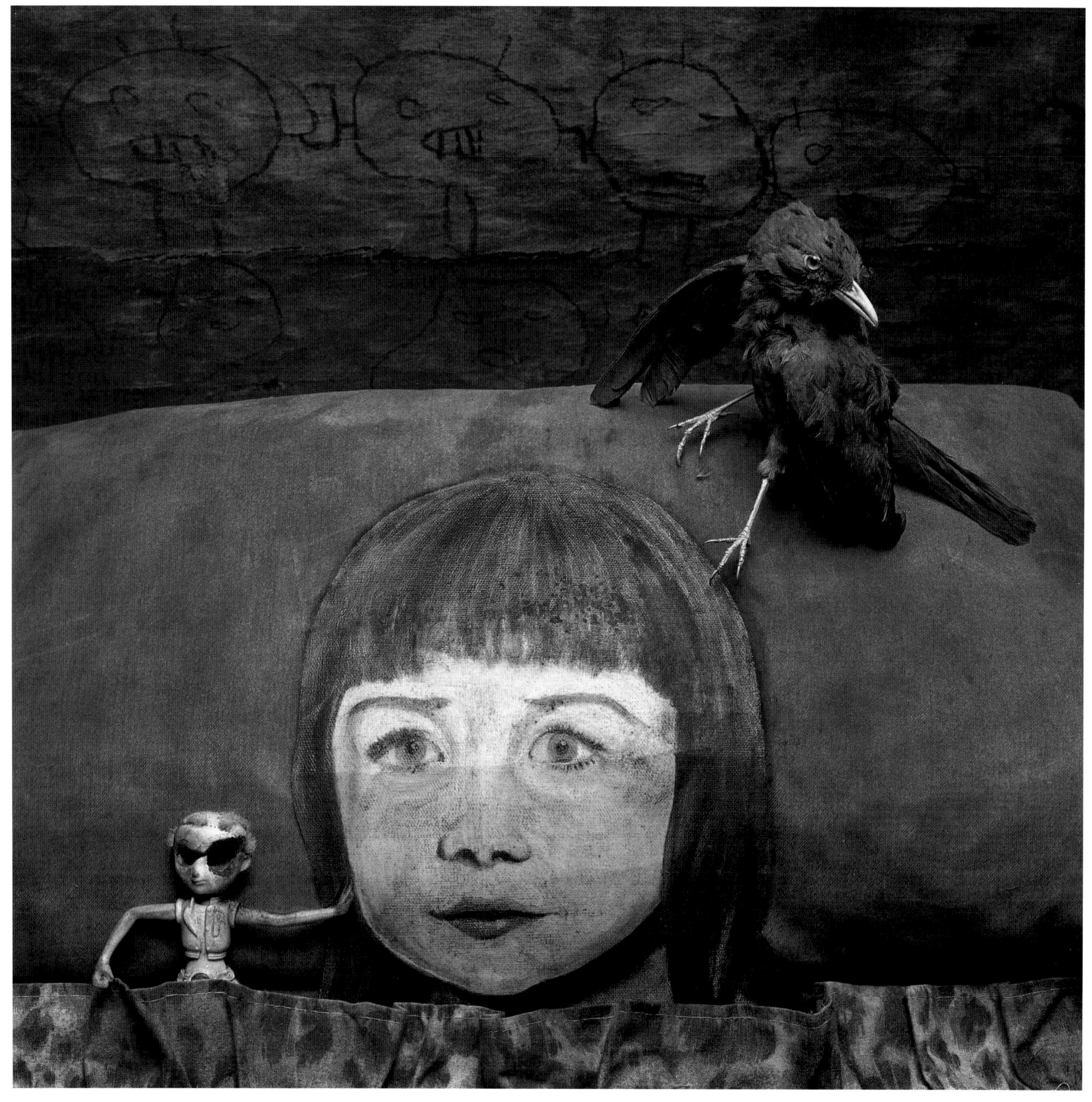

Omen 2011

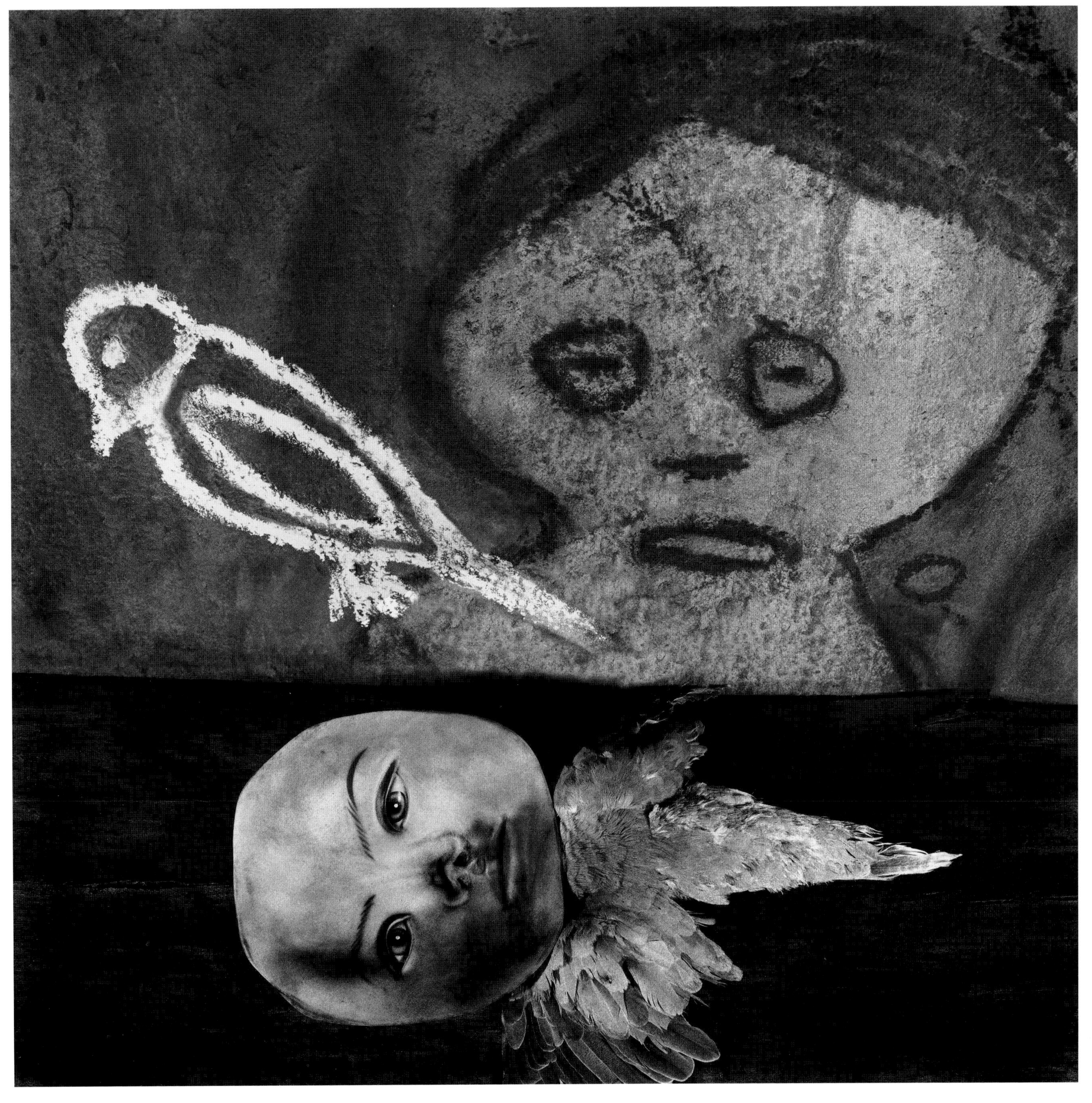

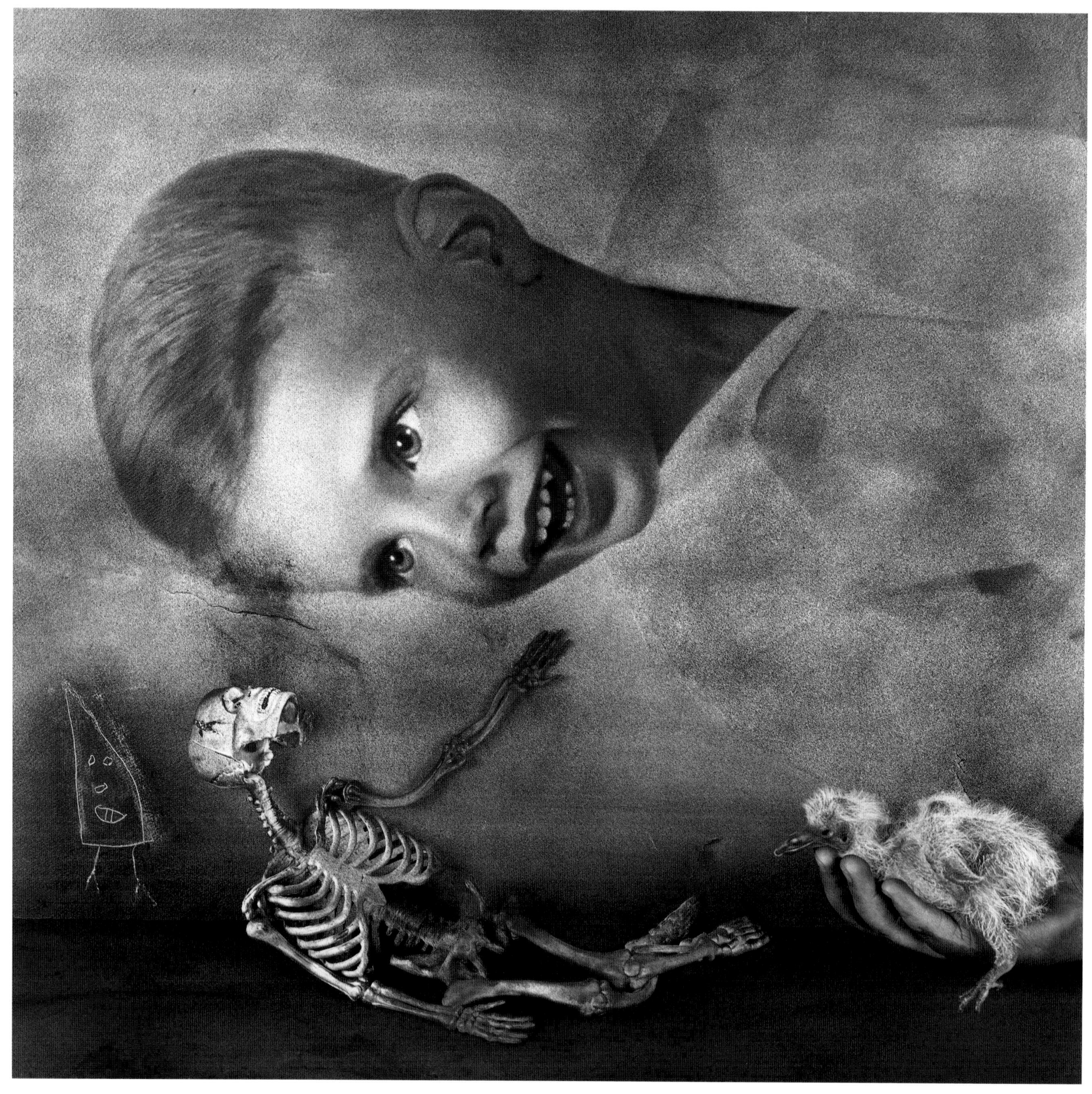

Consolation 2011

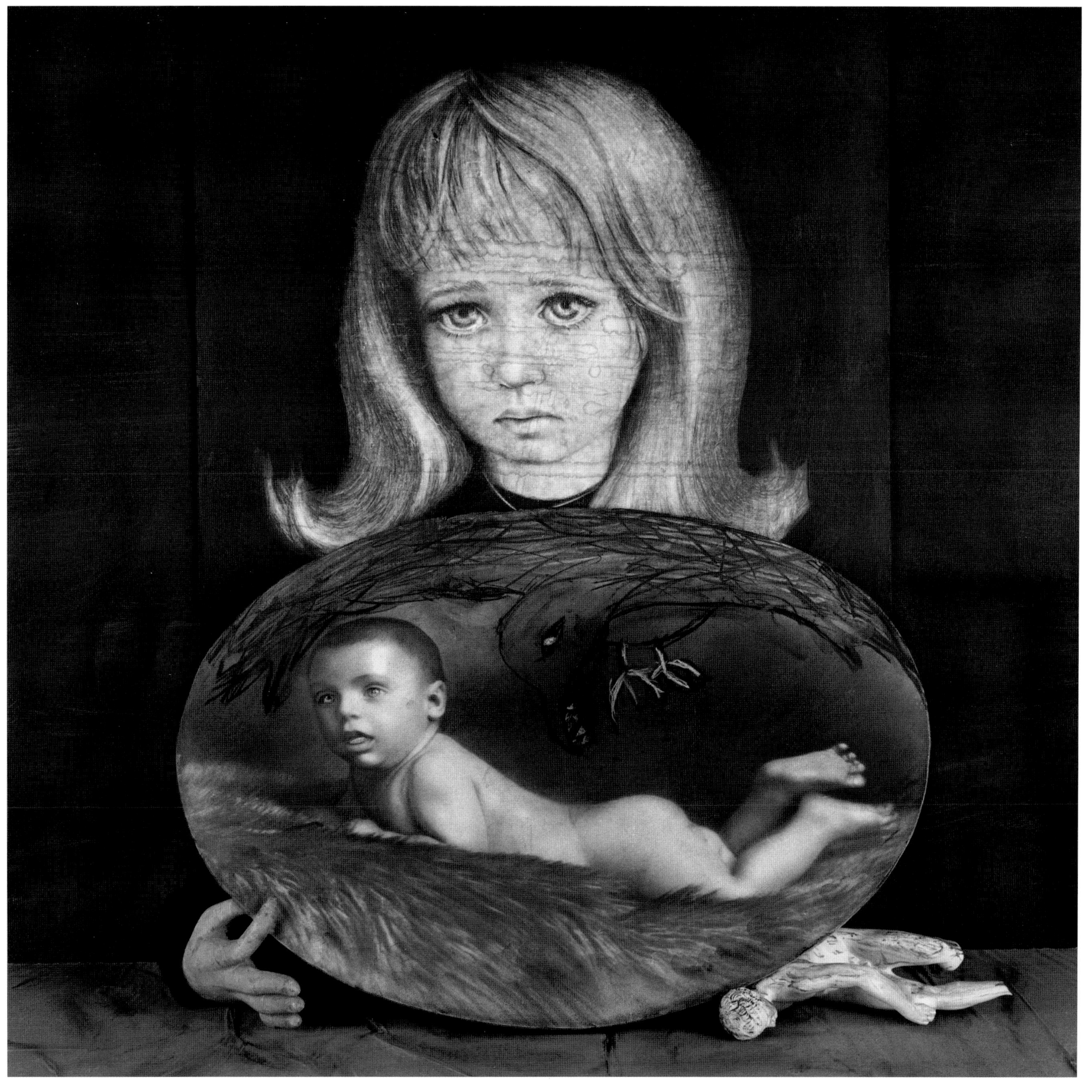

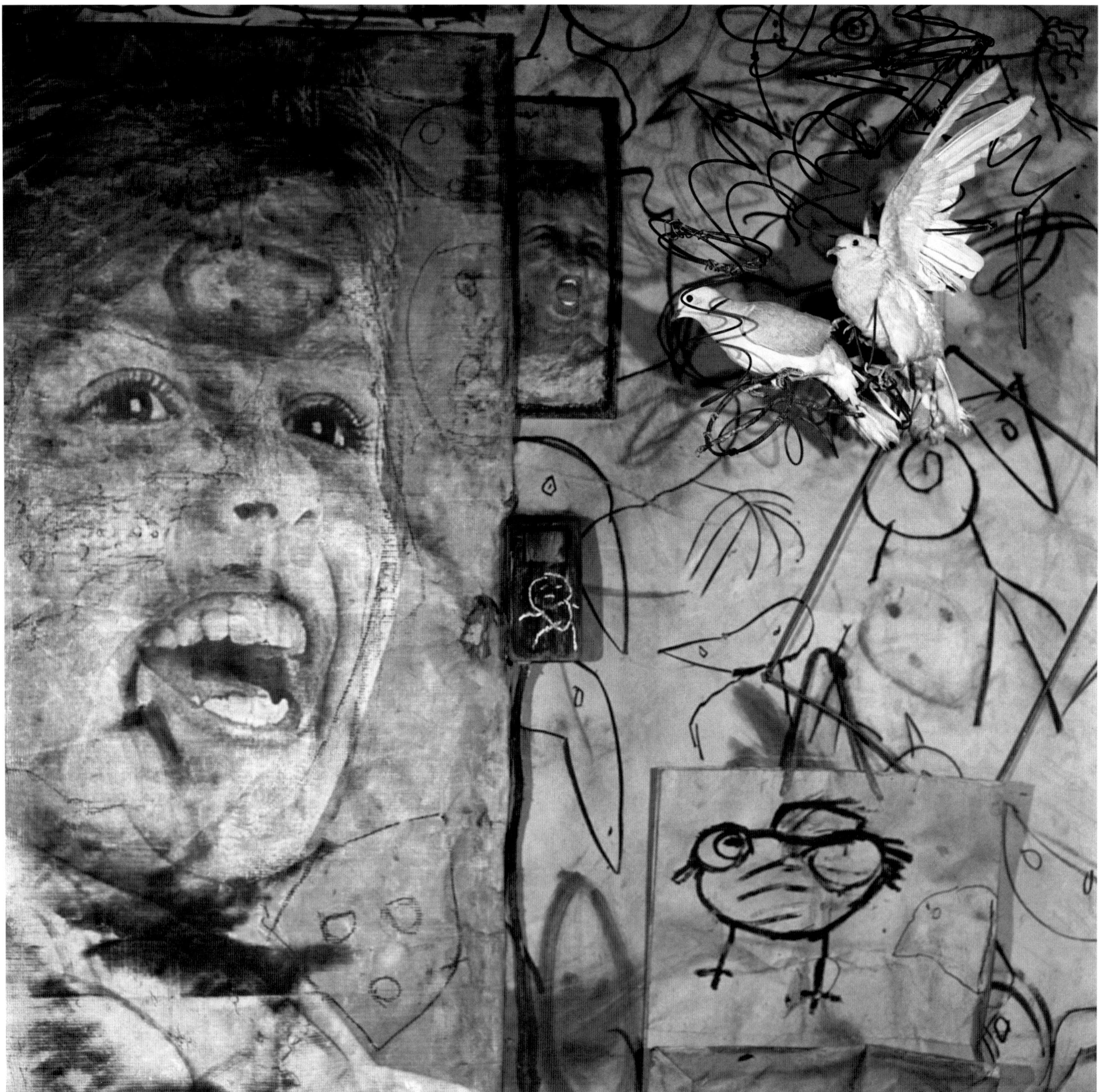

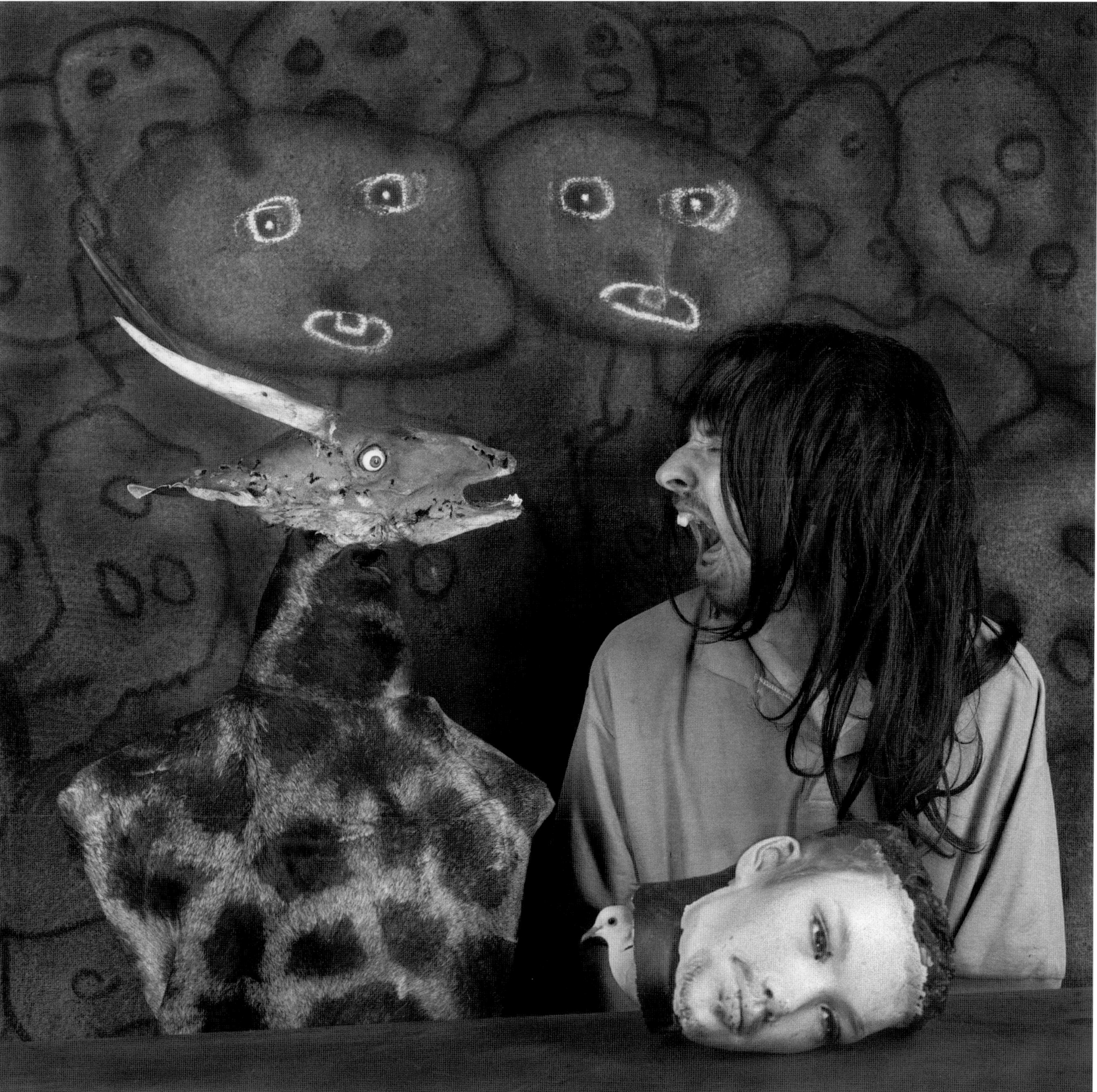

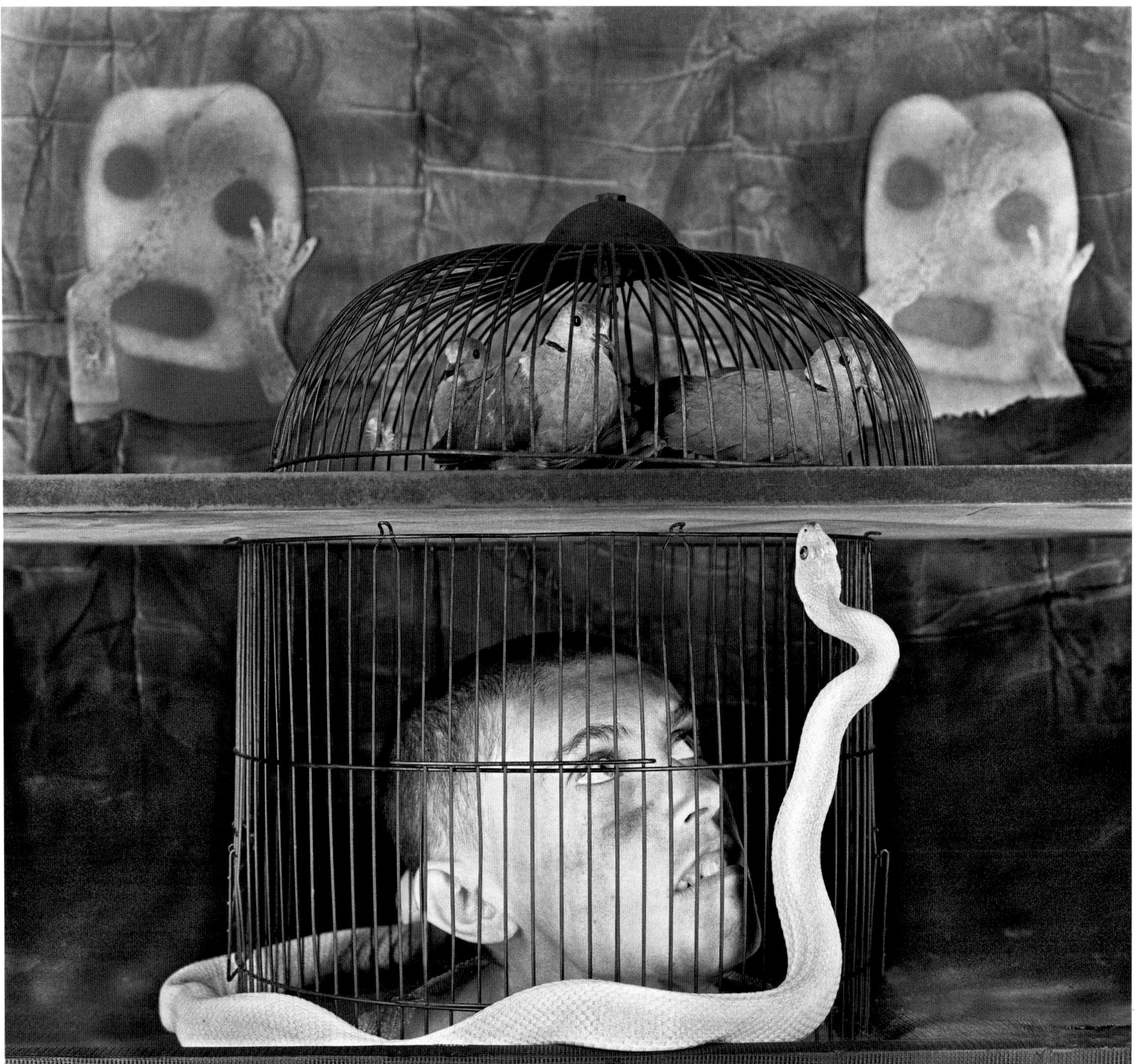

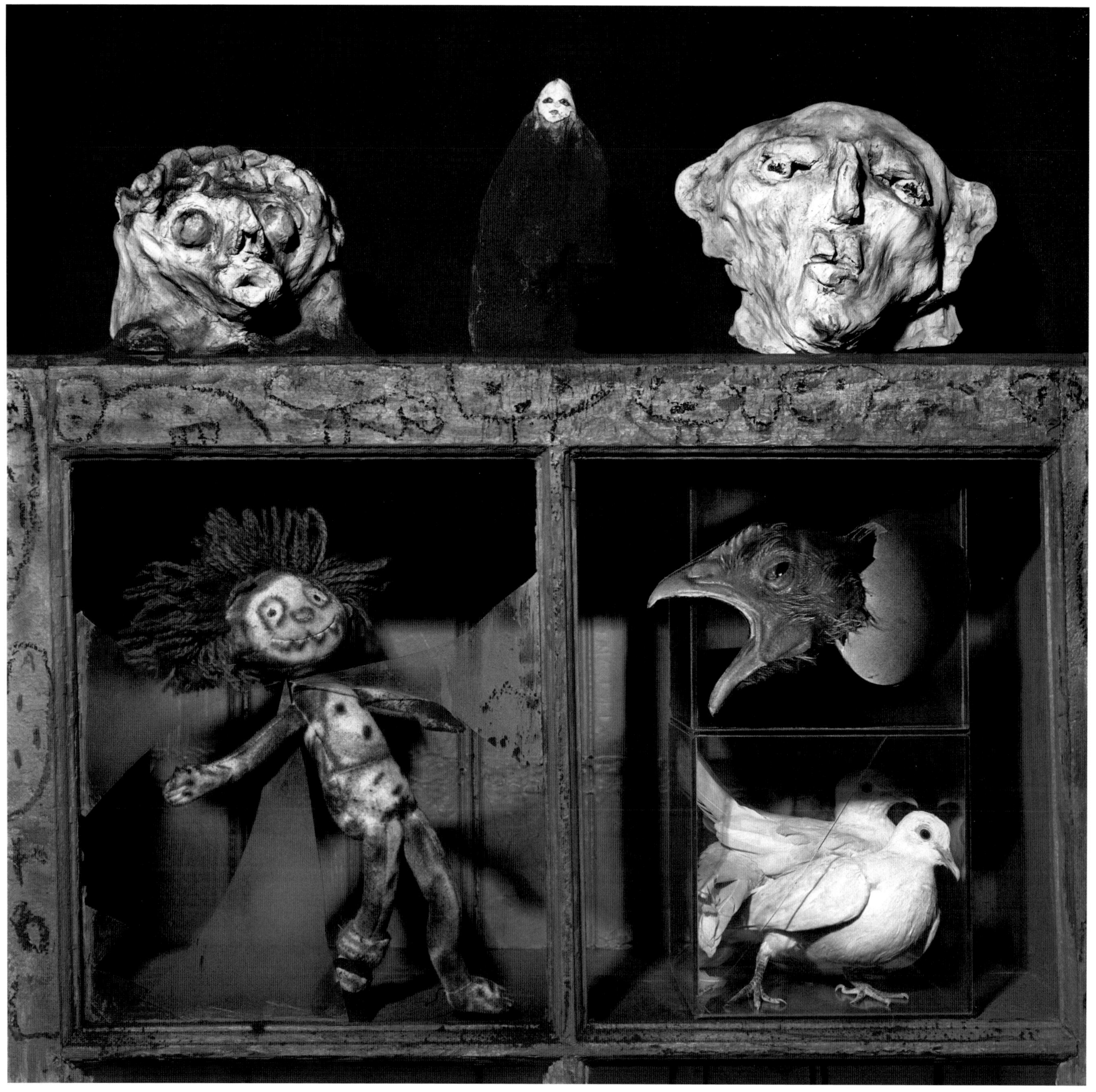

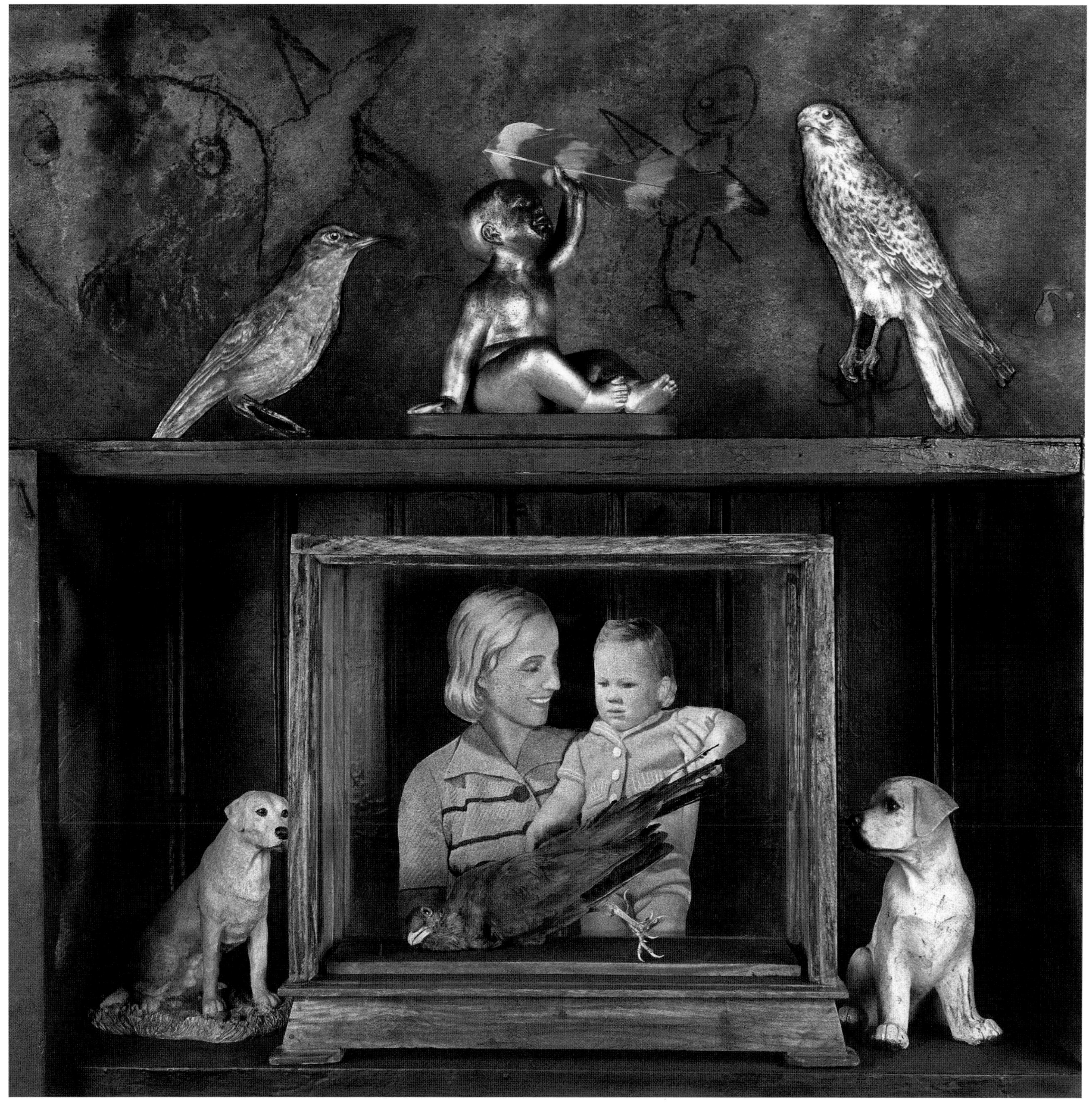

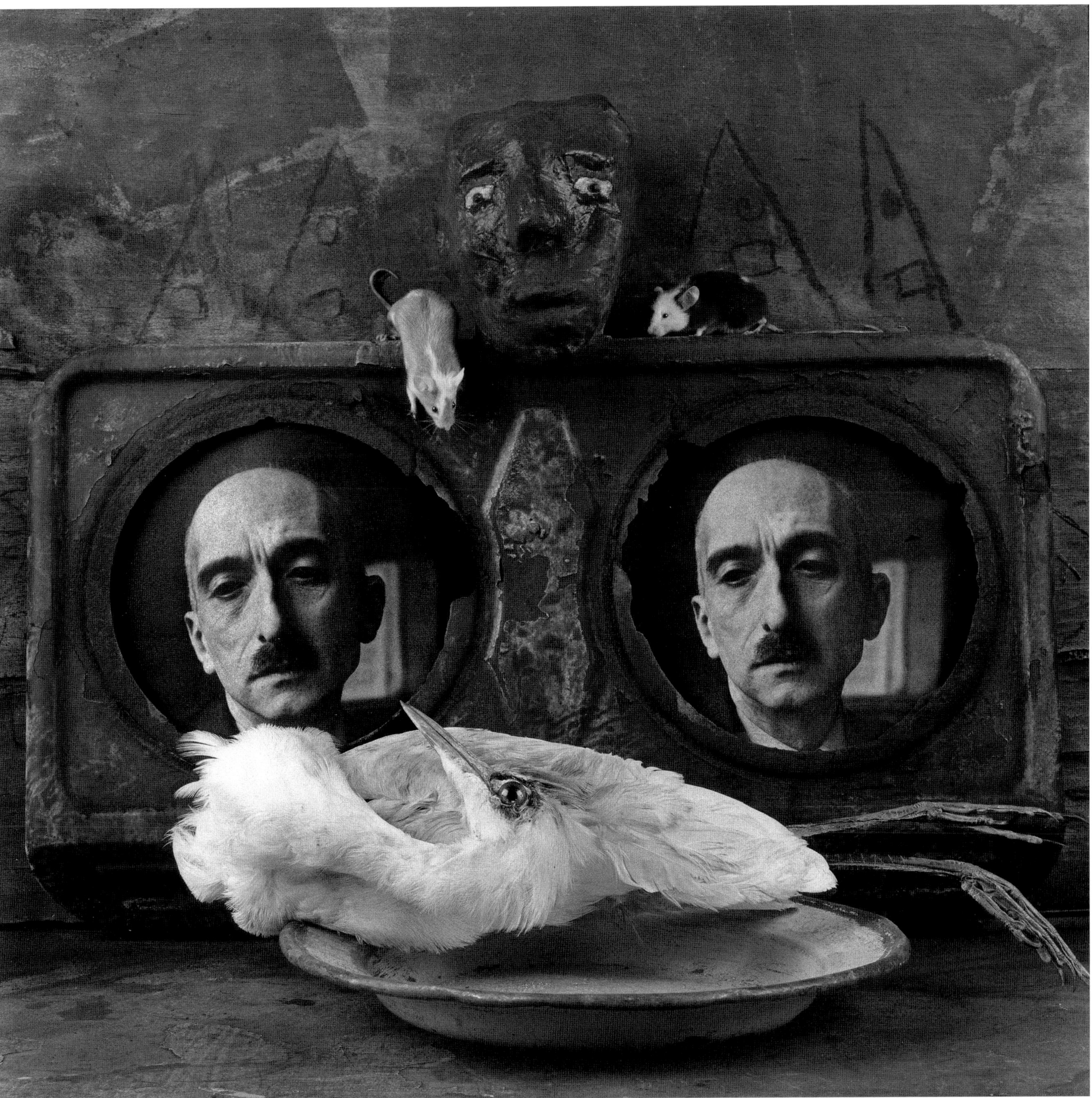

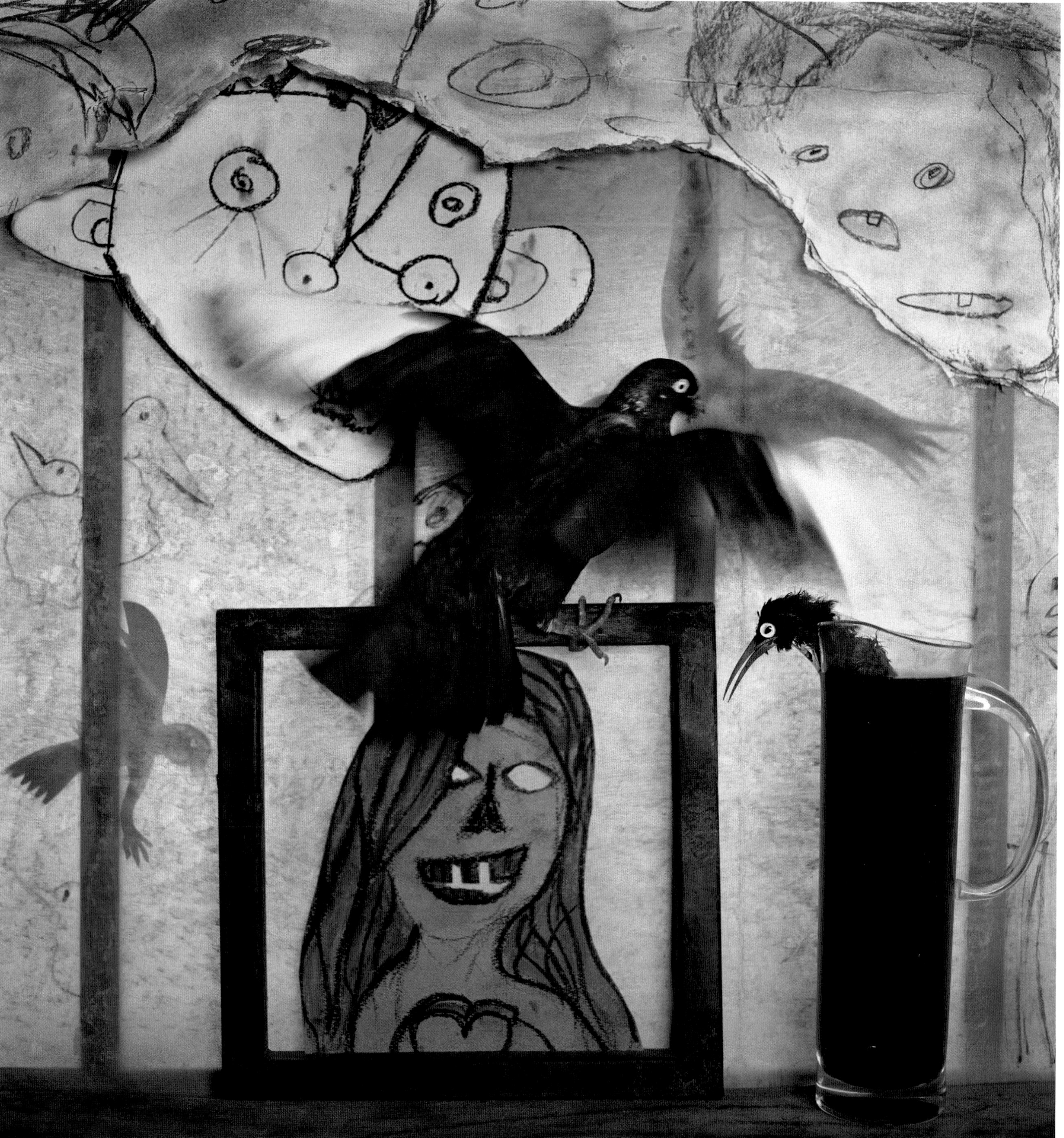

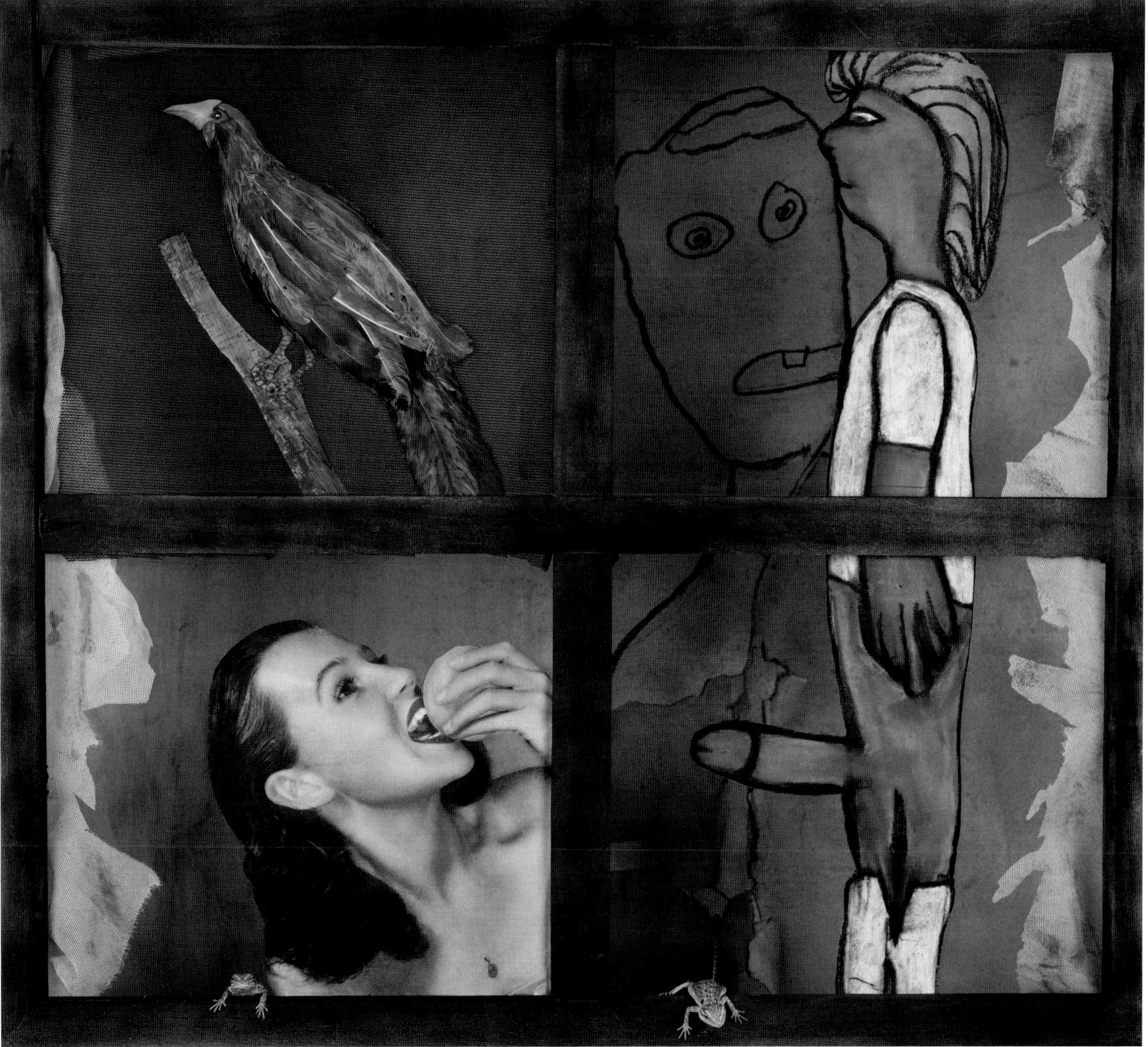

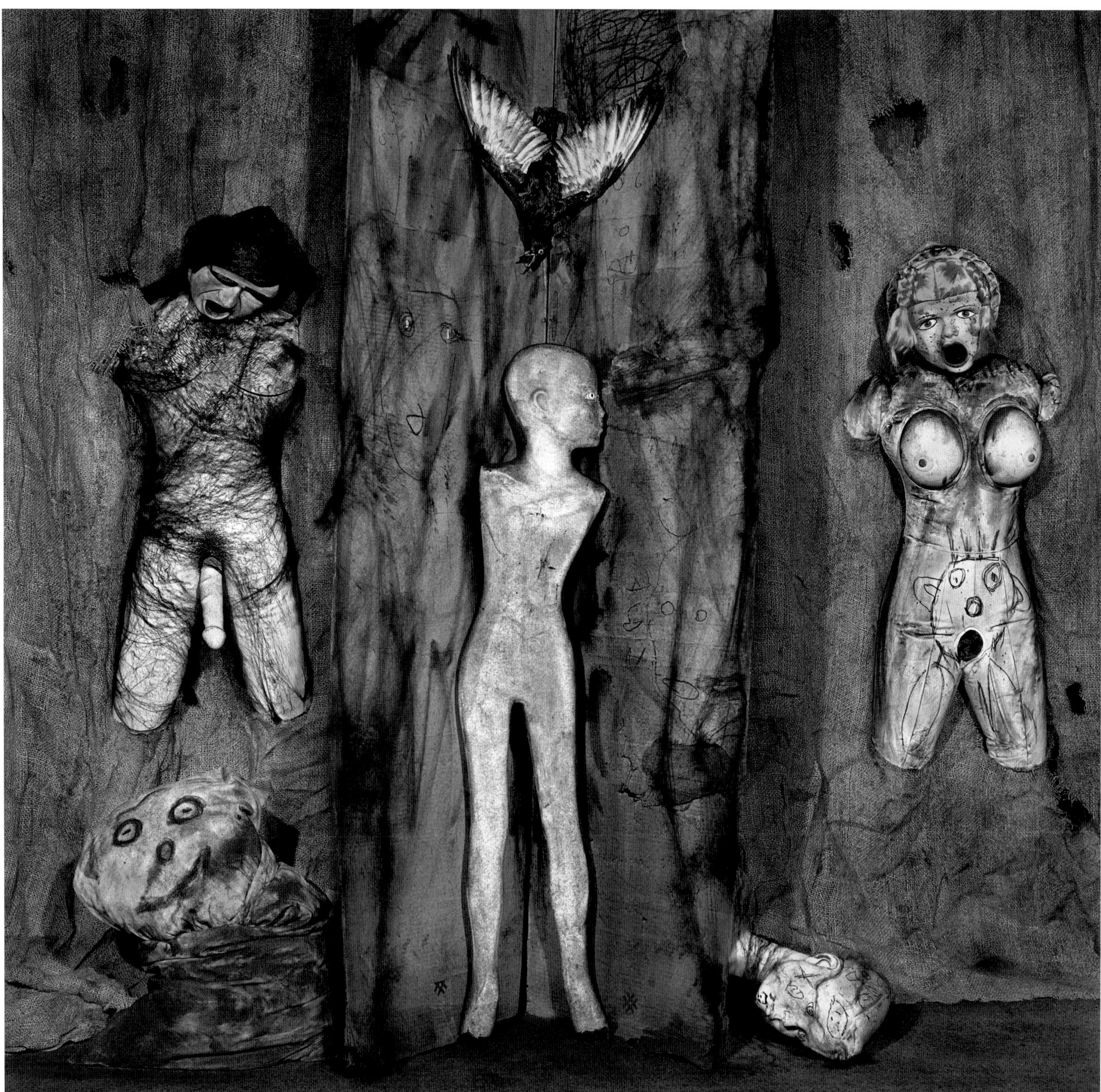

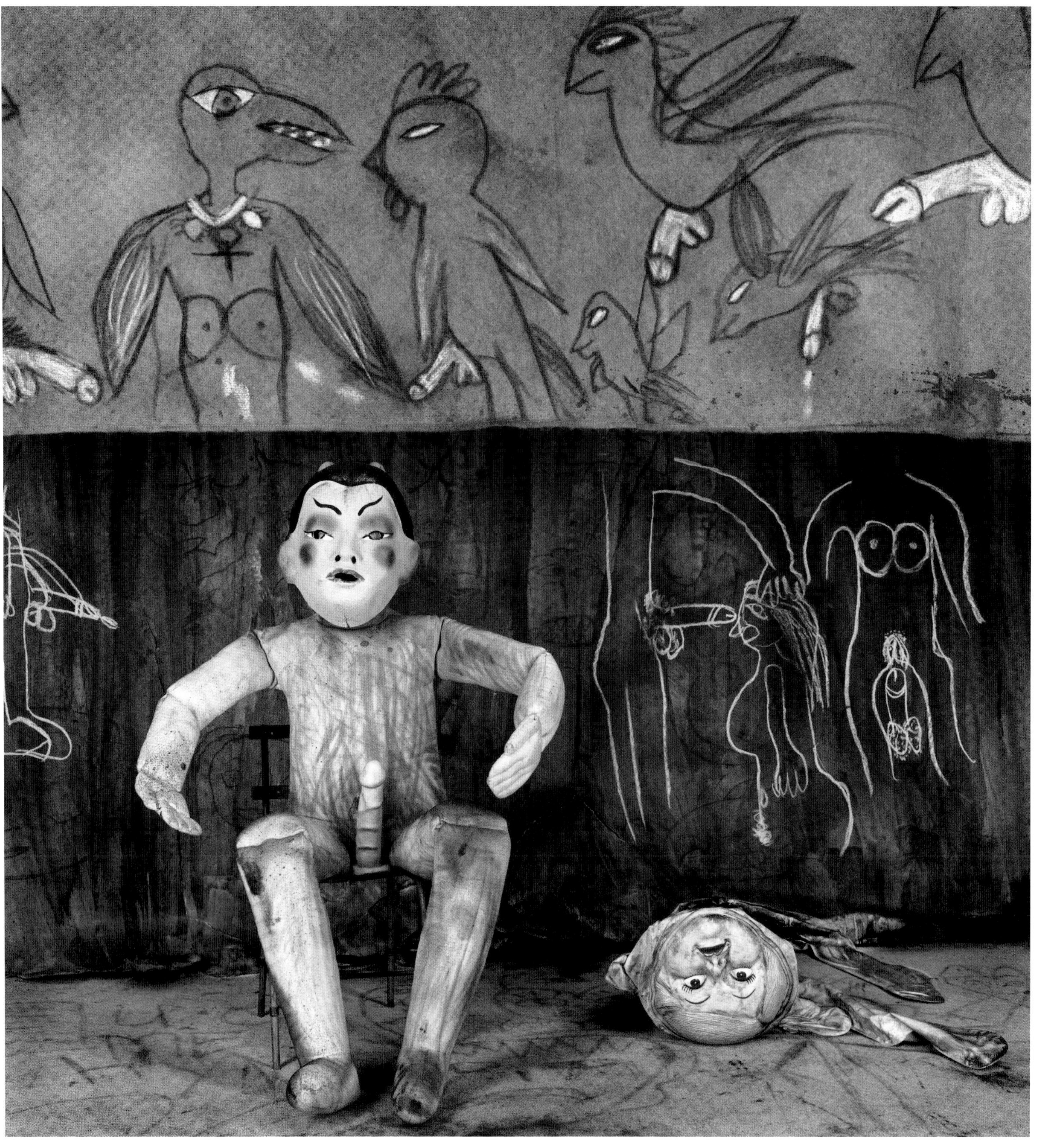

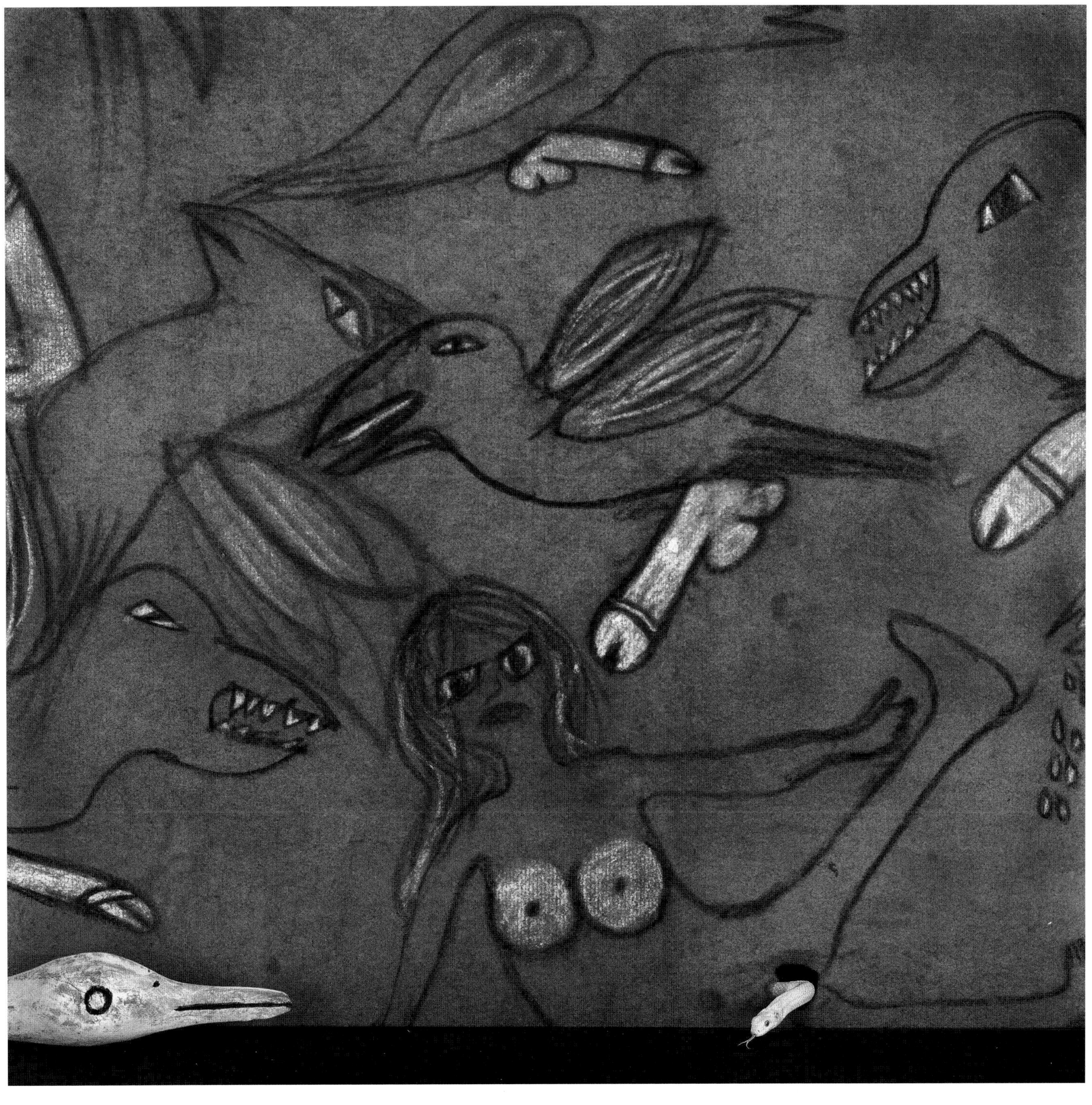

Slithering 2012

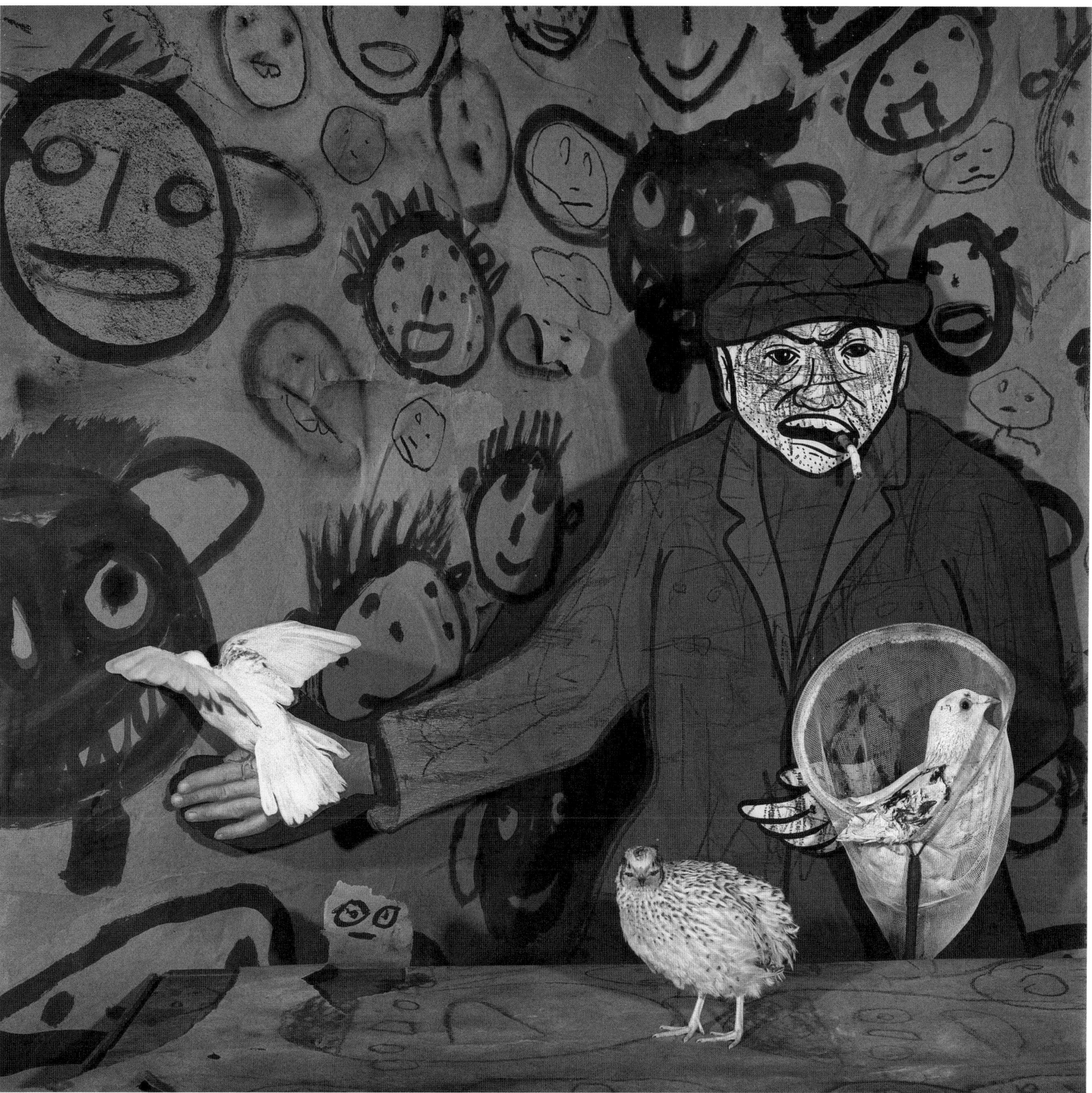

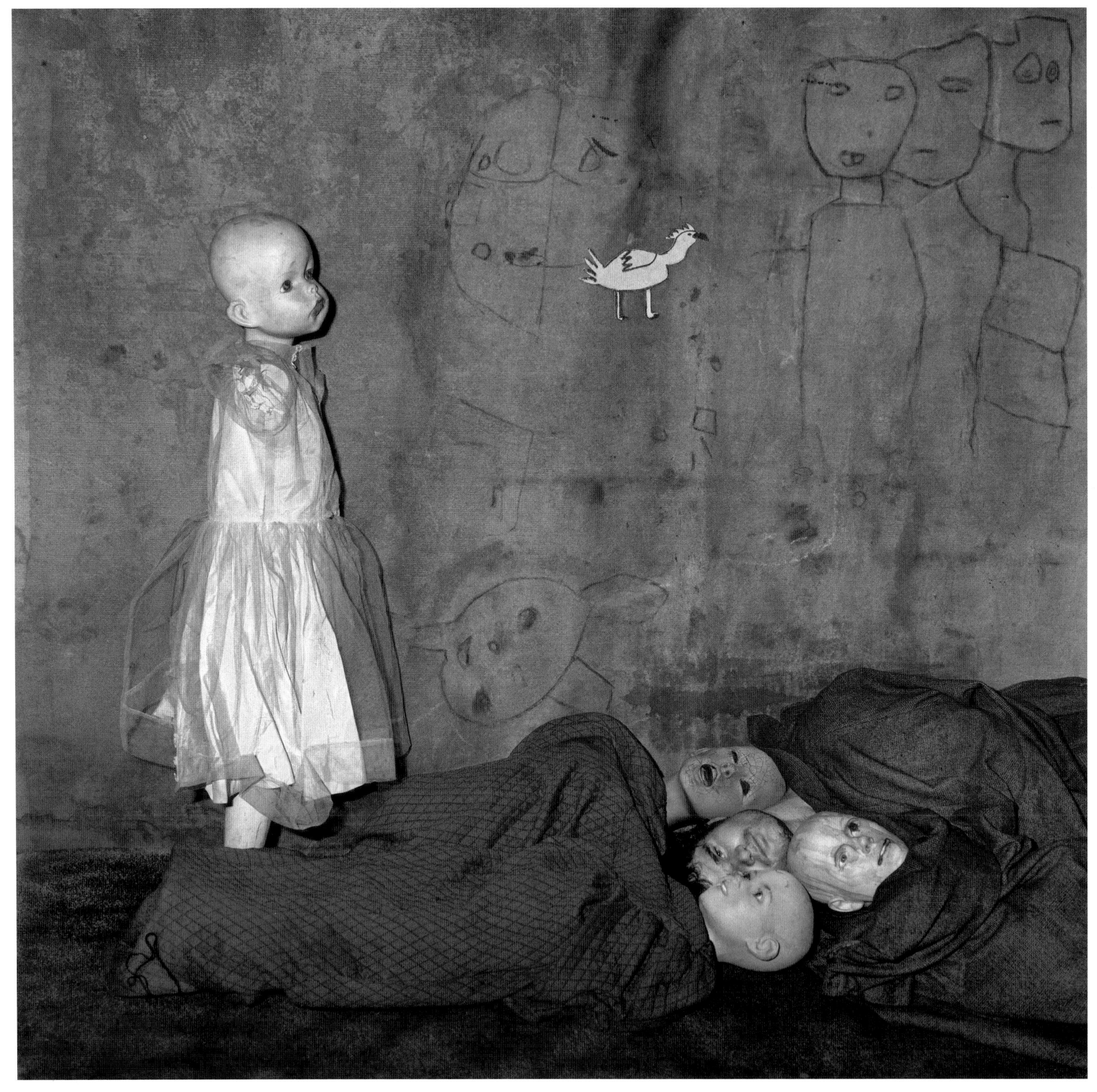

Assimilated 2004

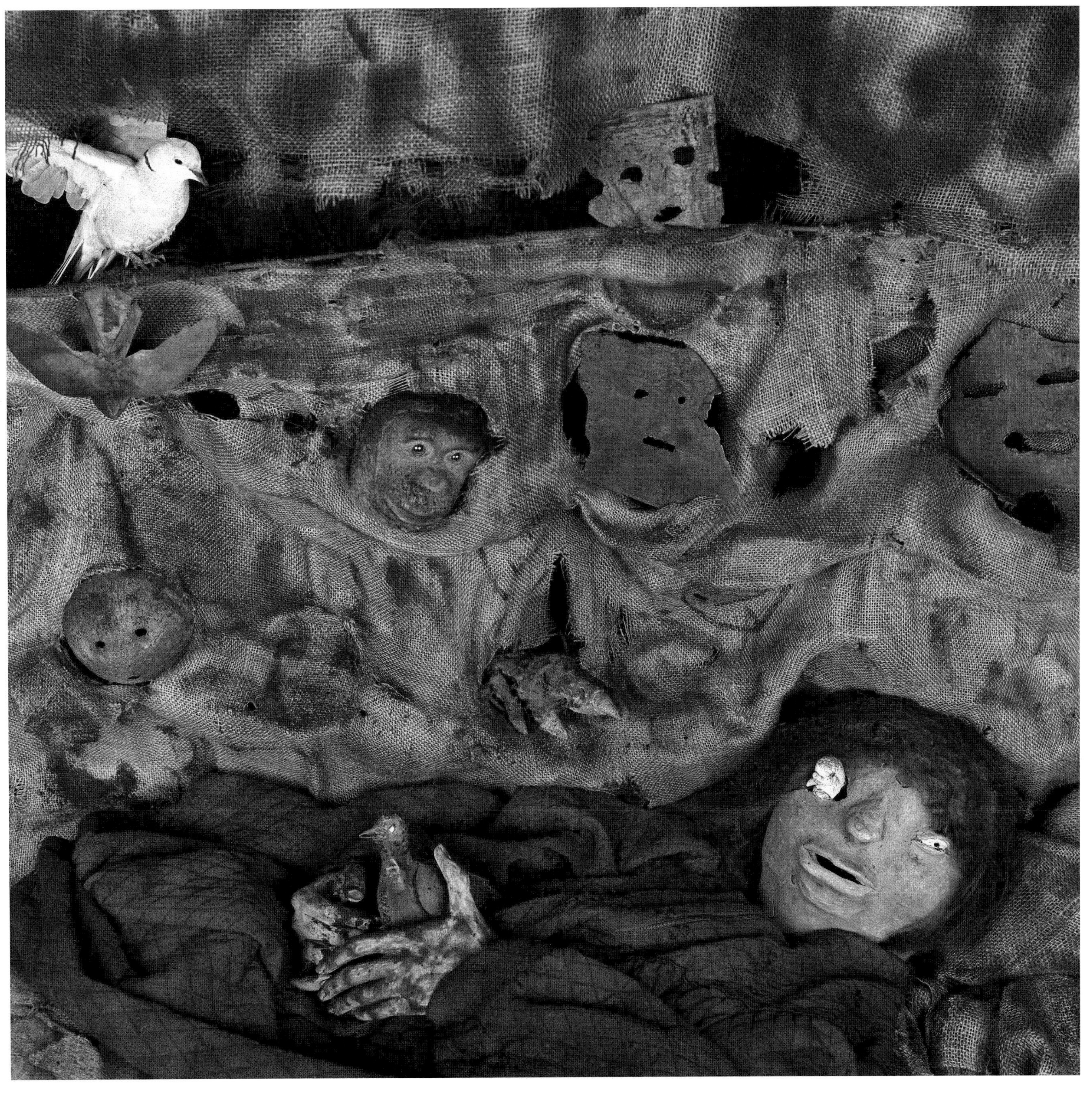

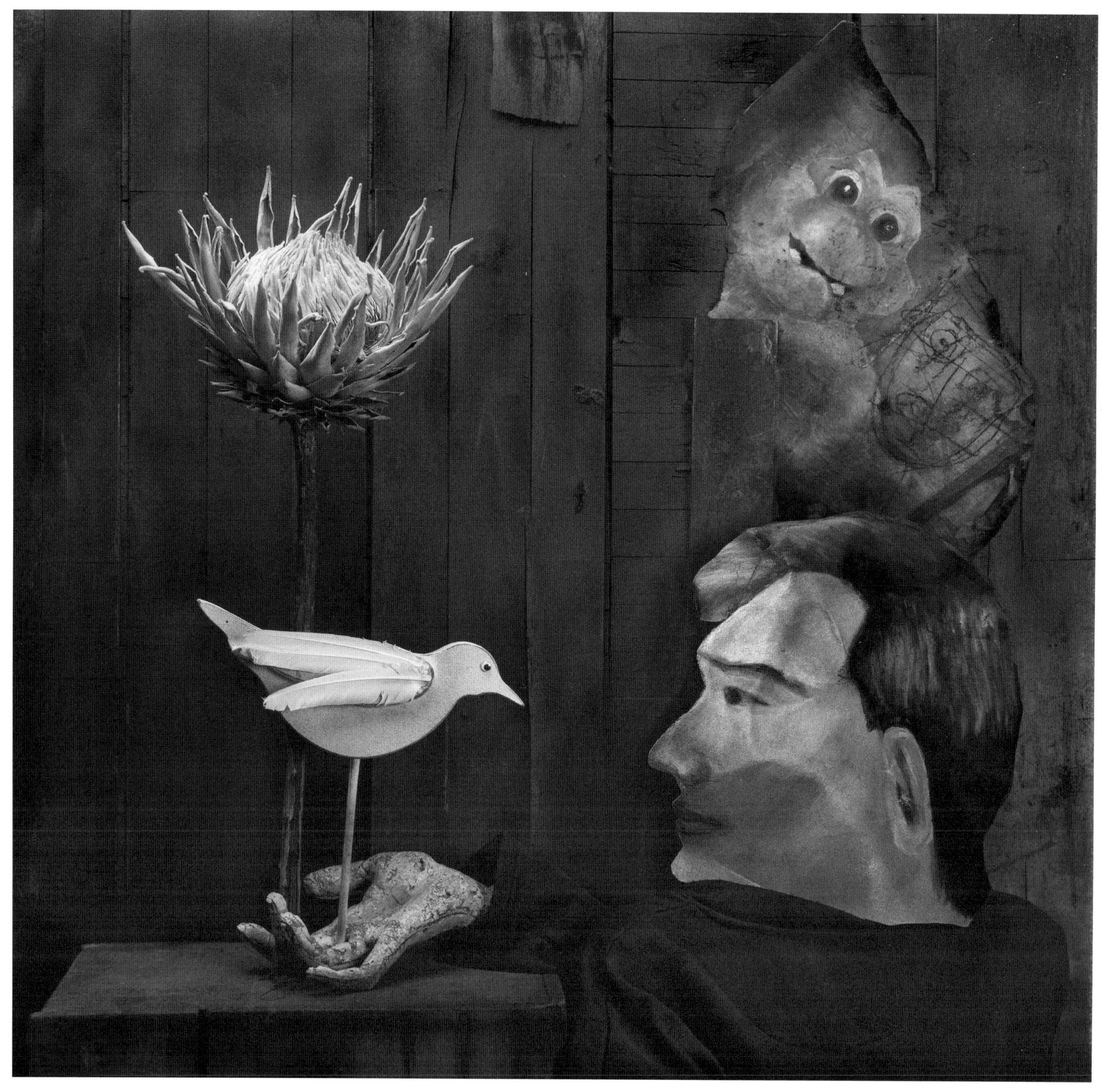

Eye to Eye 2011

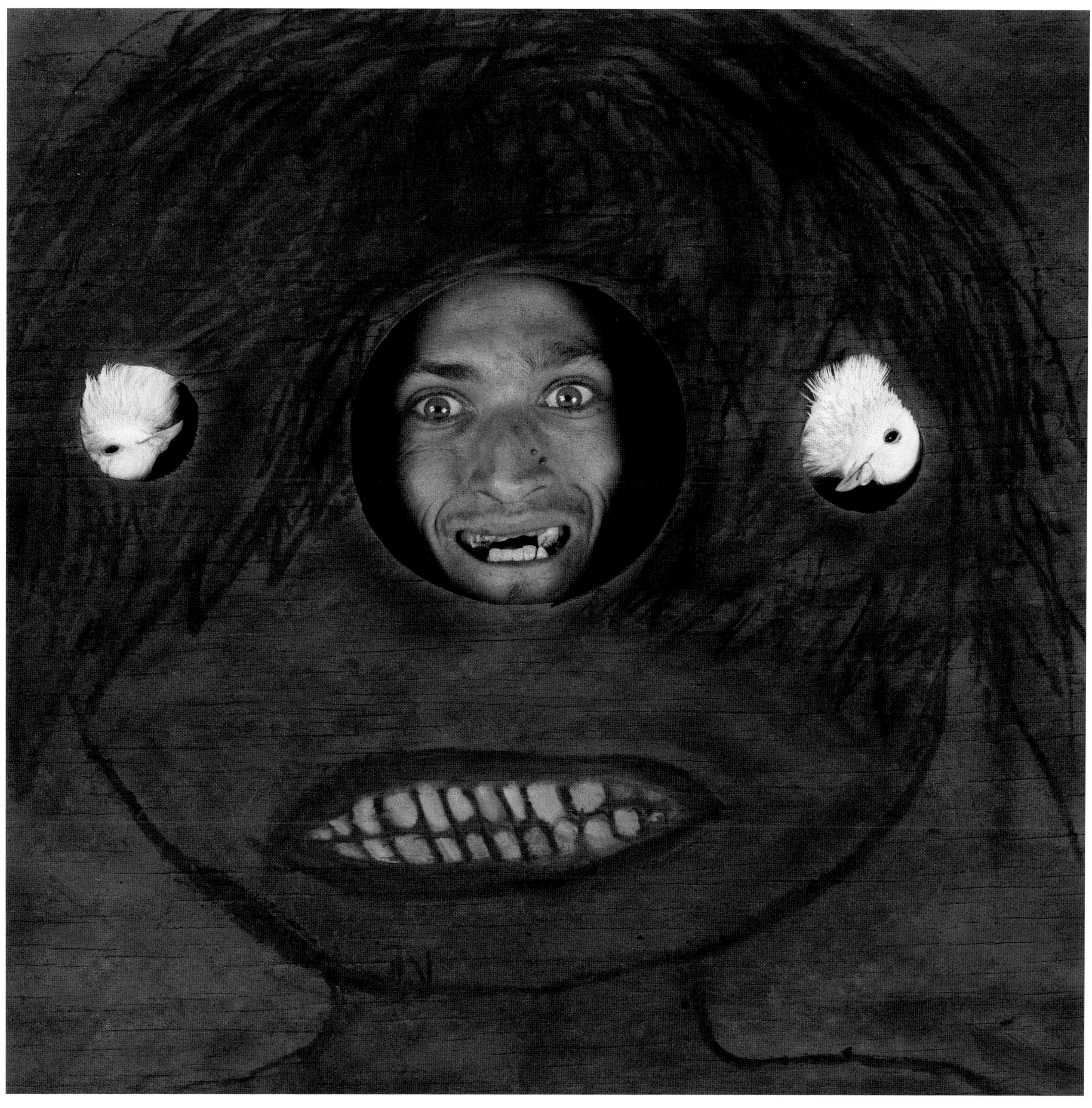

Demented 2012

Threat 2010

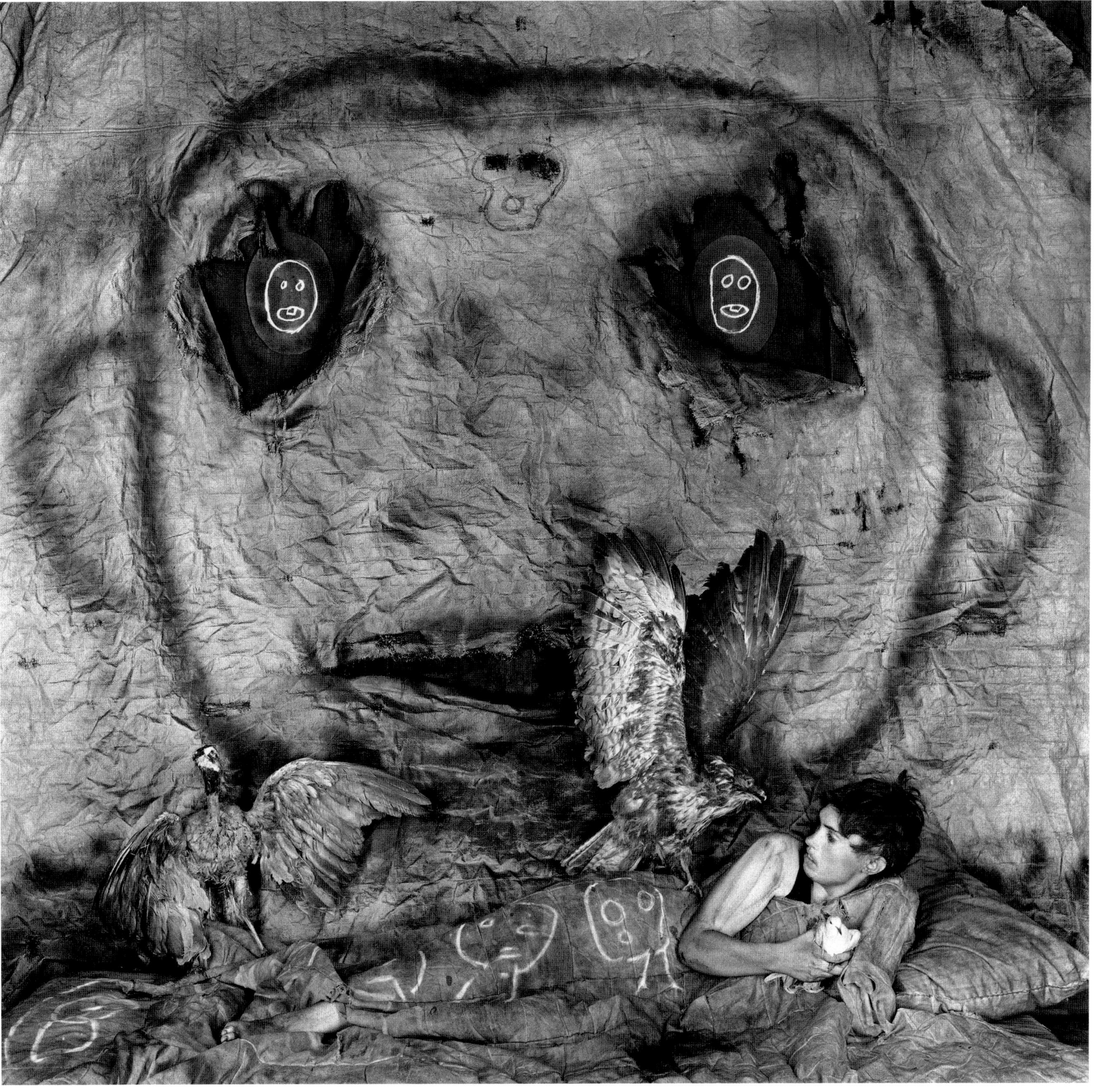

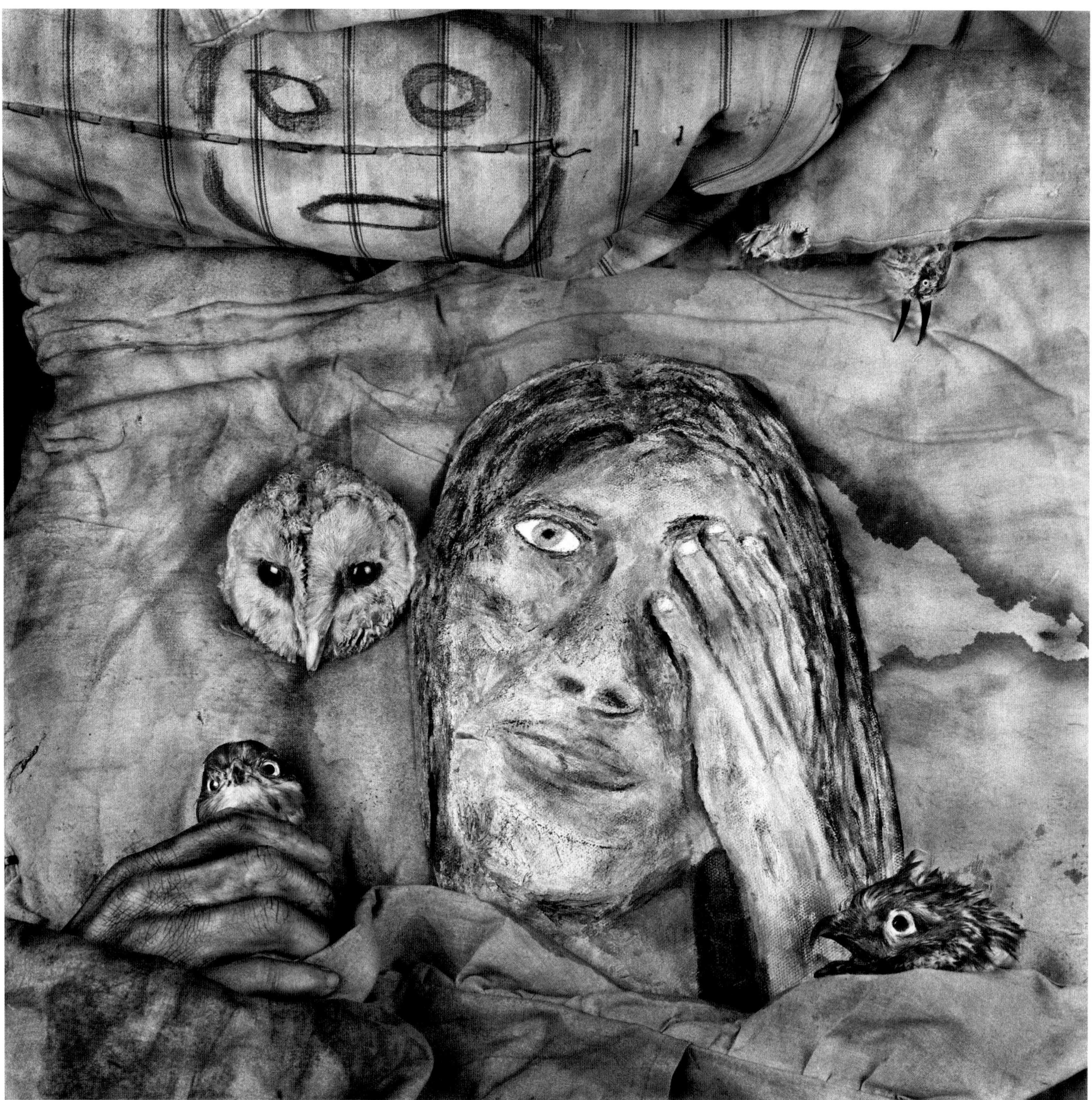

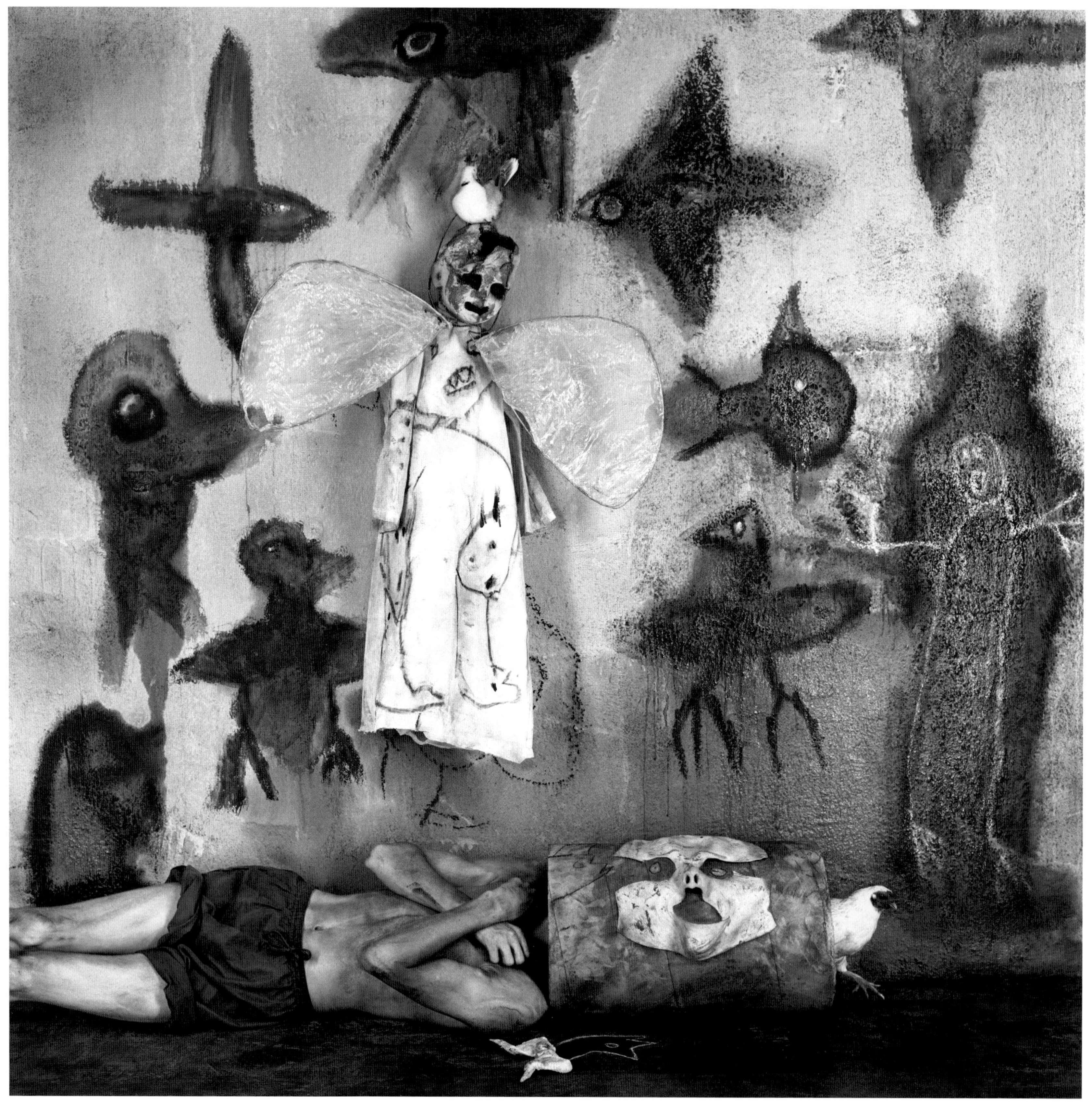

Suspended 2012

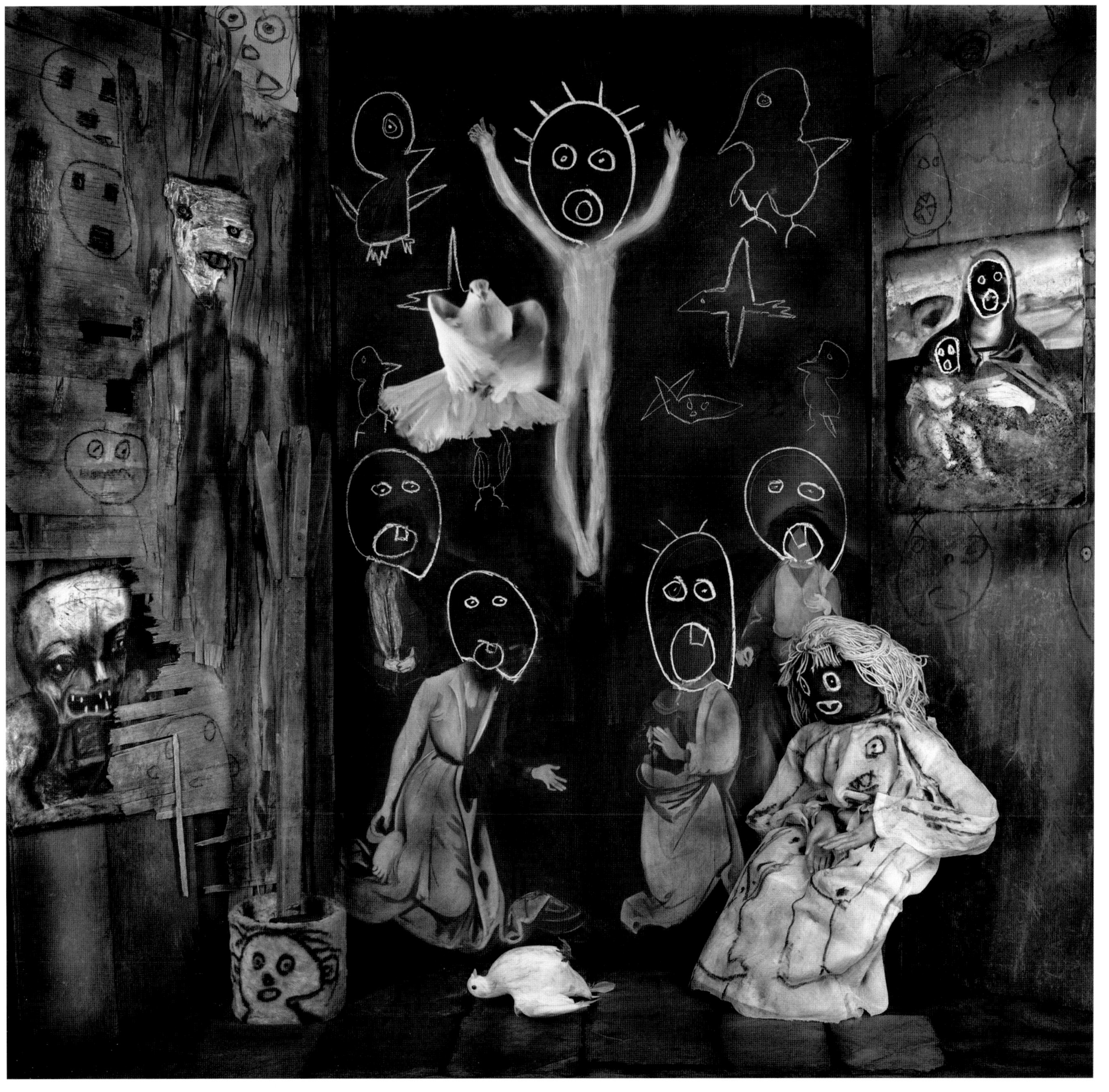

Ascension 2013

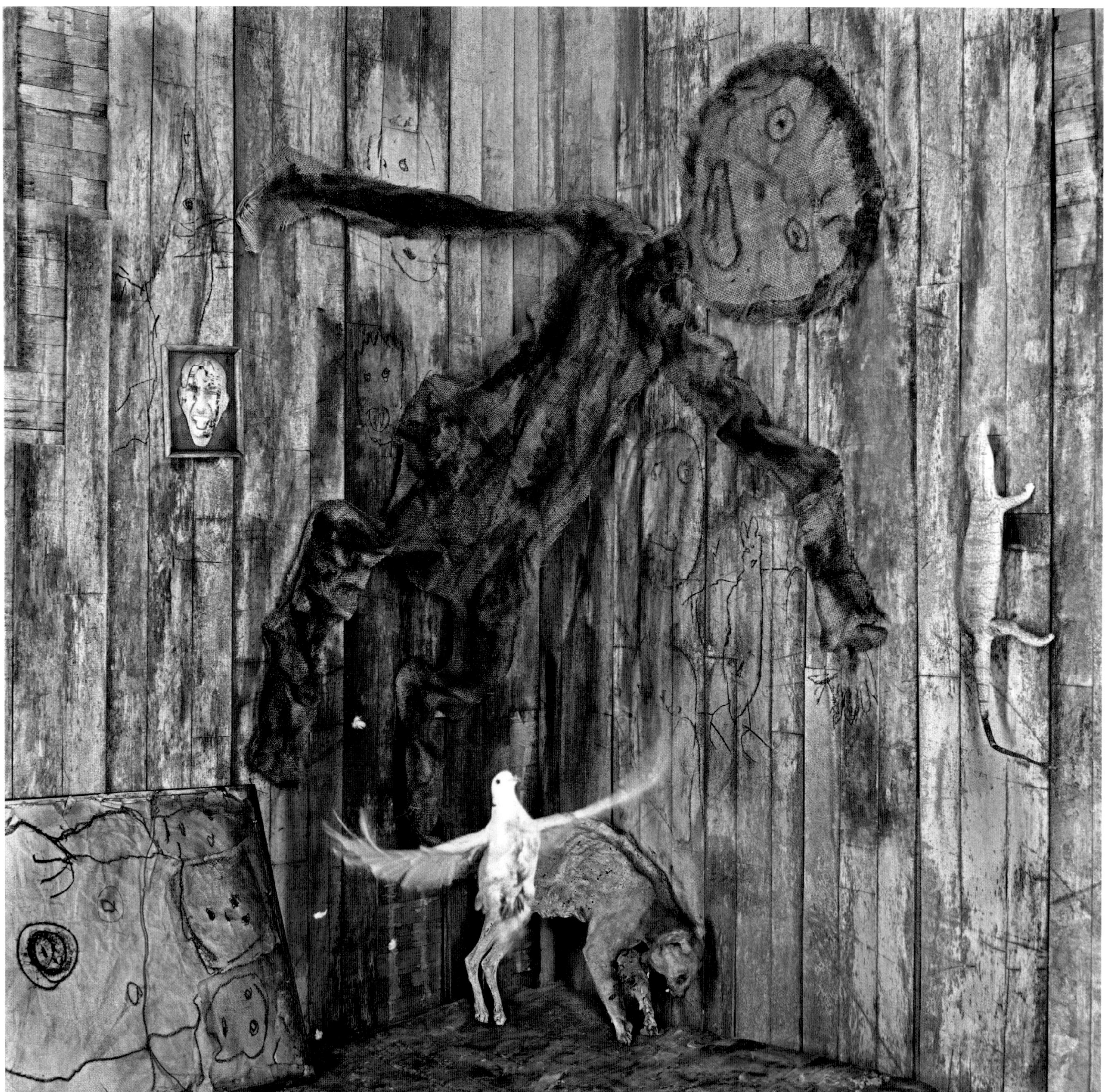

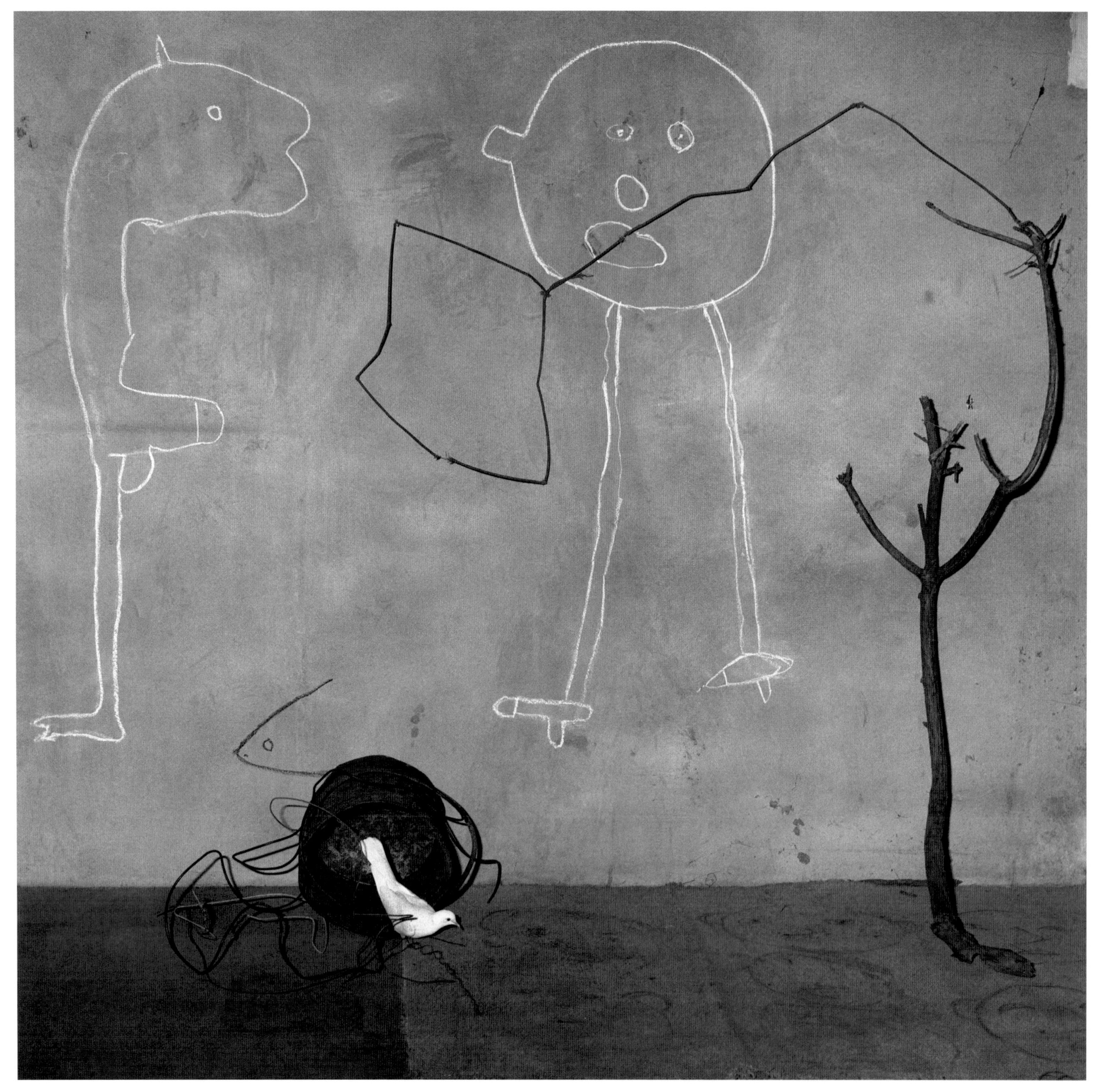

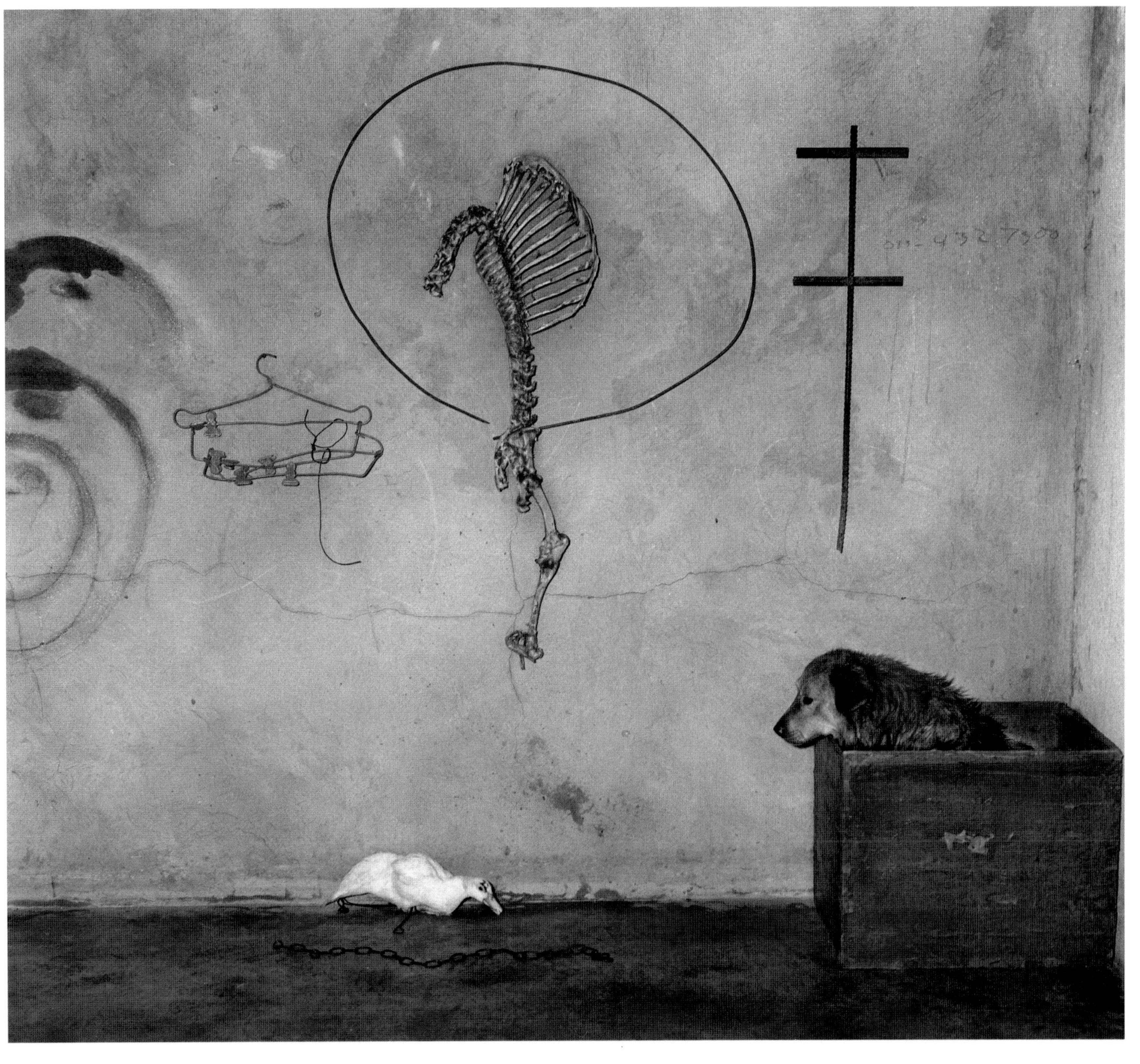

Dog Box 2003

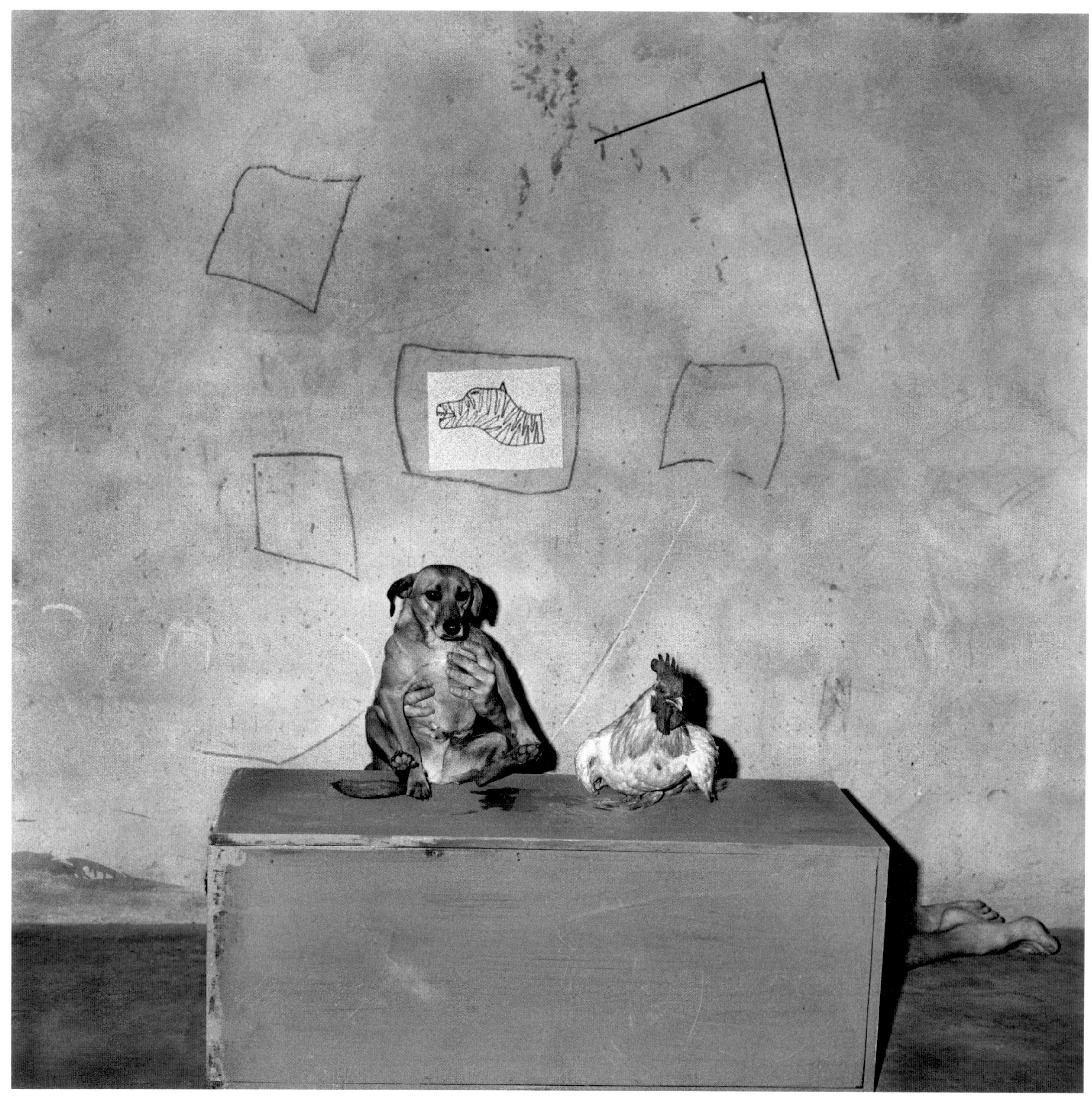

Podium 2003

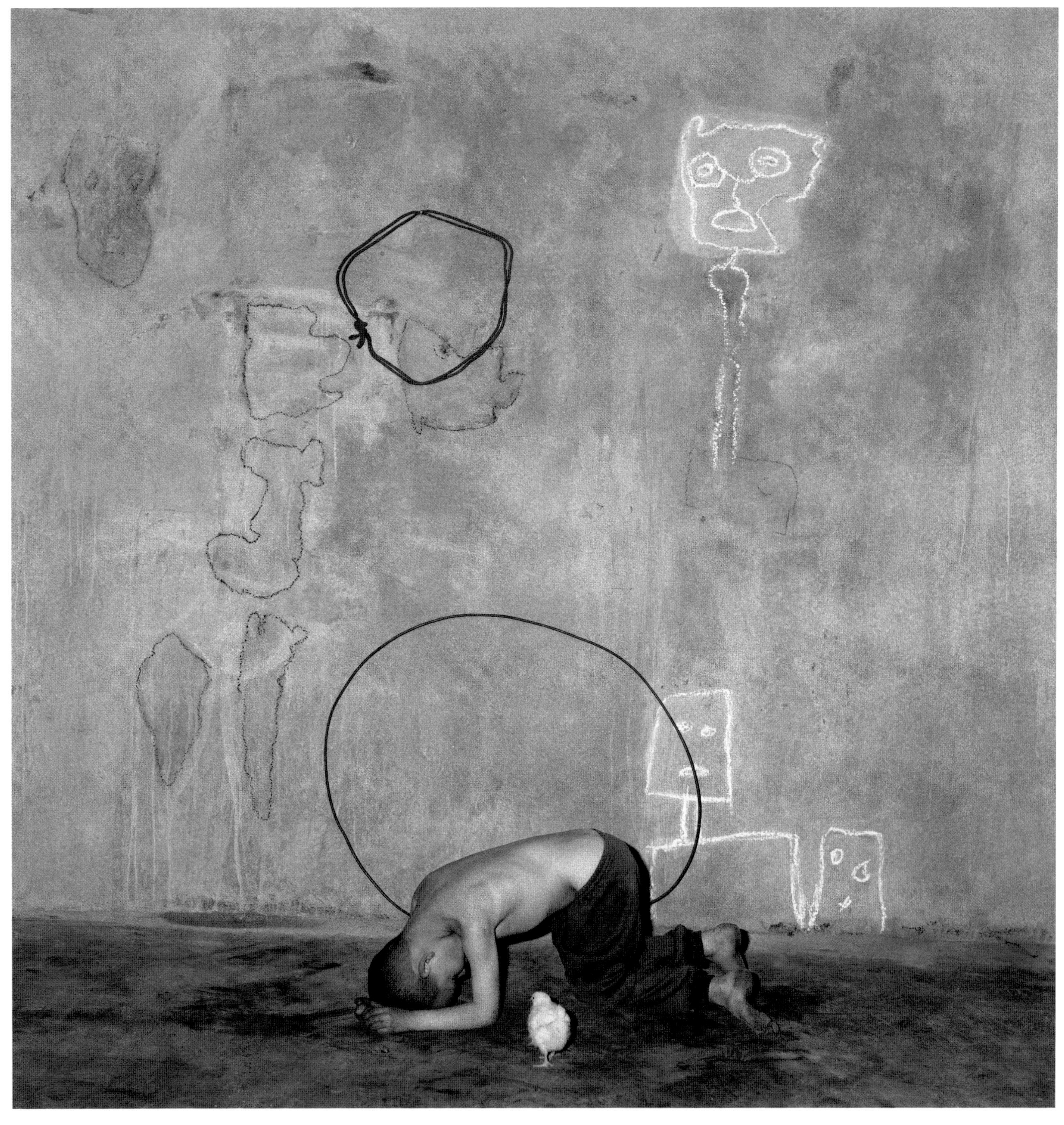

Invitation 2003

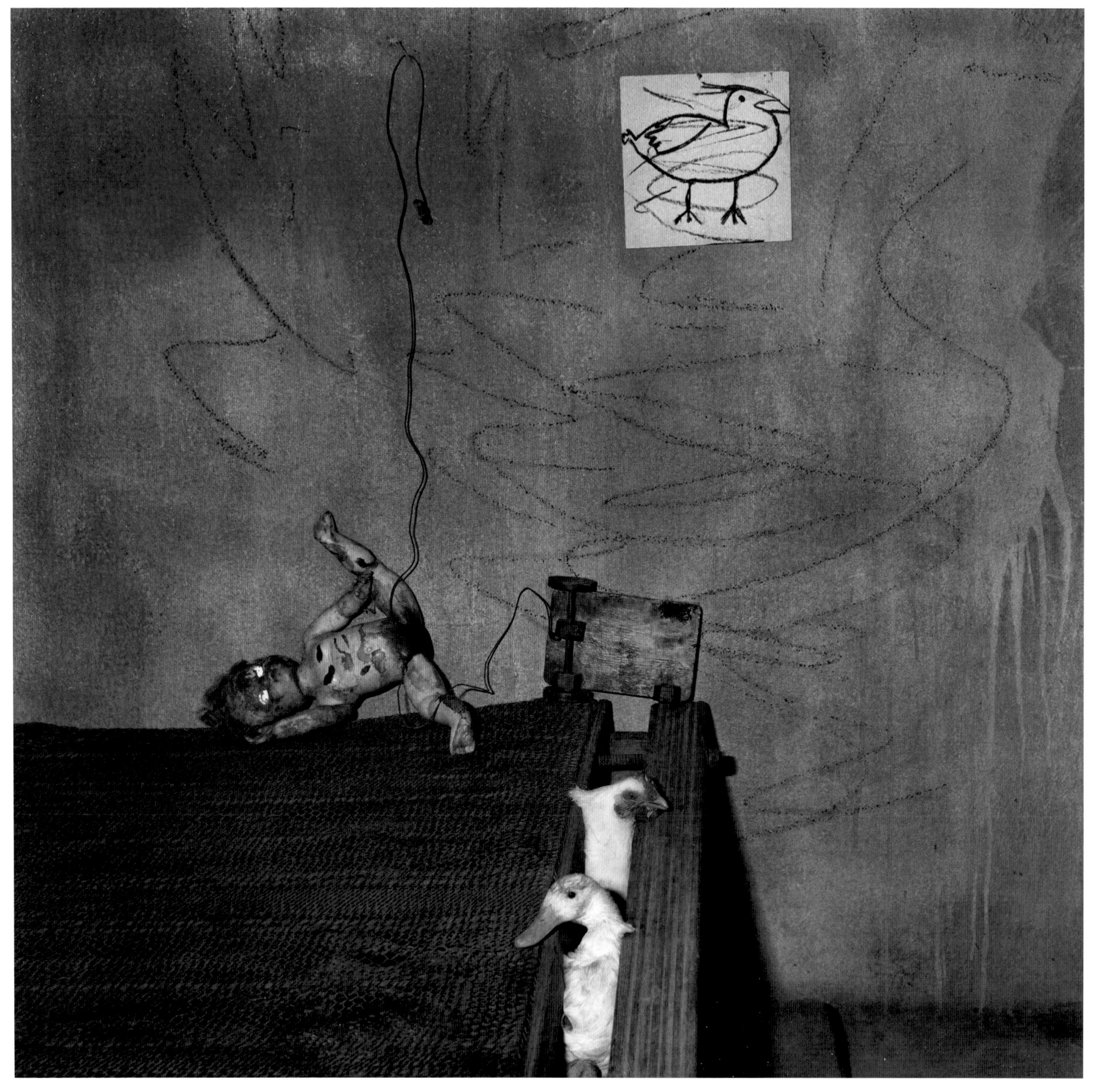

Stuck 2004

94

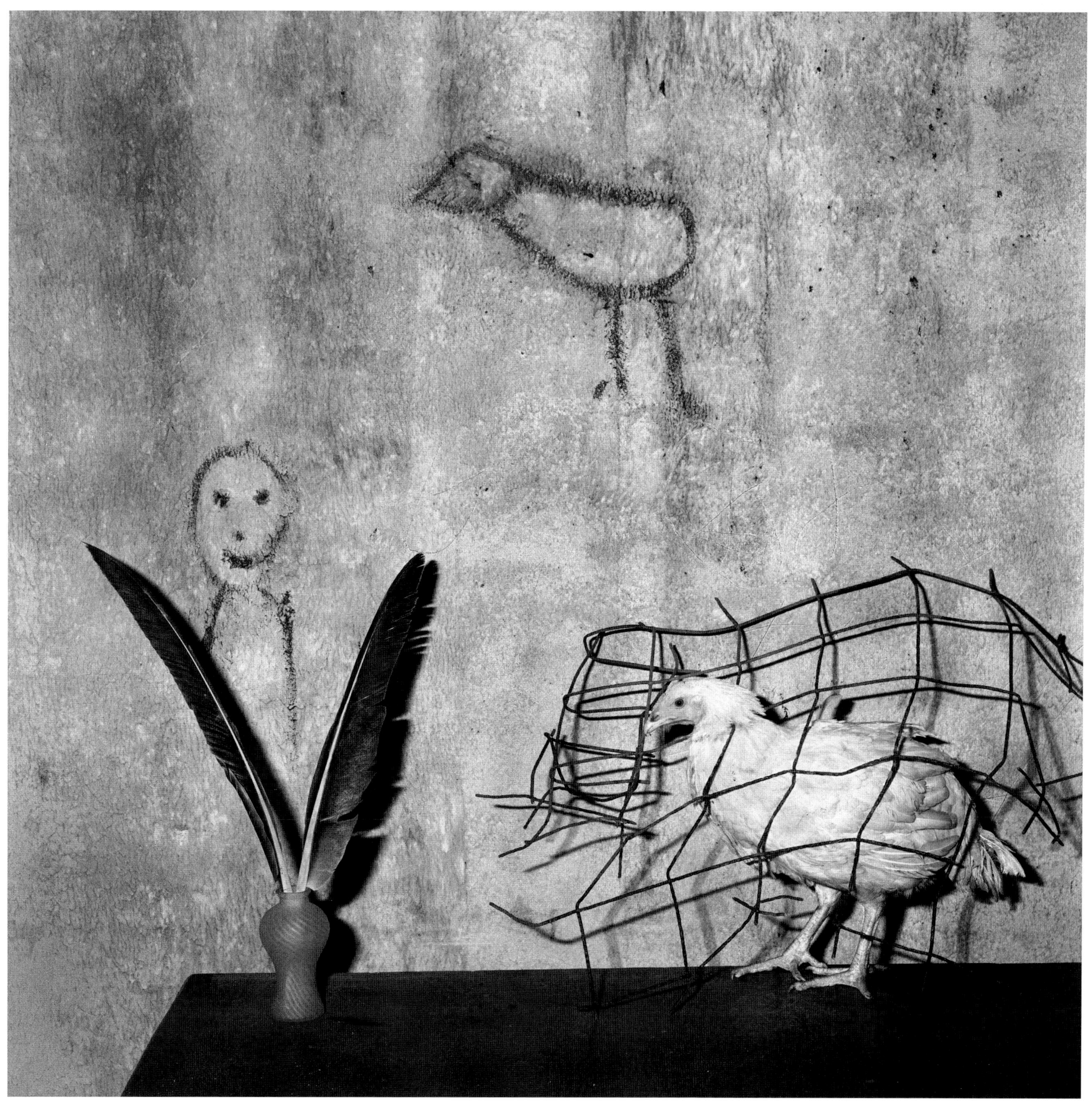

Ensnared 2005

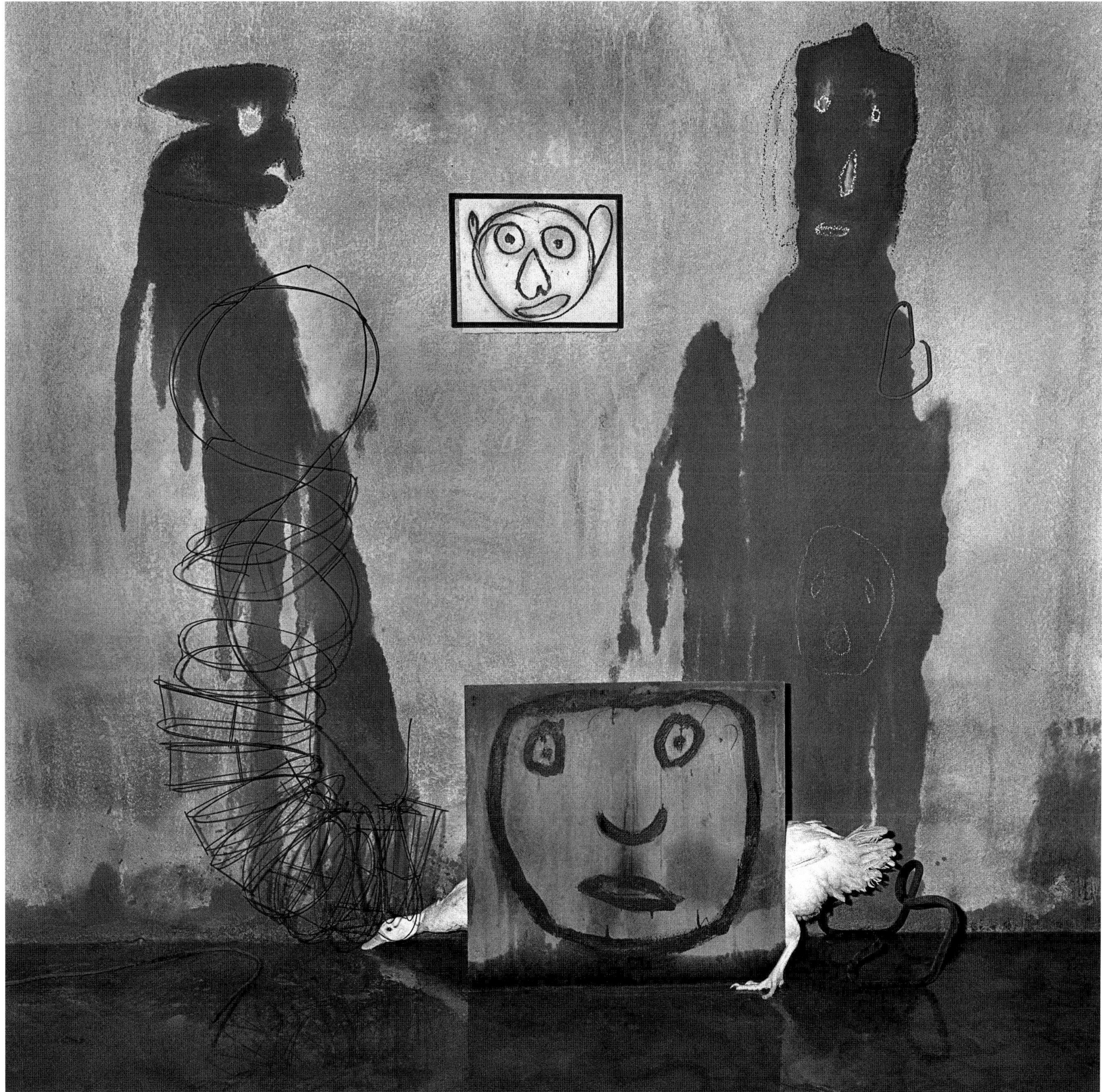

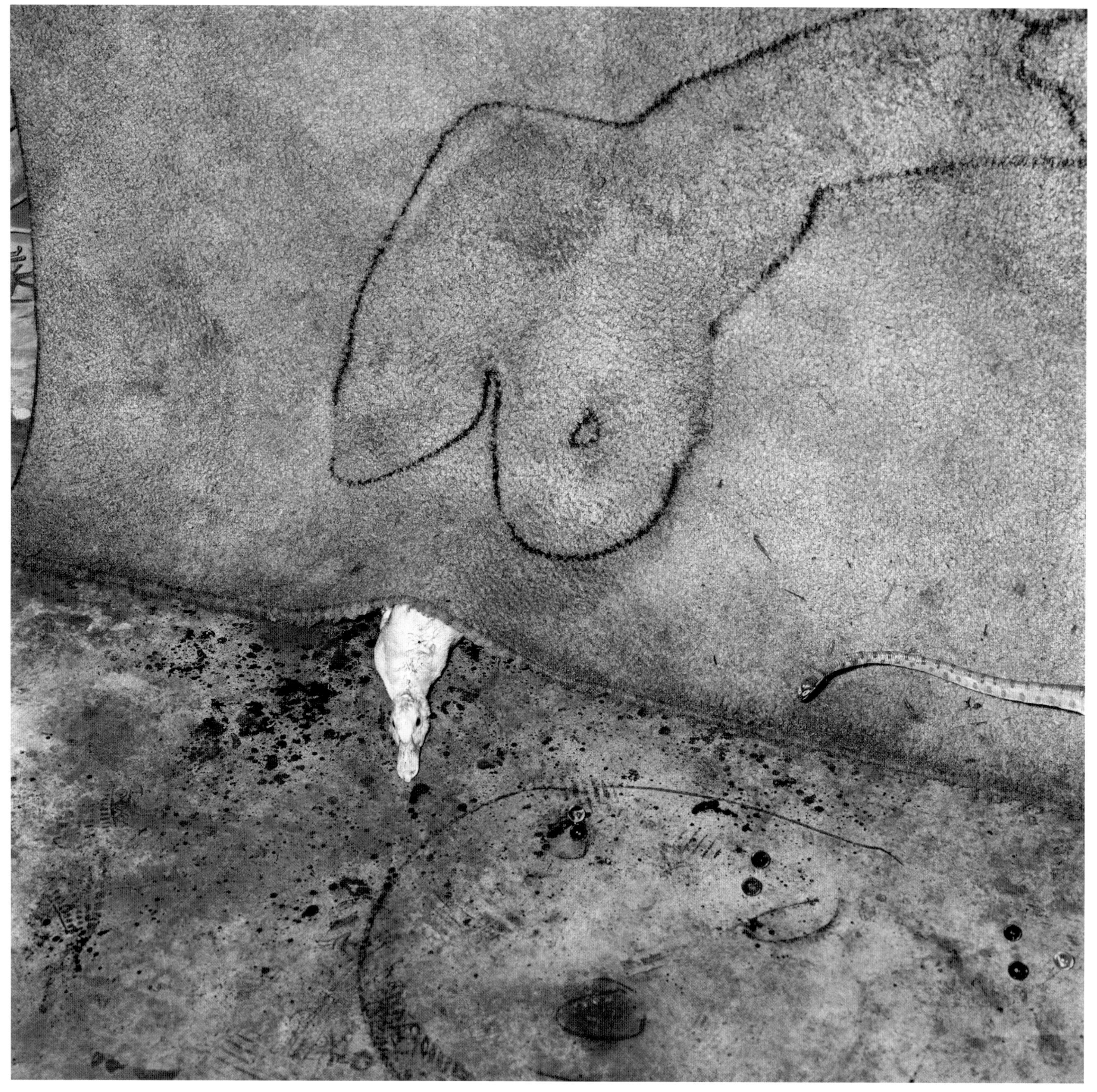

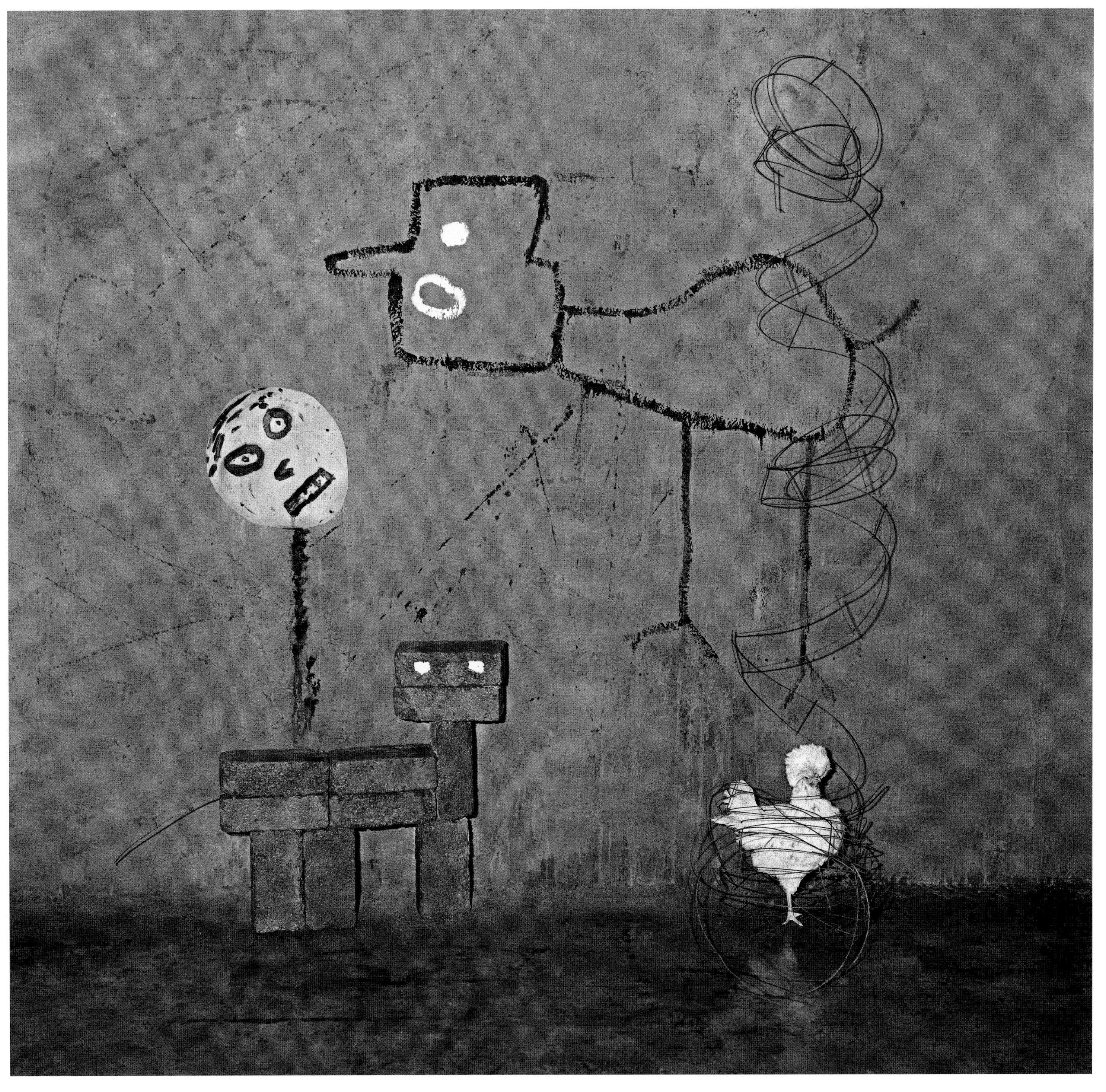

Spinning 2006

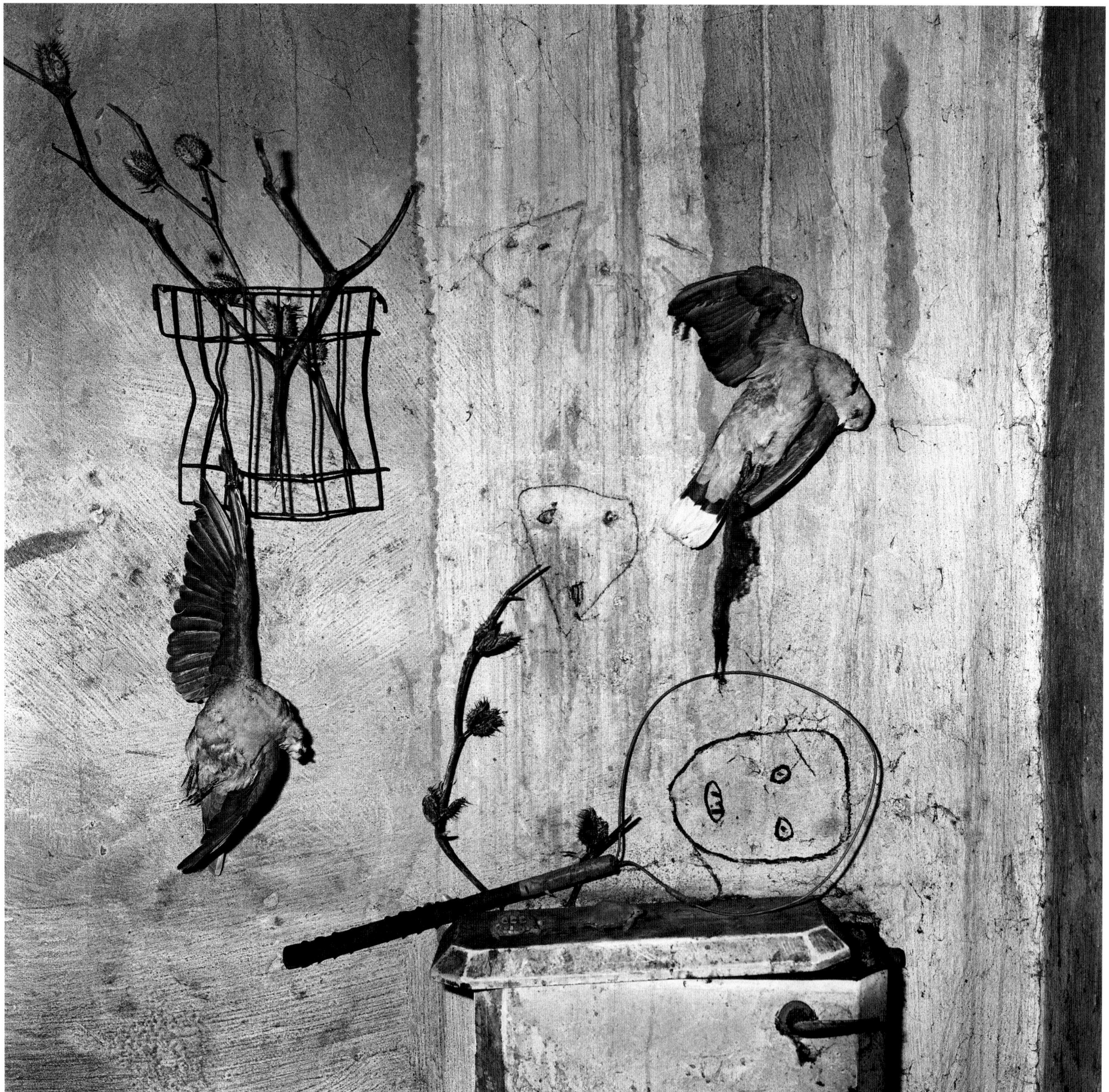

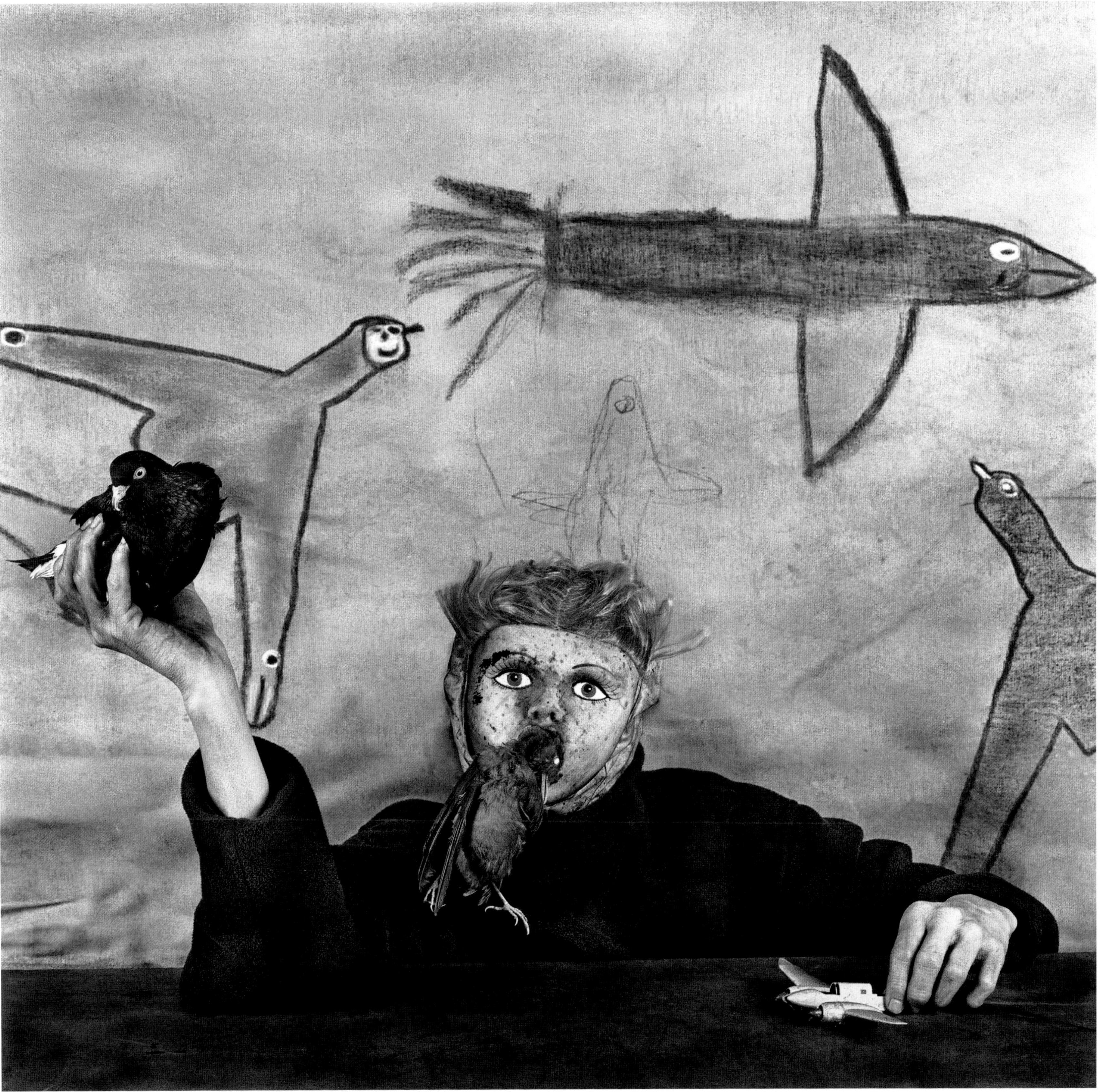

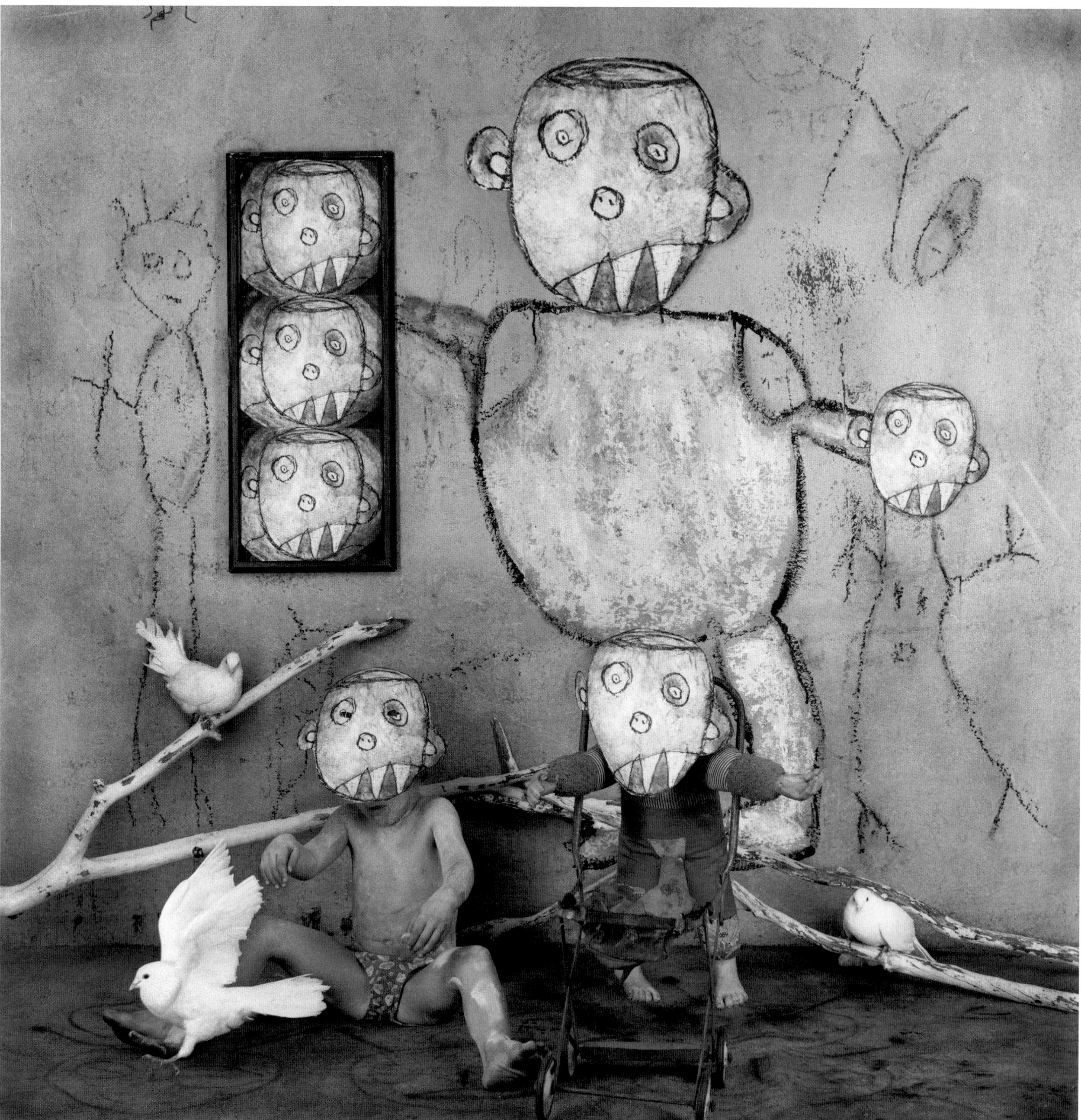

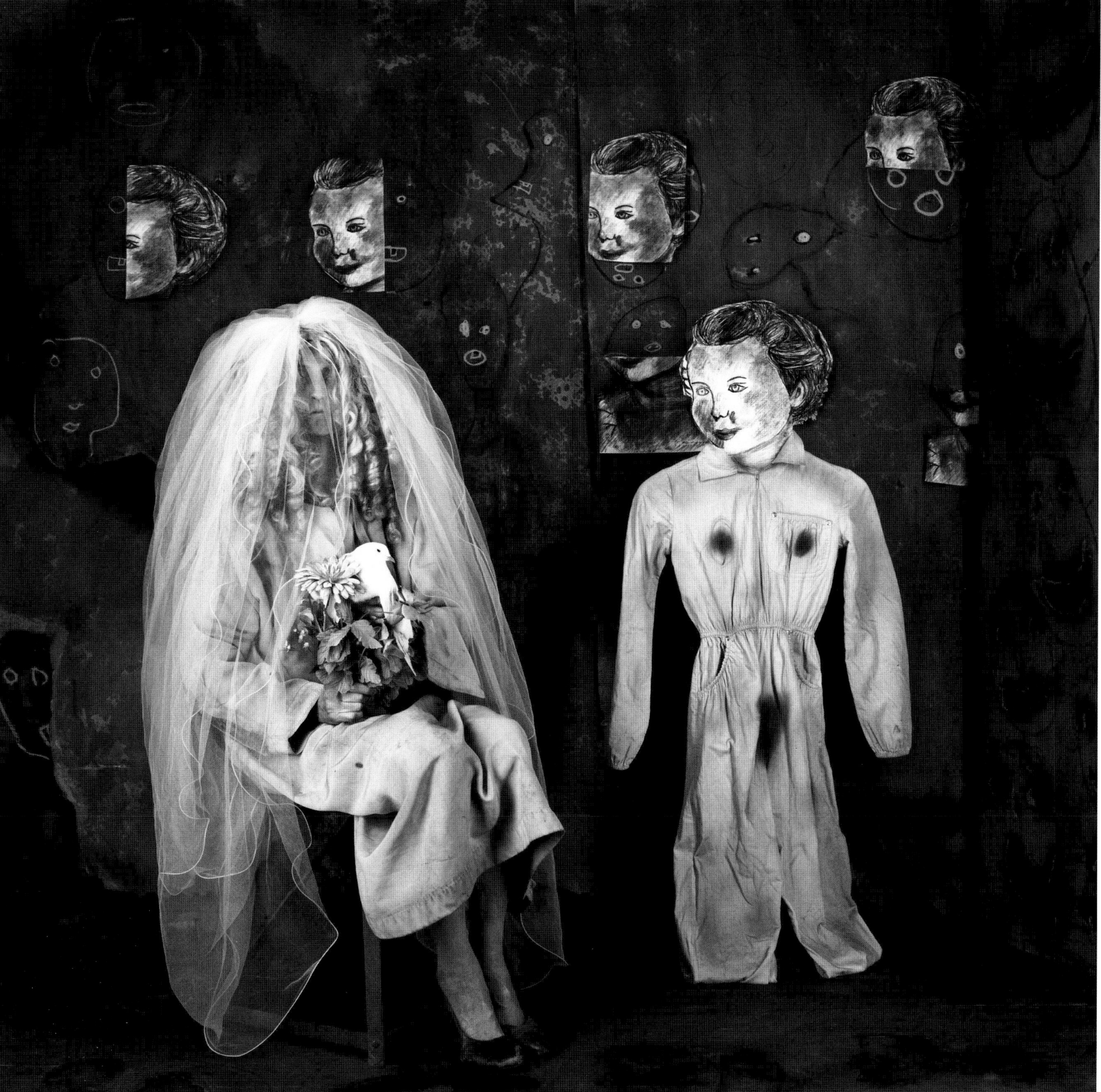

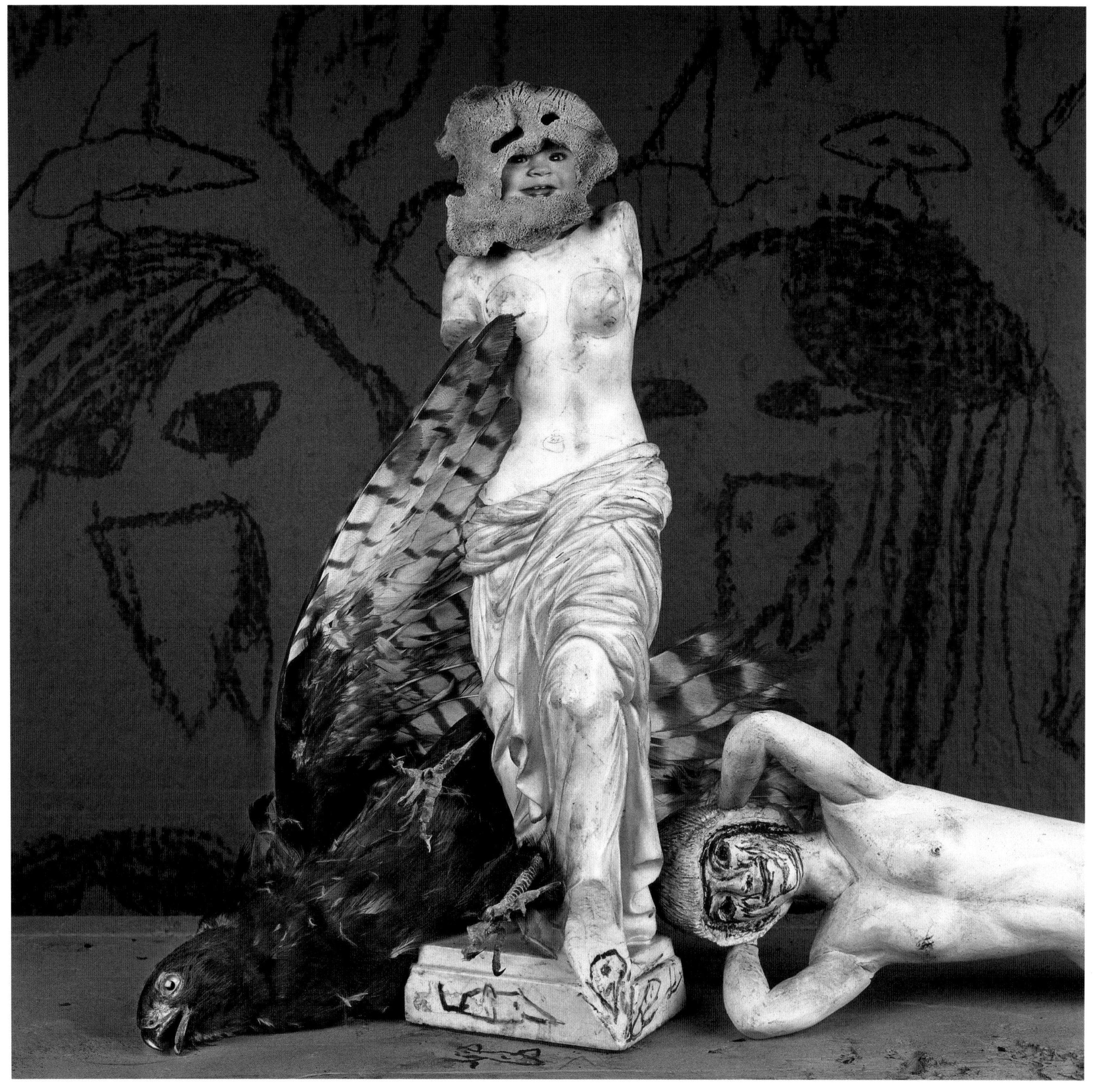

Fallen 2011

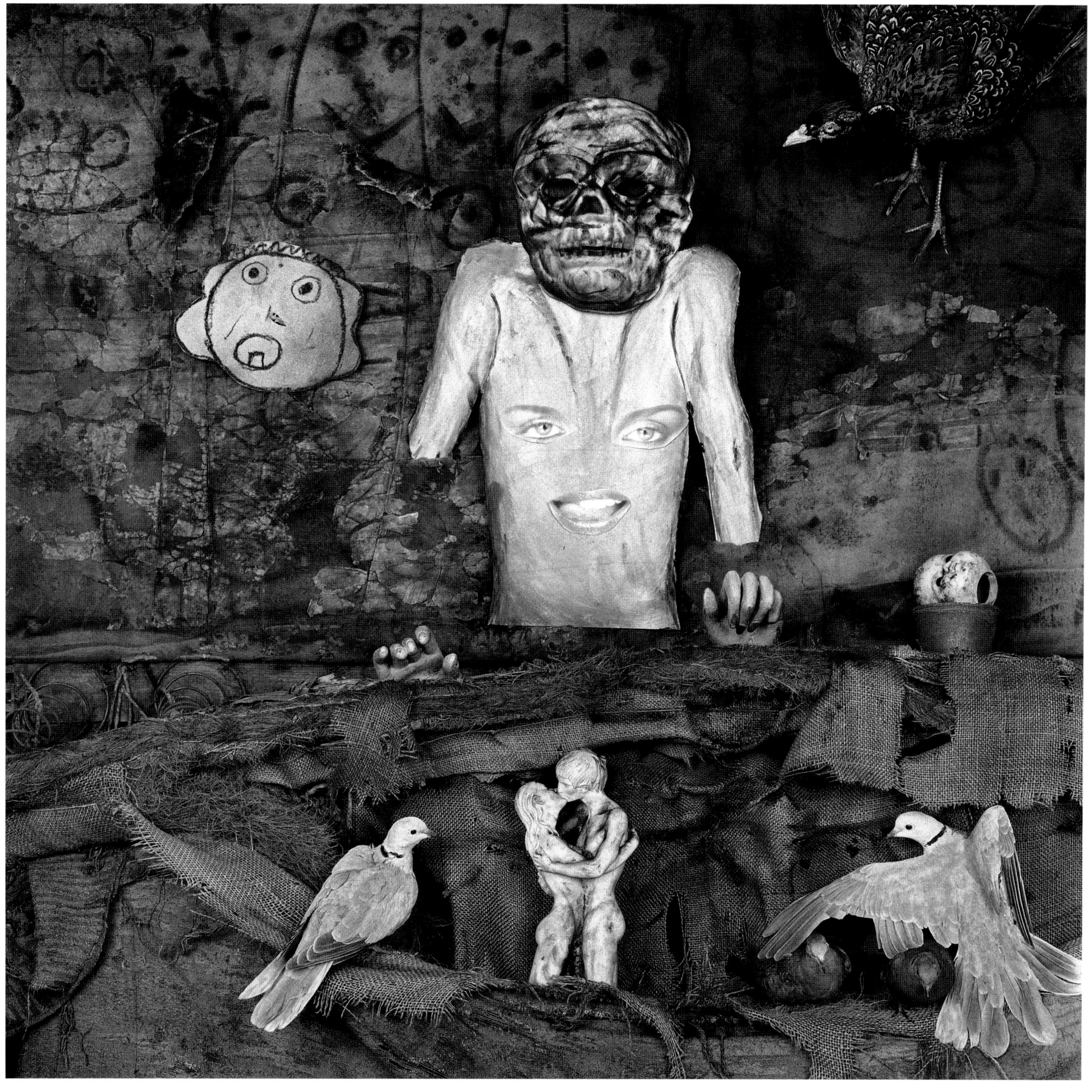

Love Scene 2010

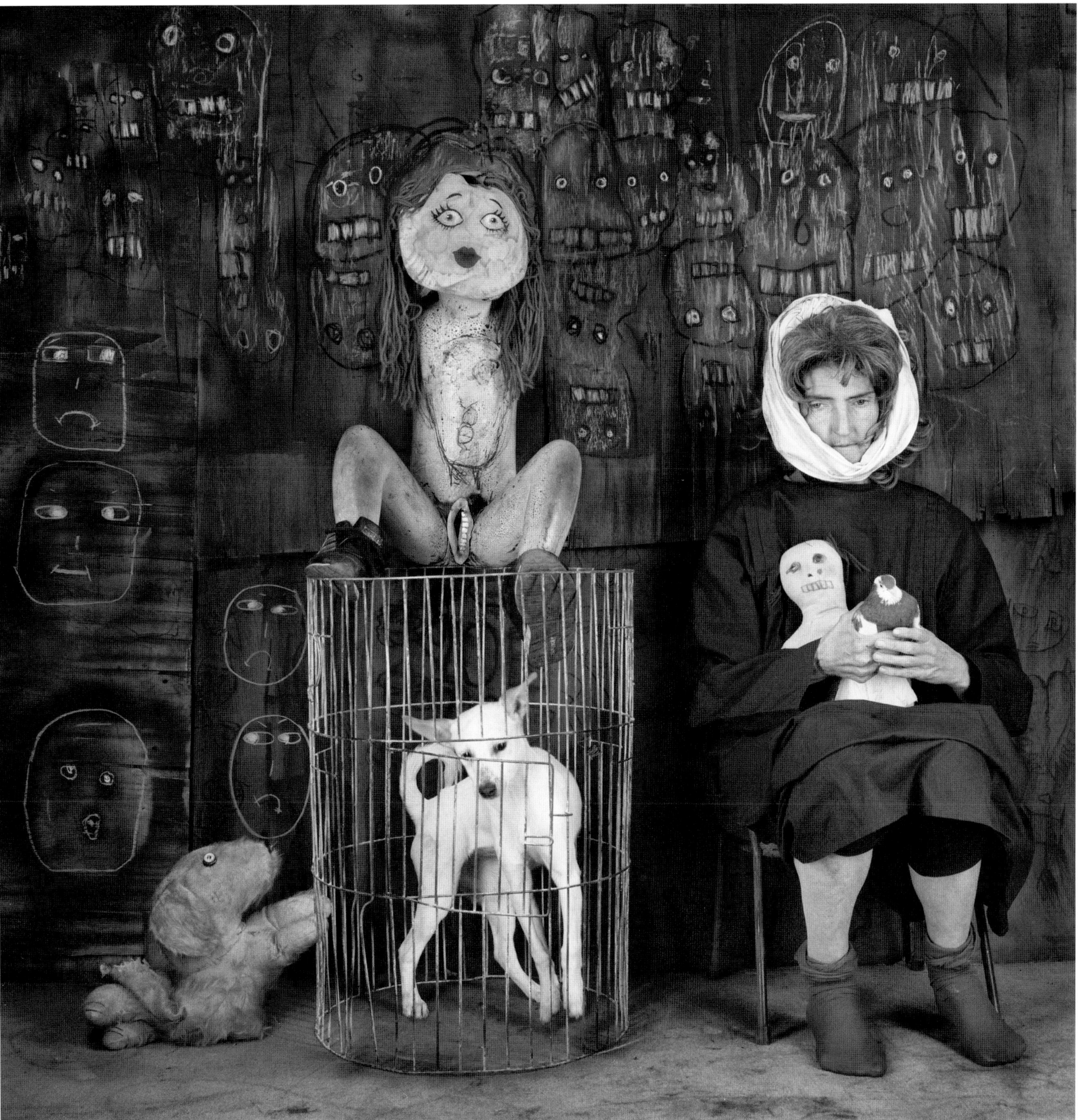

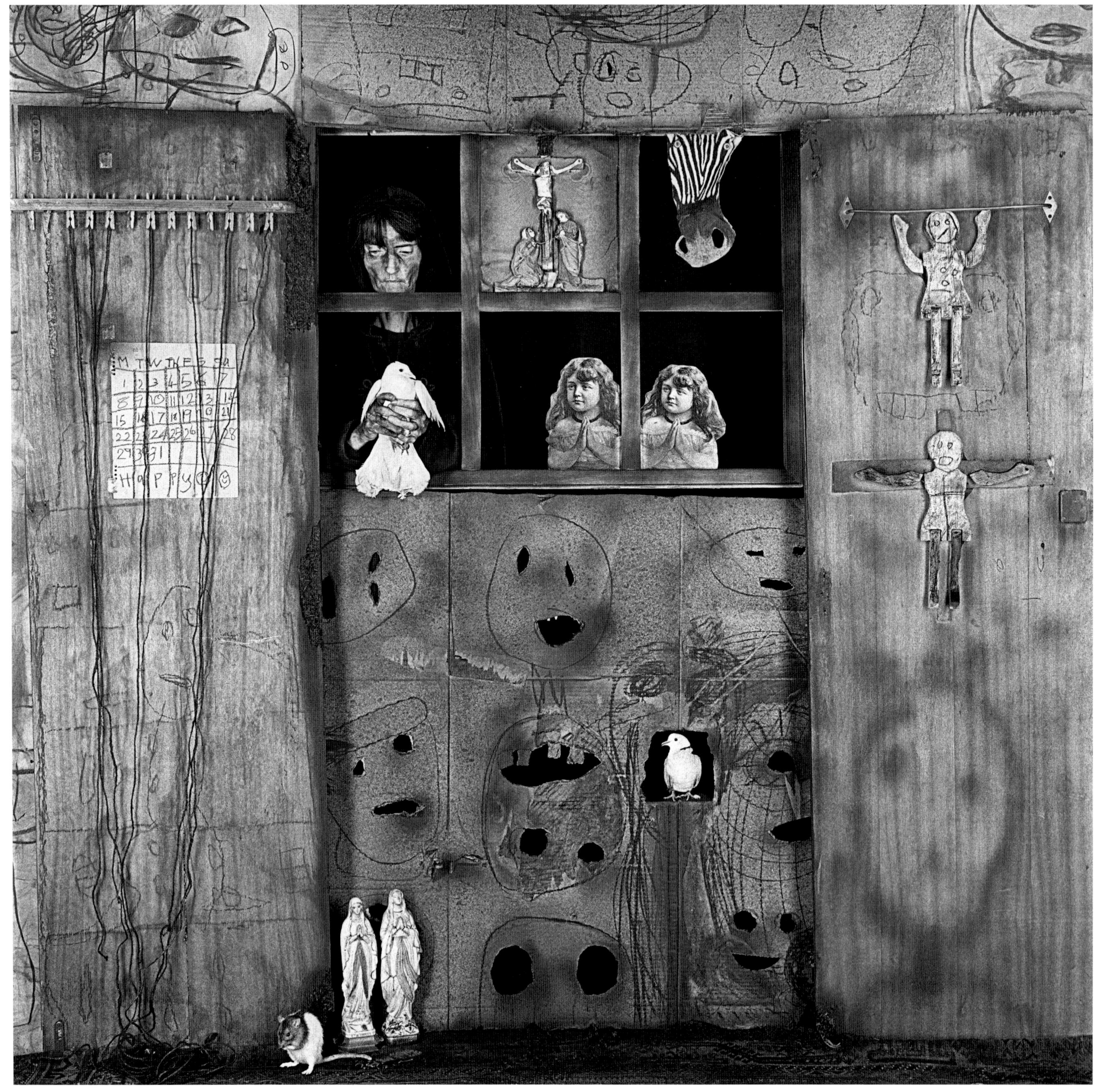

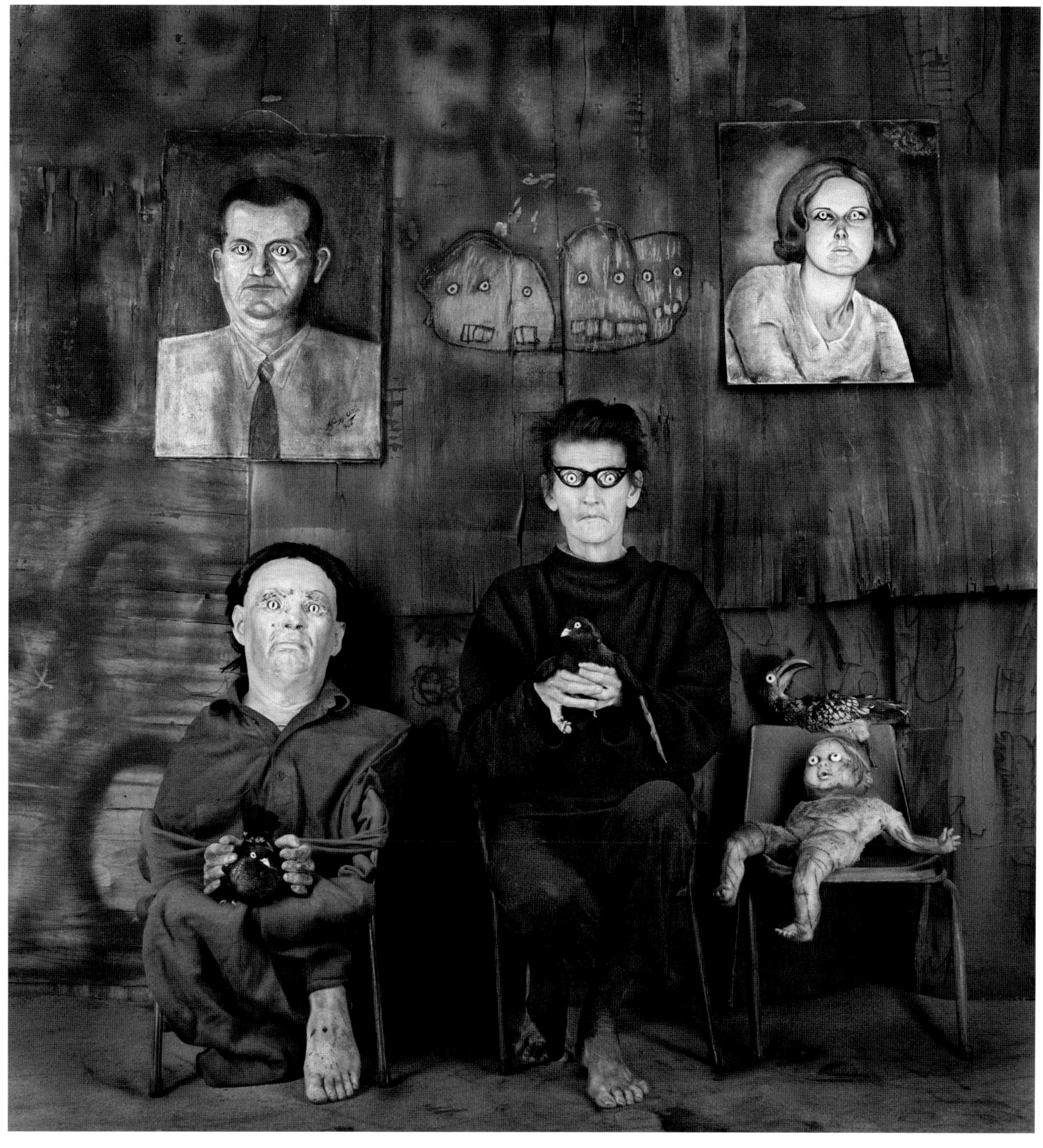

Place of the Eyeballs 2012

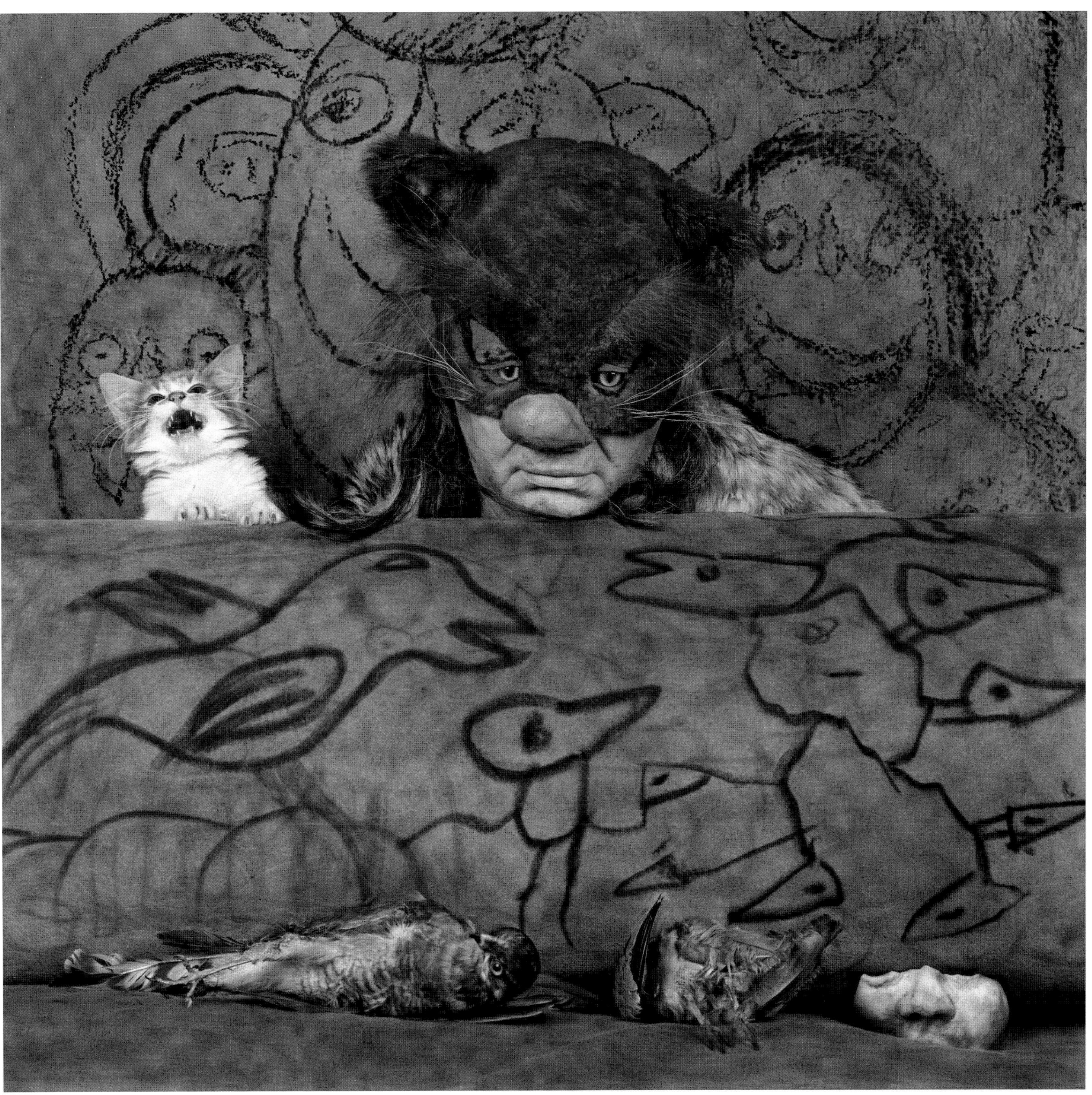

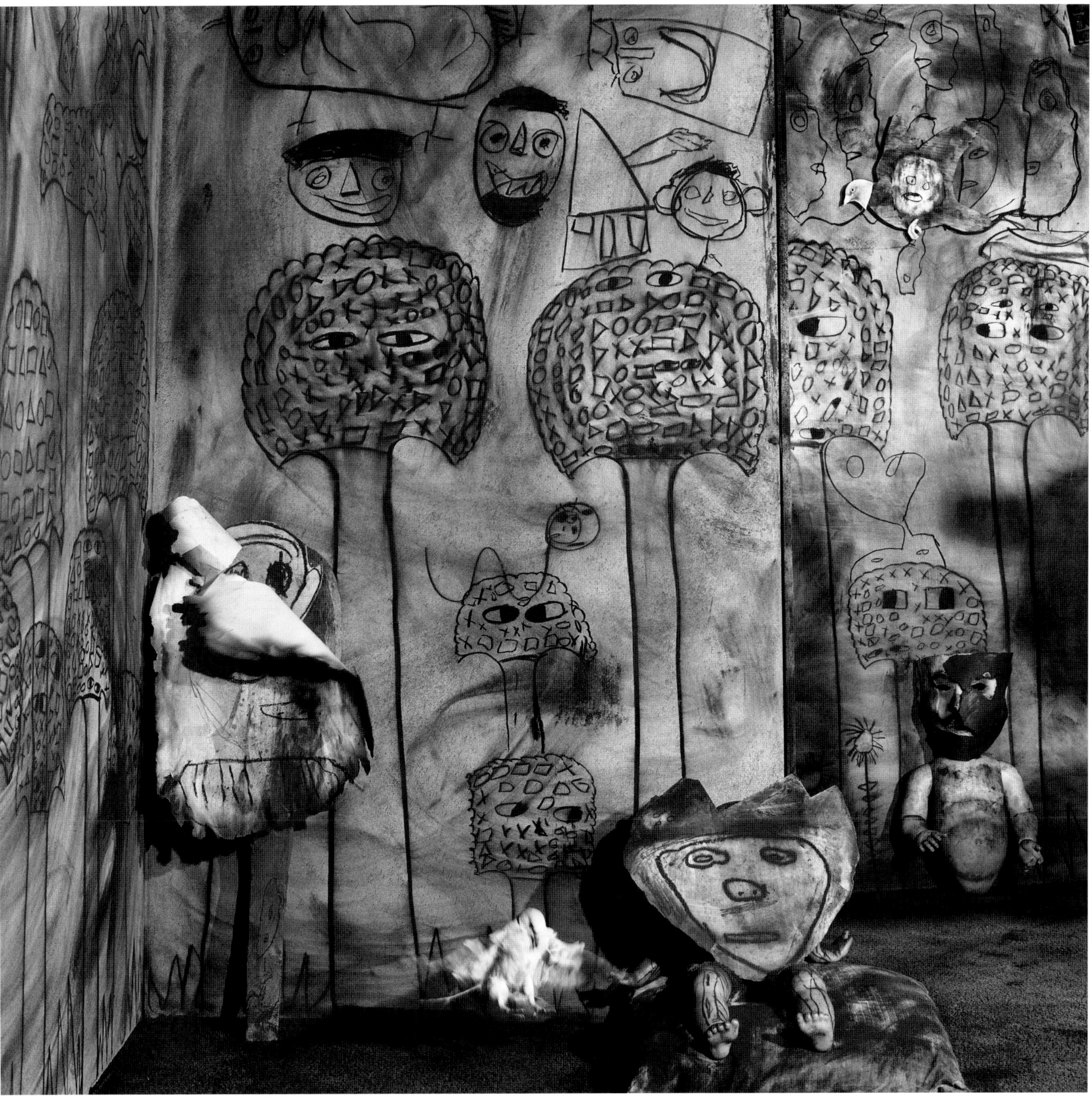

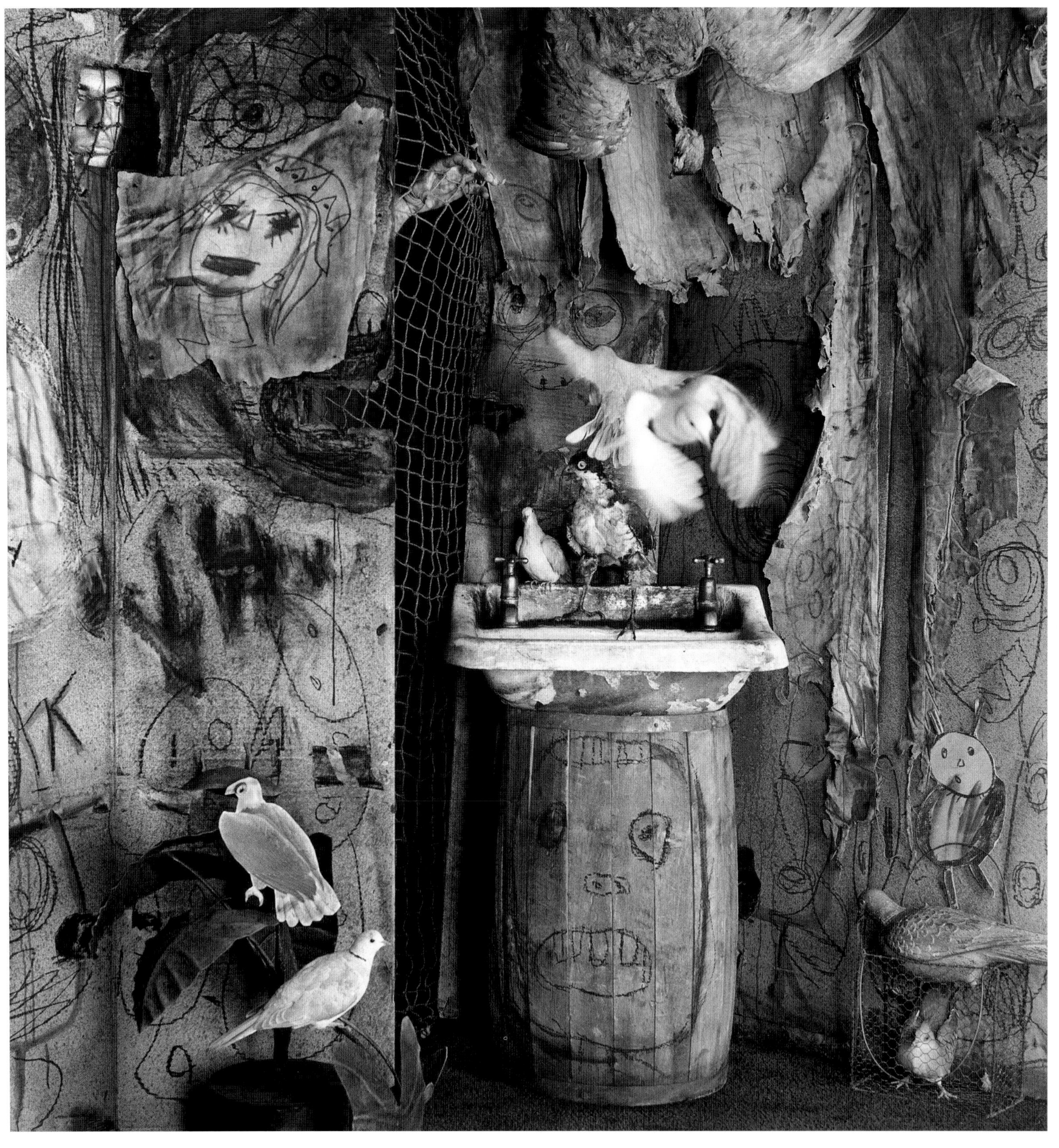

Intruder 2010

118

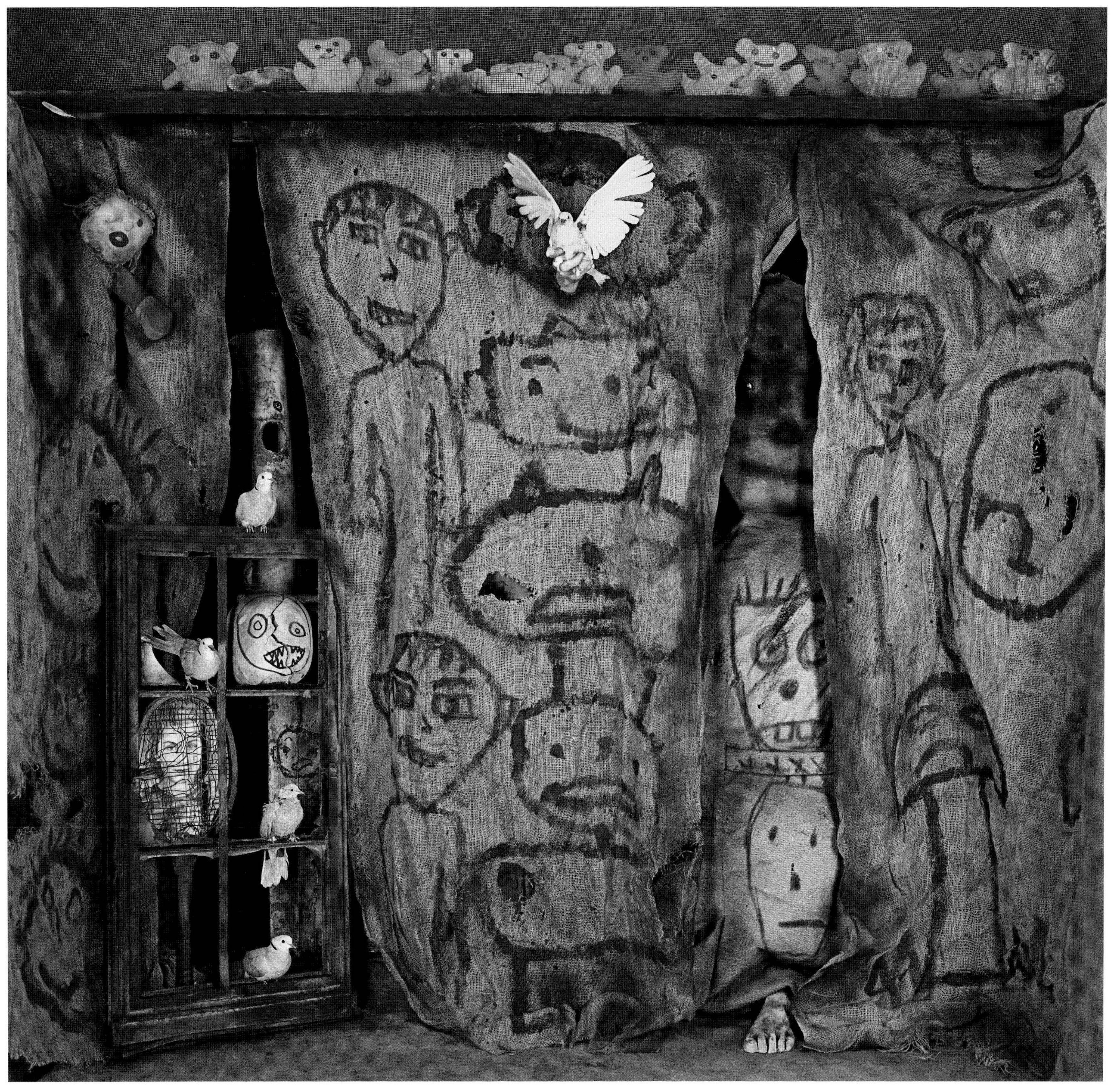

Lurking 2010

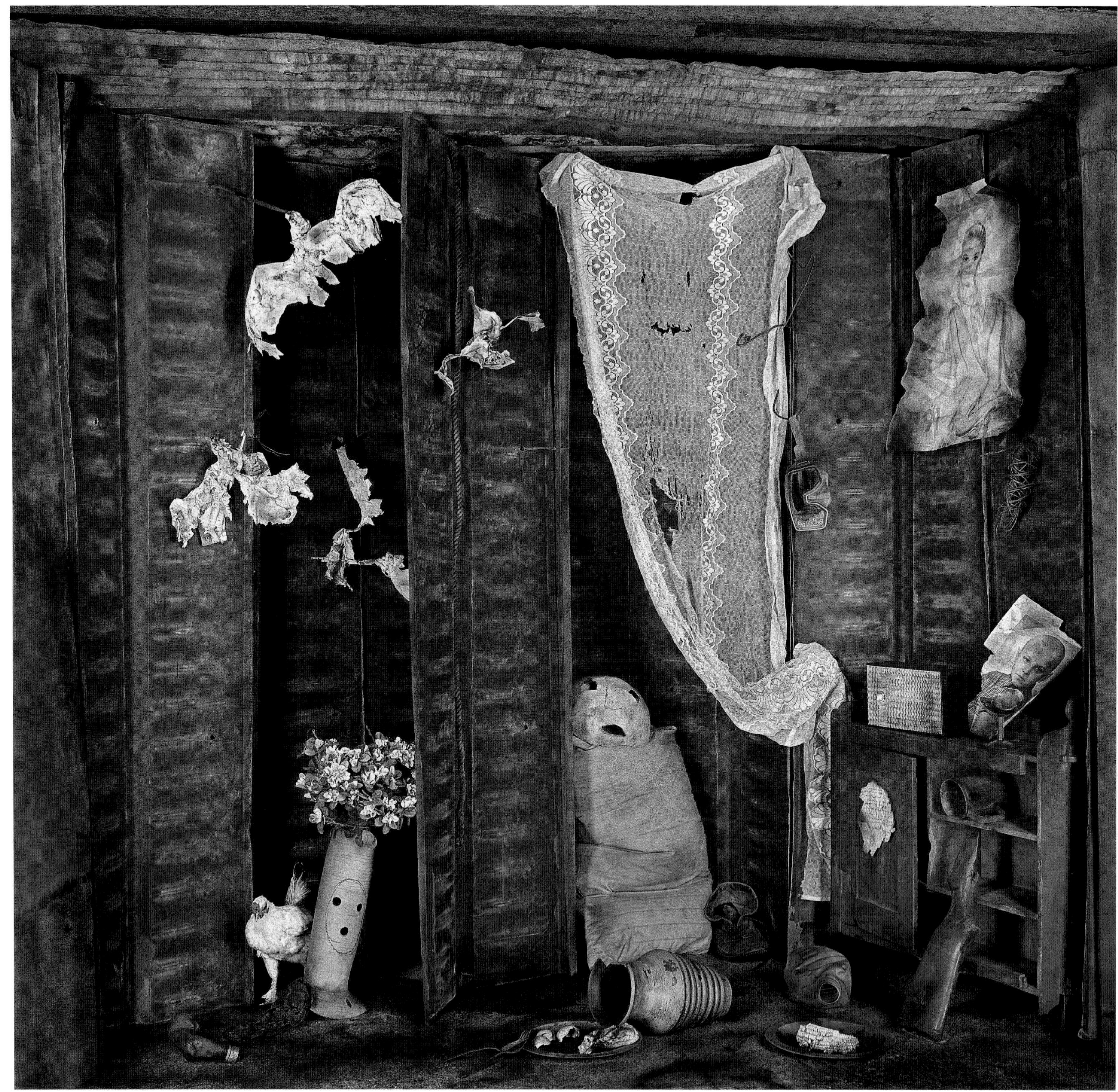

Break Through 2010

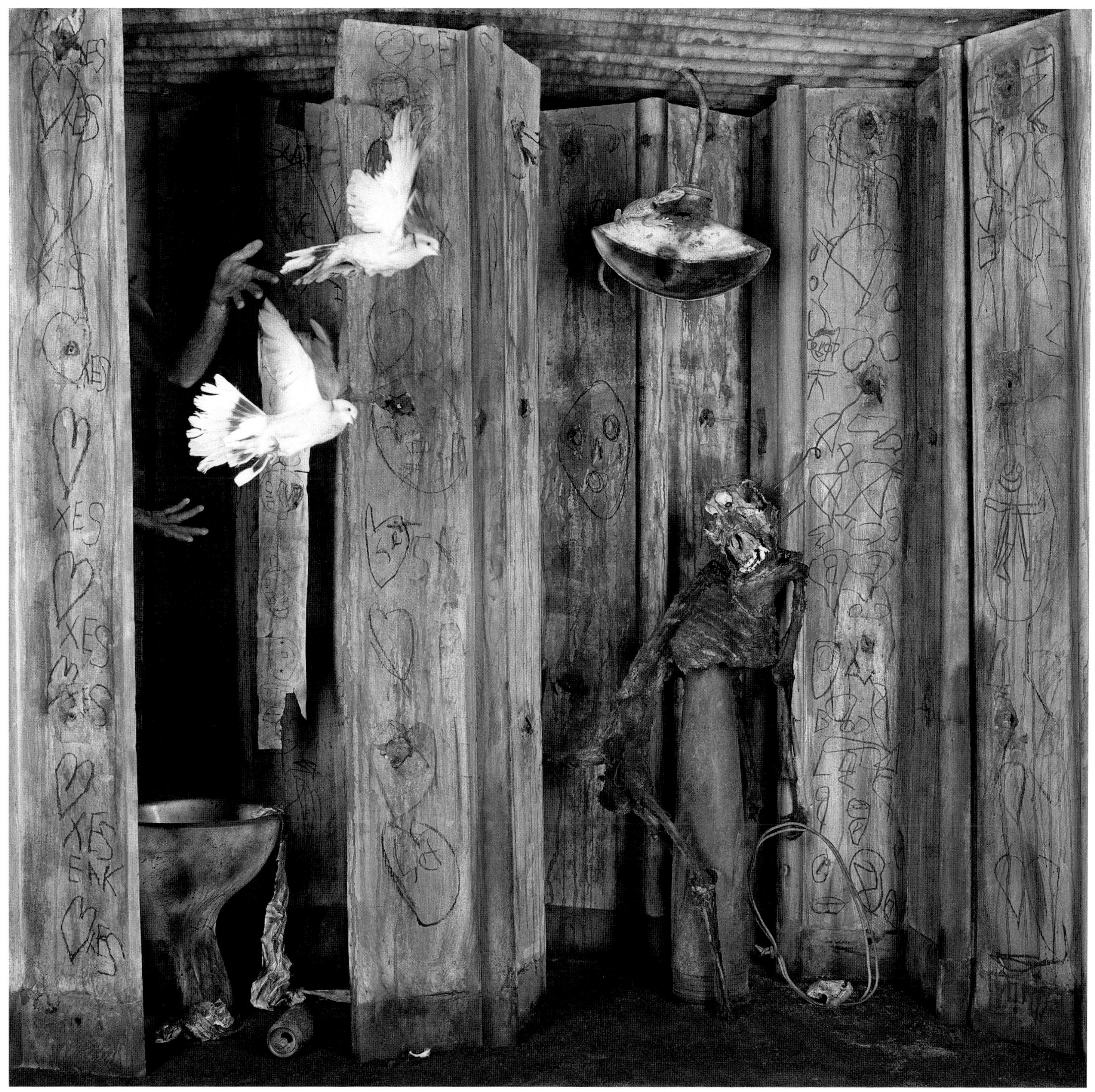

Relinquished 2010

121

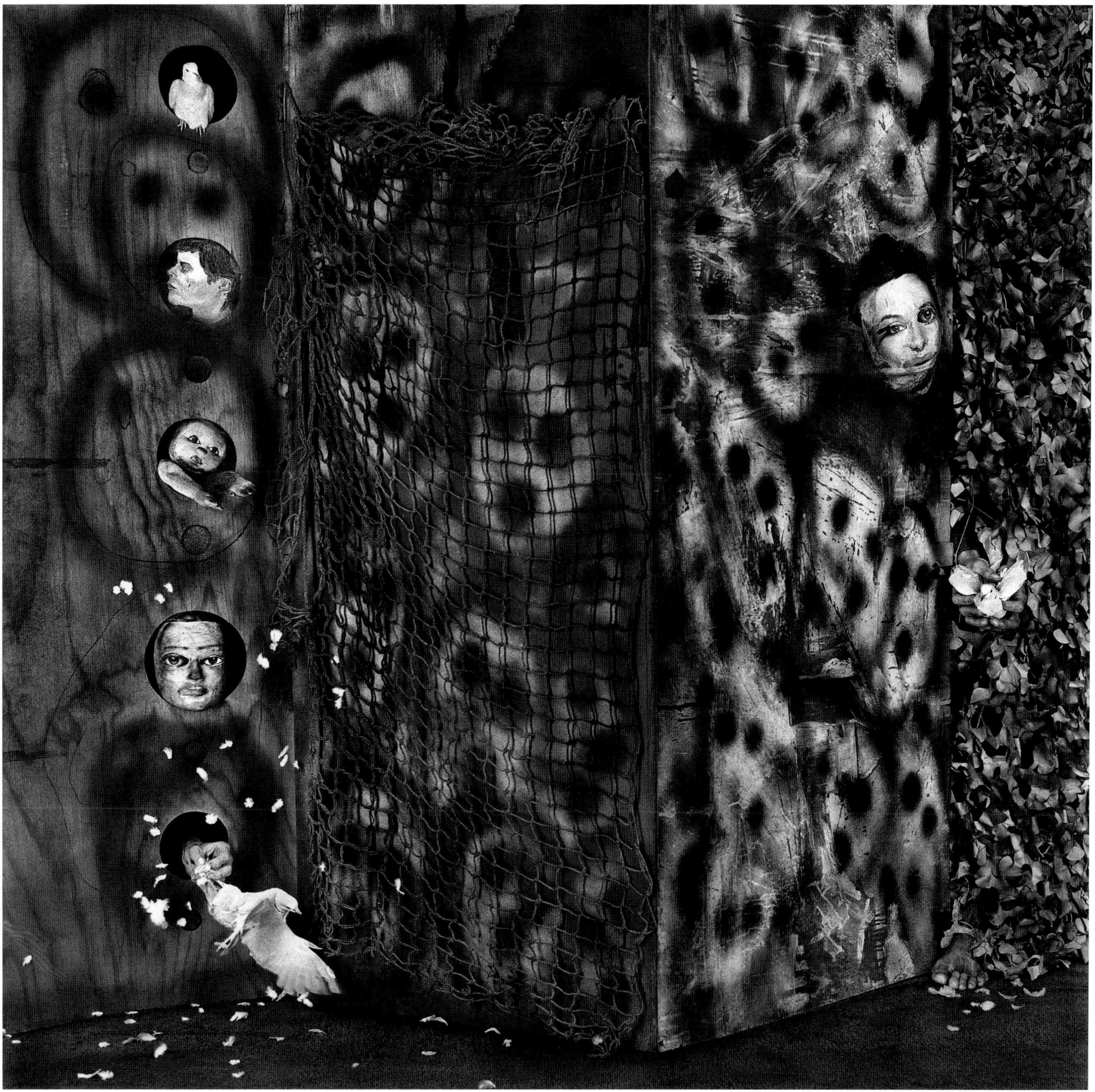

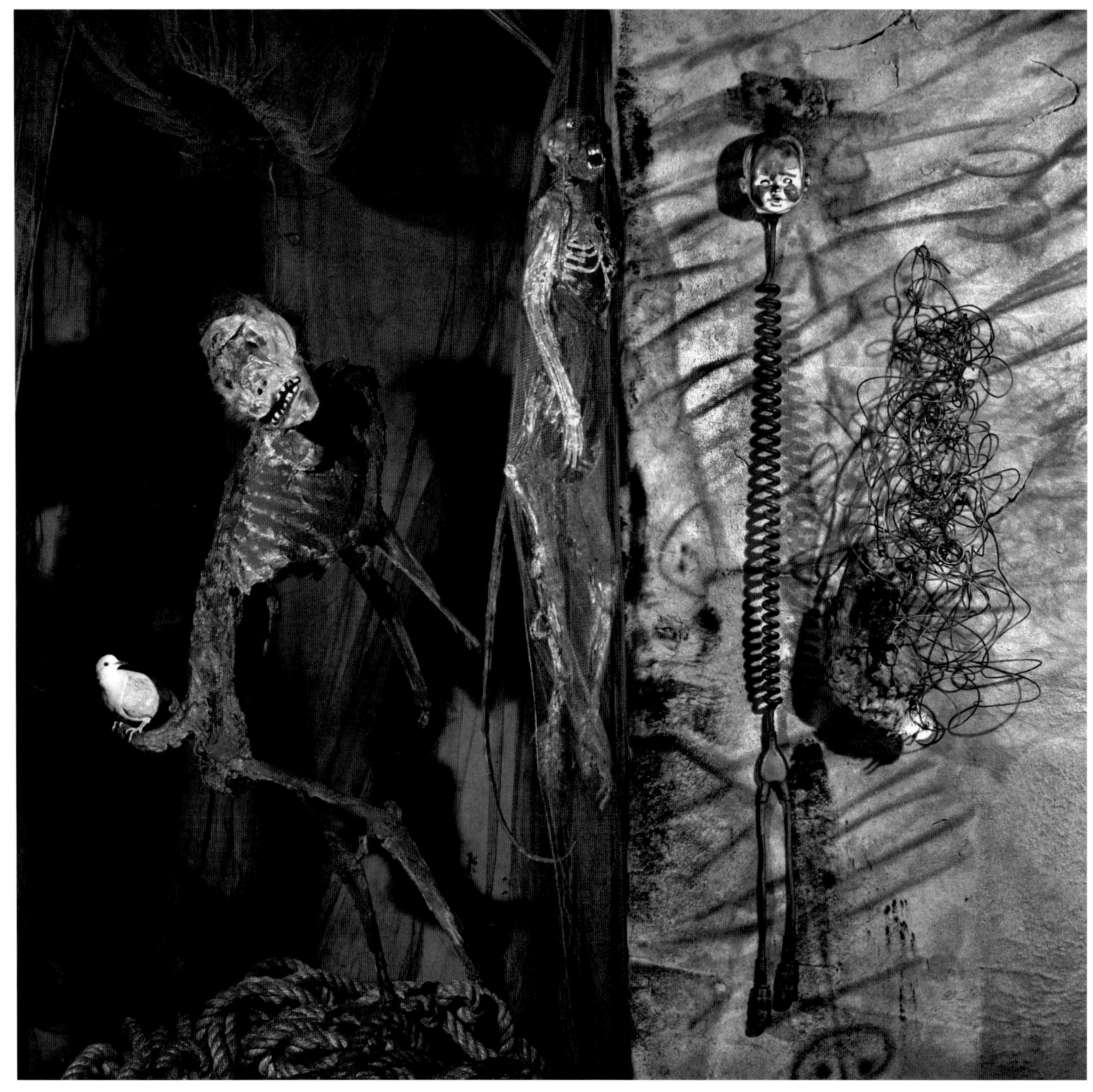

Encounter 2009

124

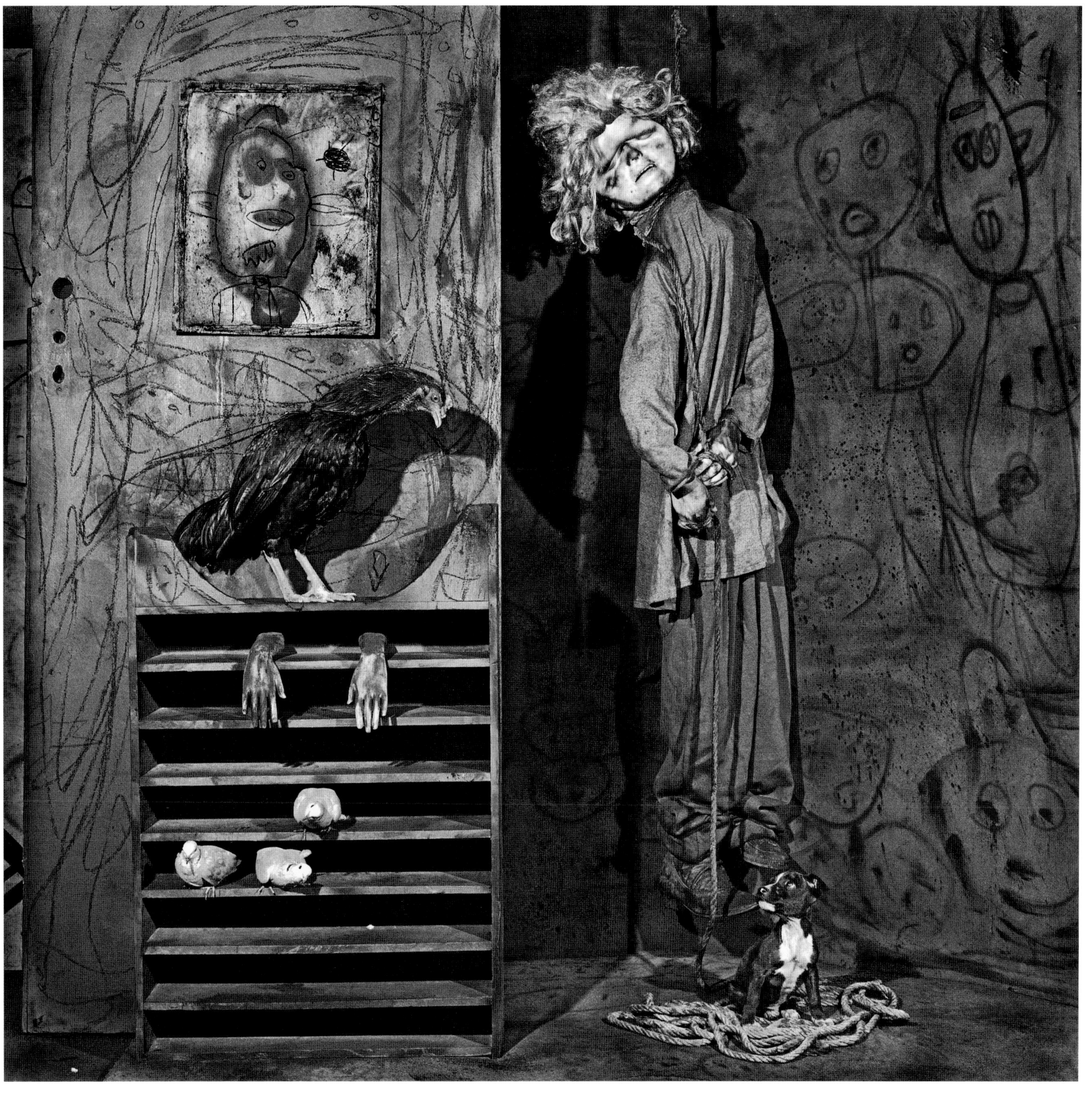

Hanged 2009

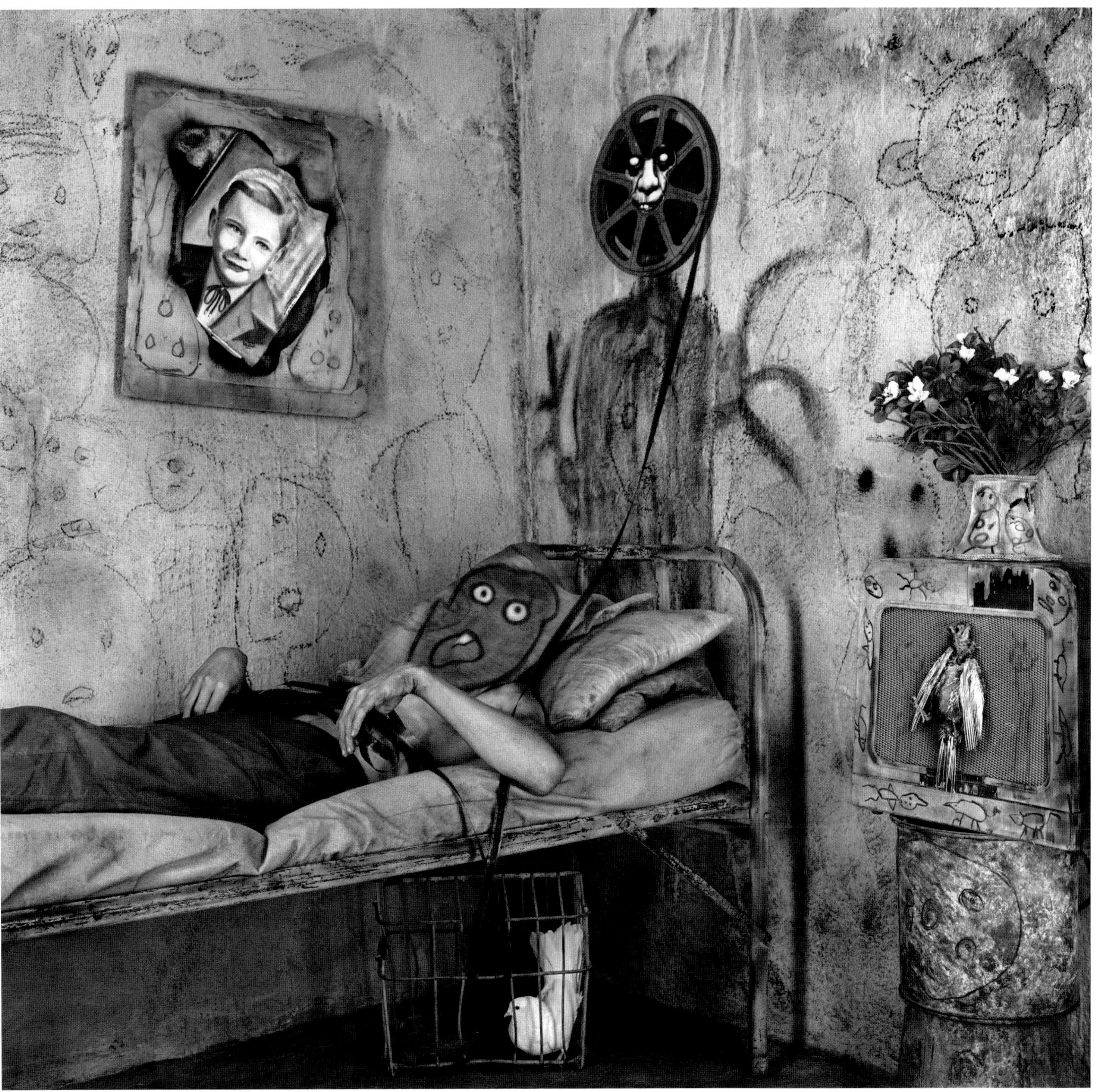

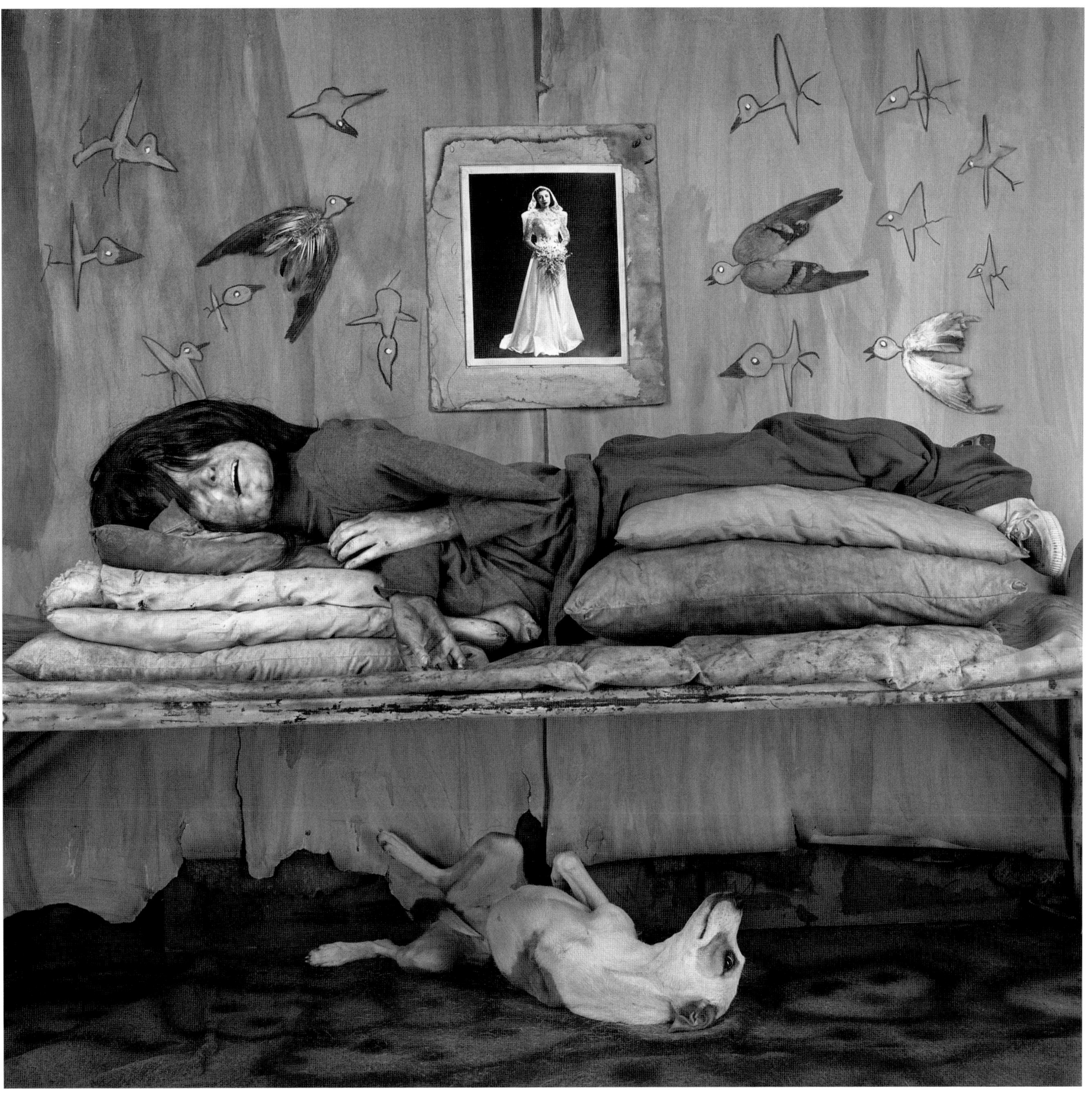

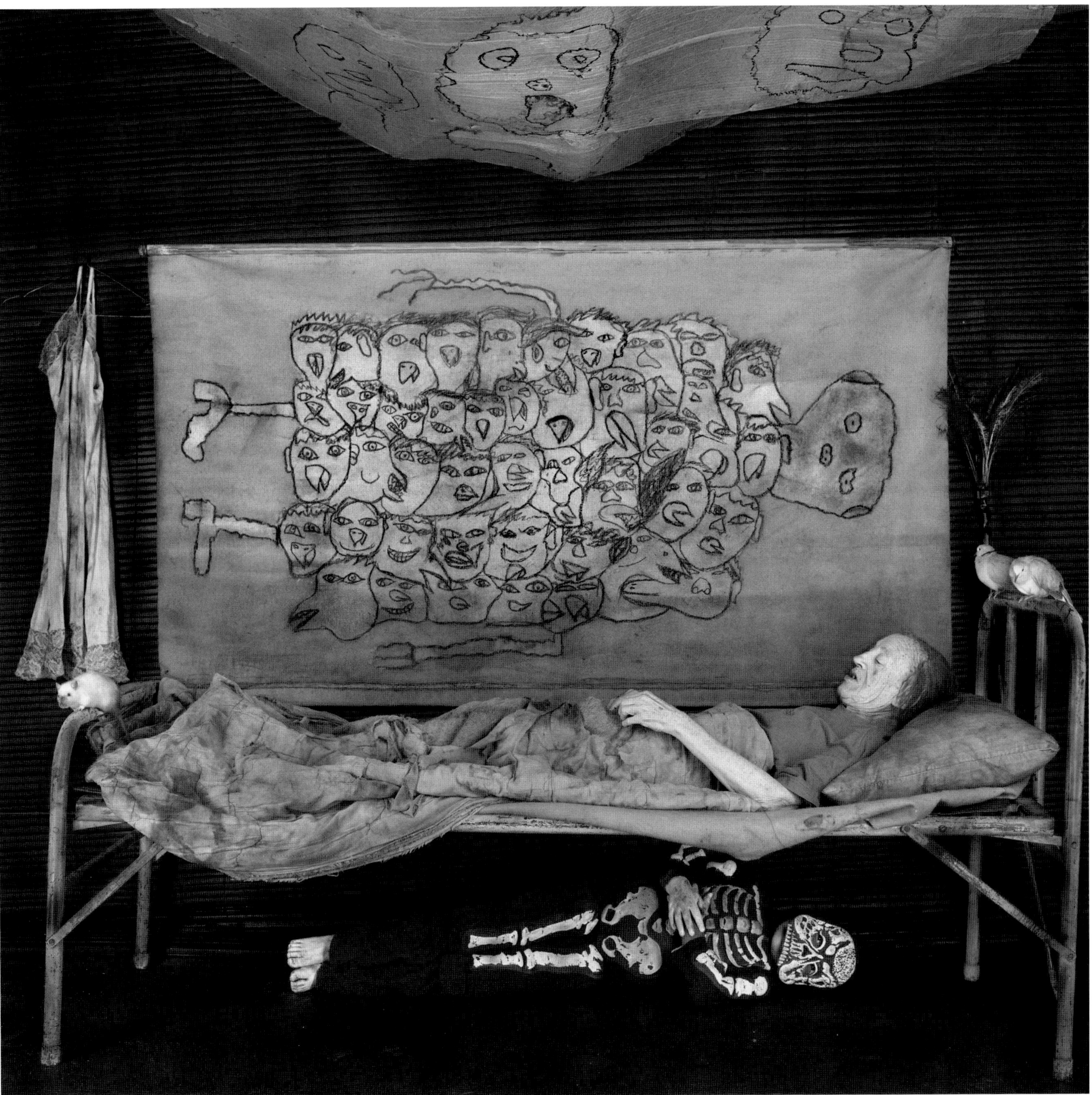

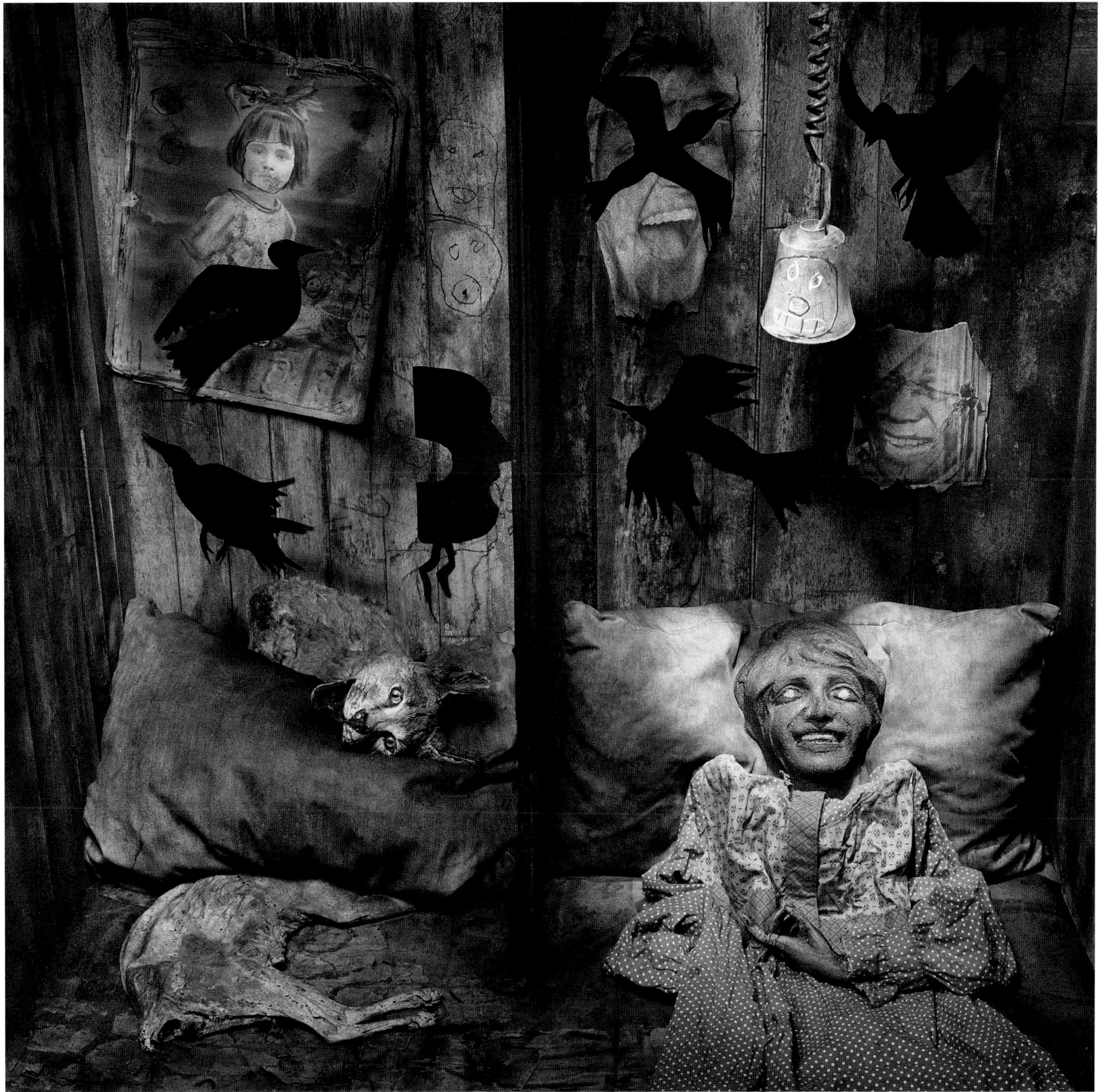

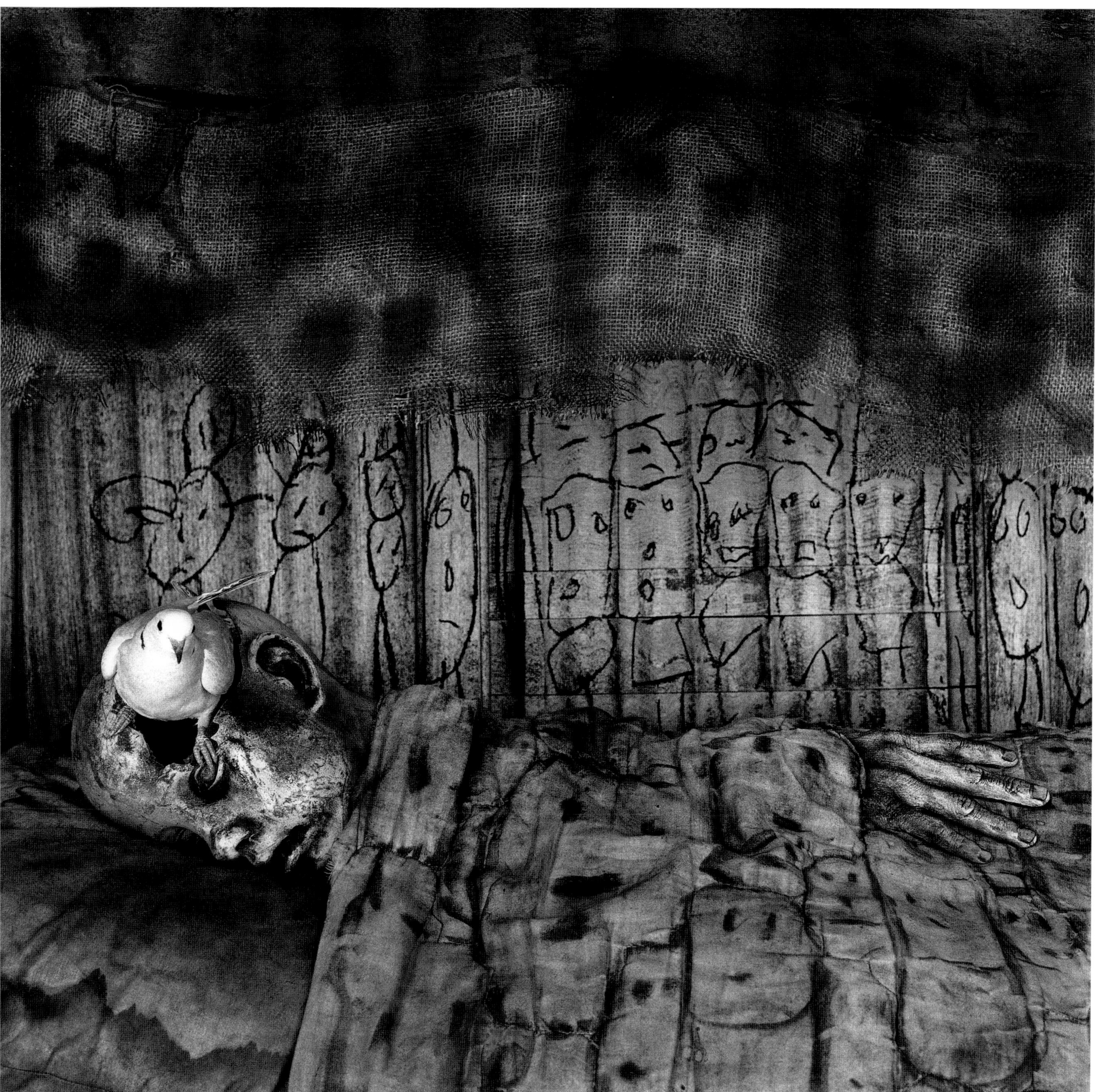

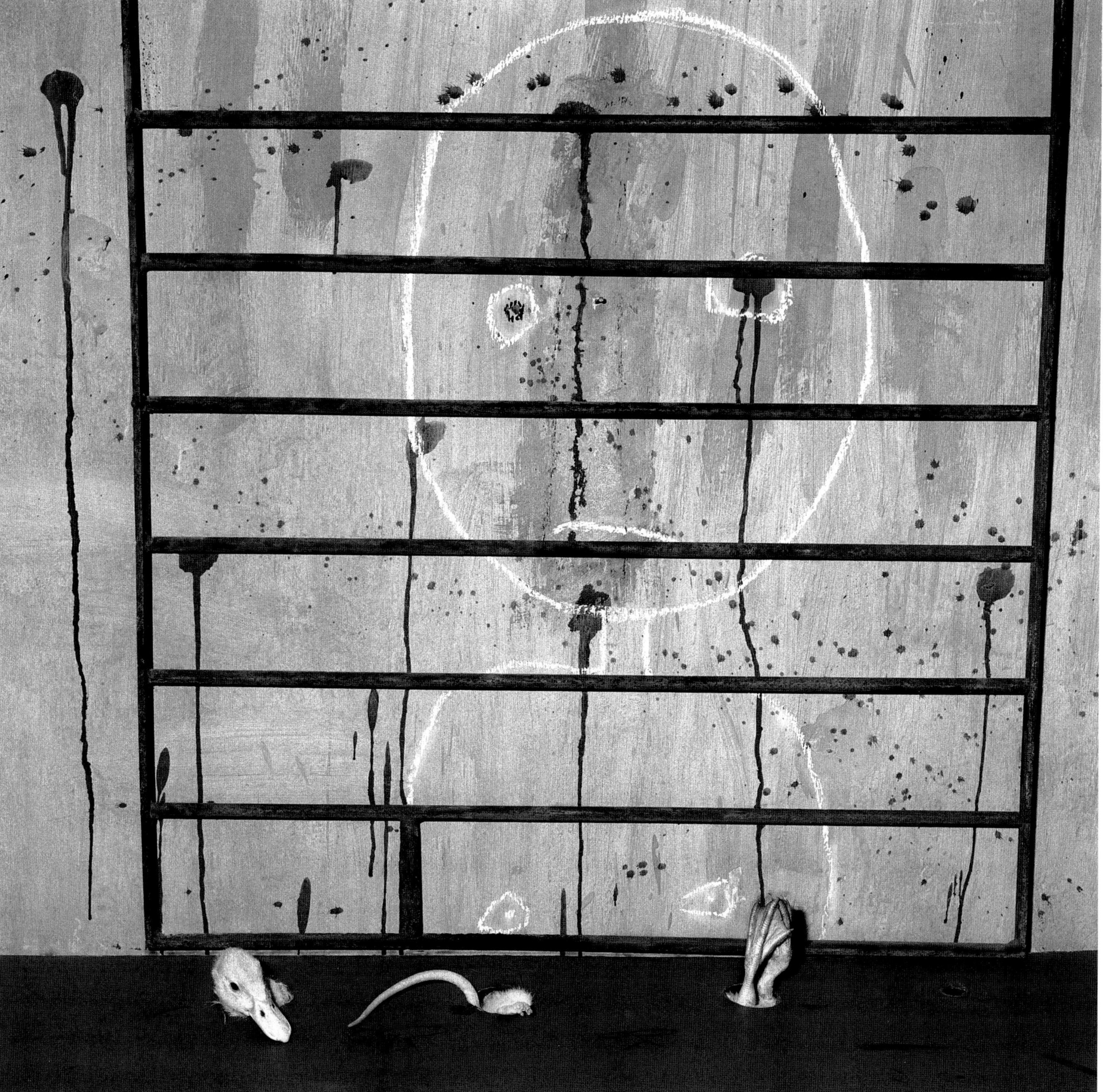

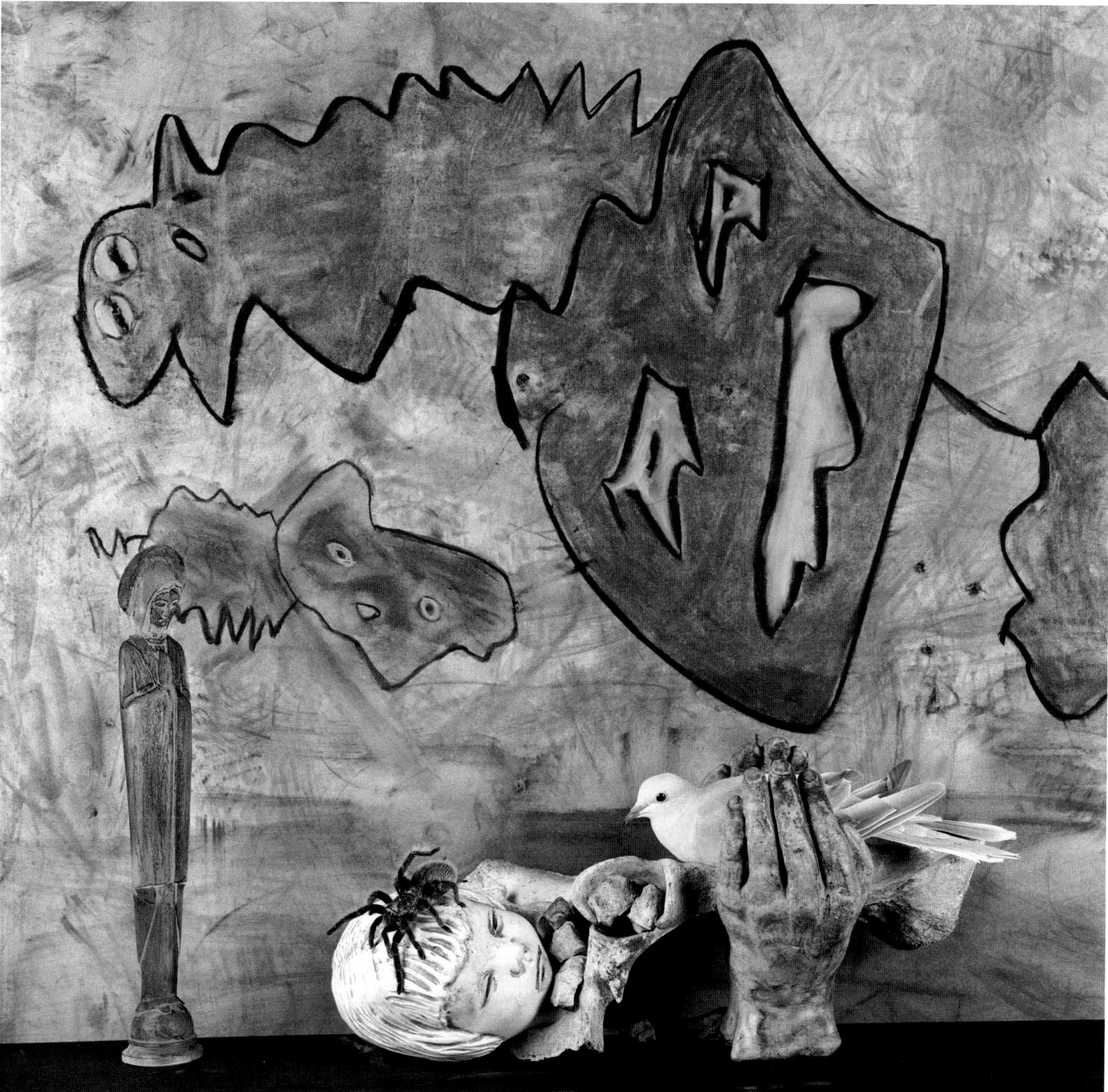

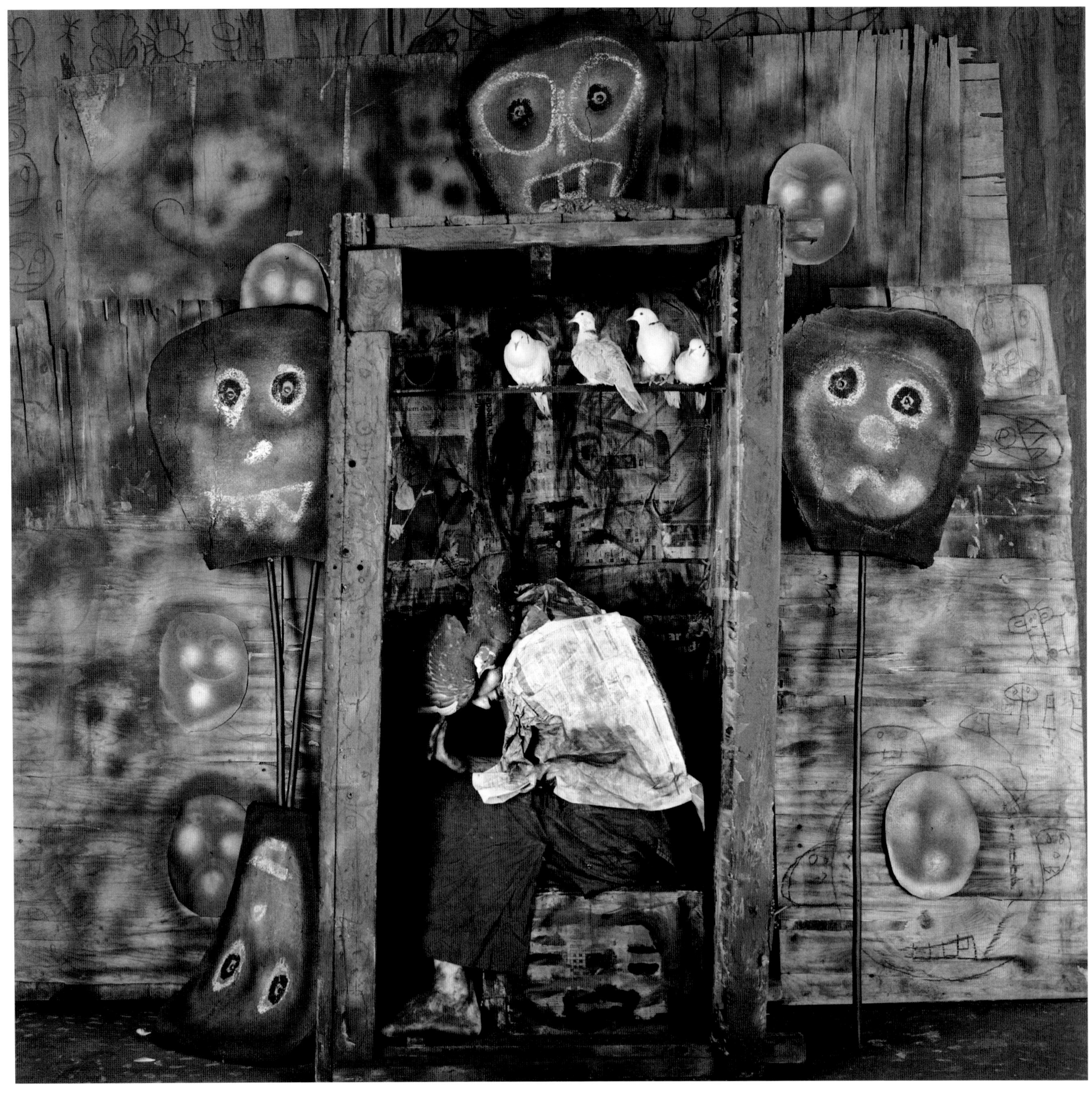

Confession 2010

140

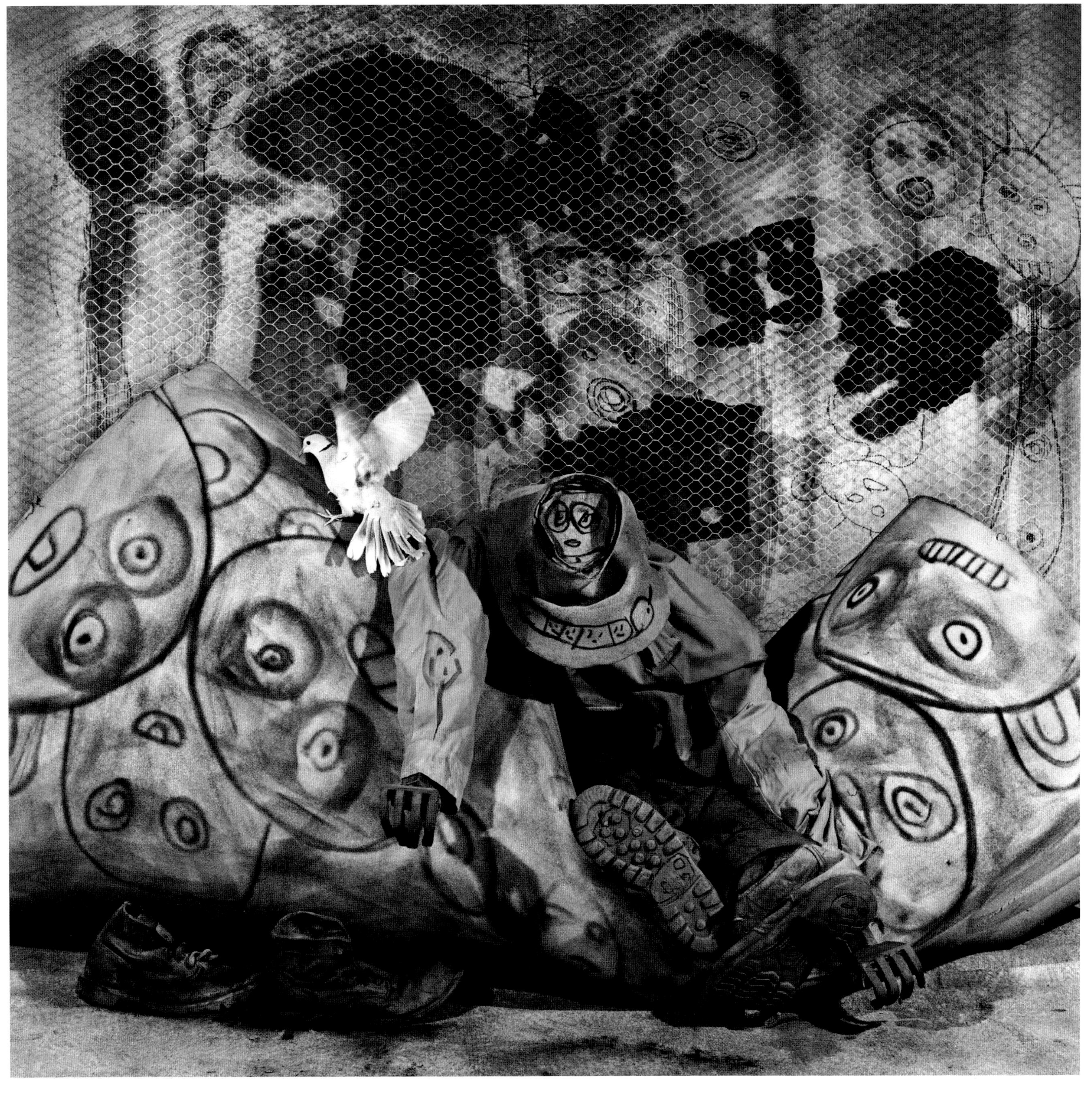

Collapsed 2009

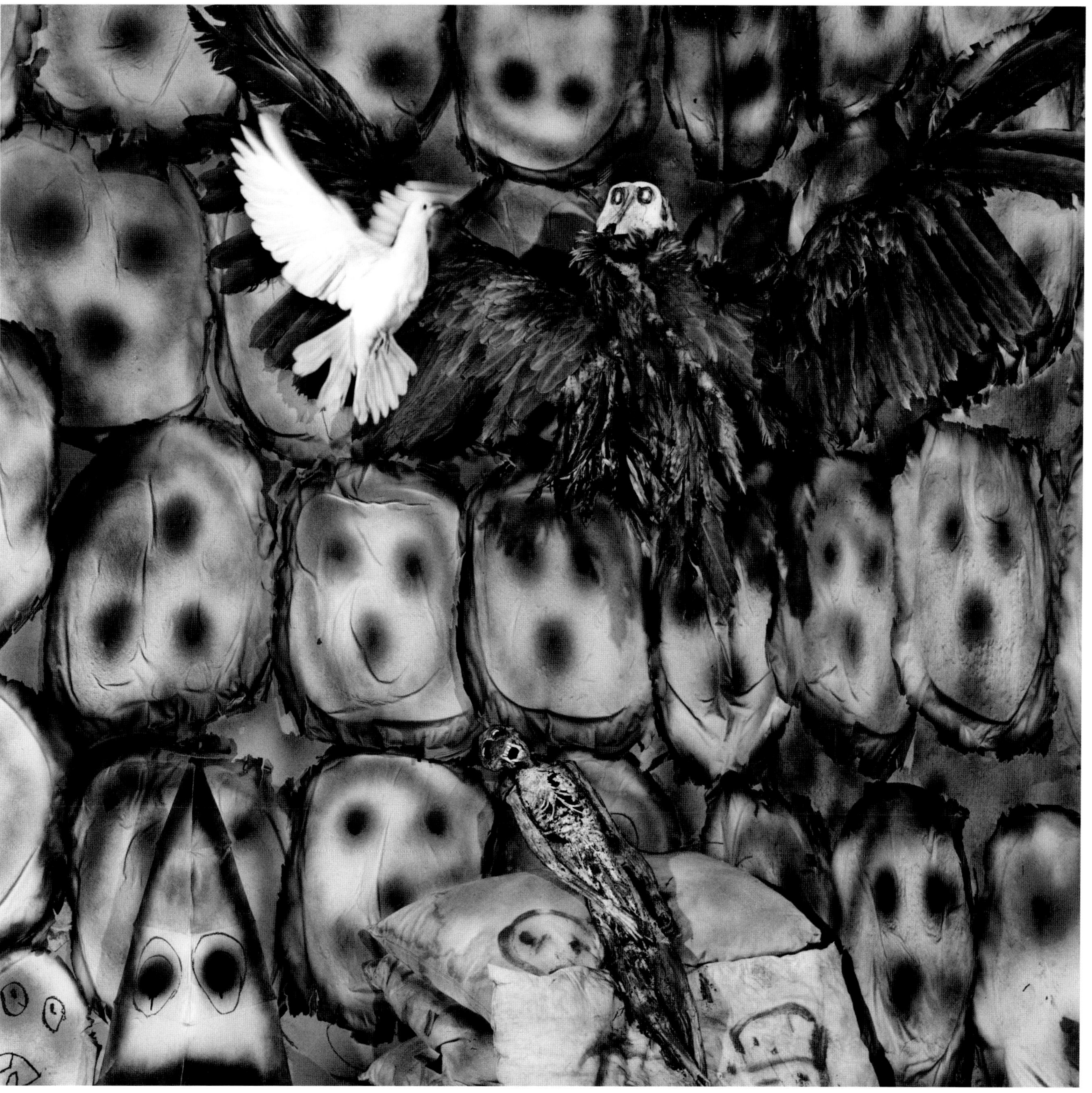

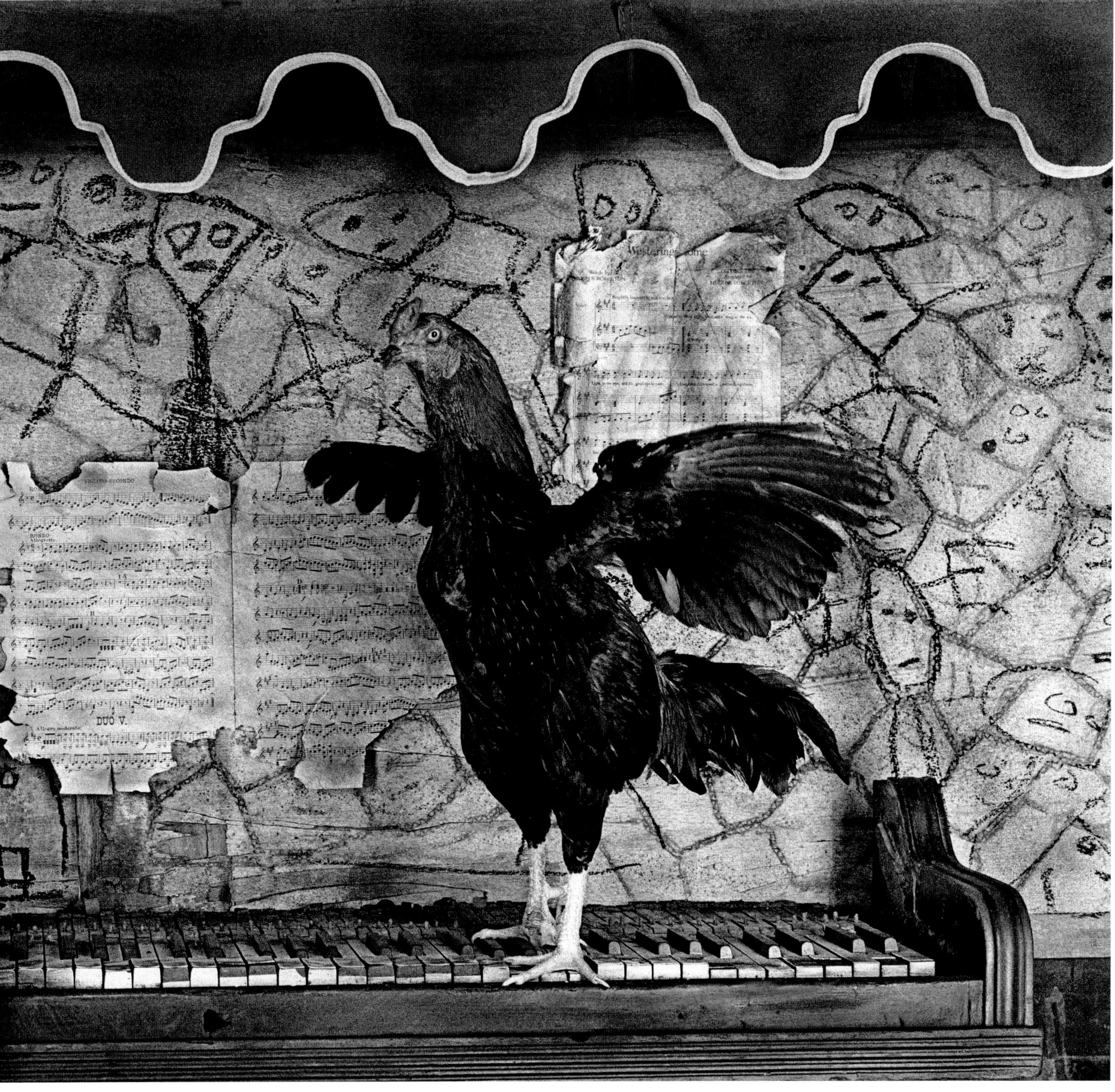

Westering Home
VIOLINO SECONDO
RONDO
Allegretto
DUO V.
Allegro moderato

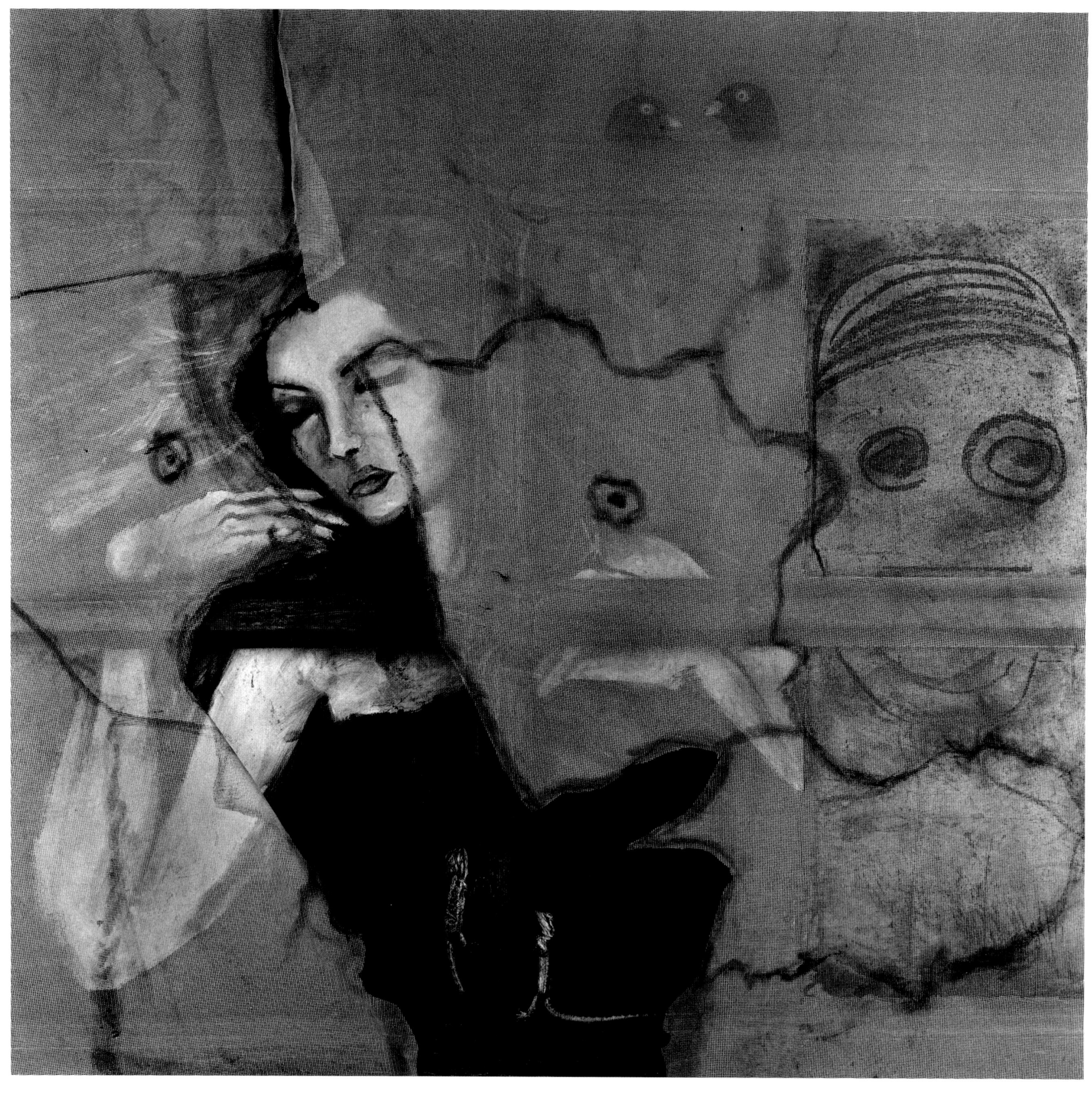

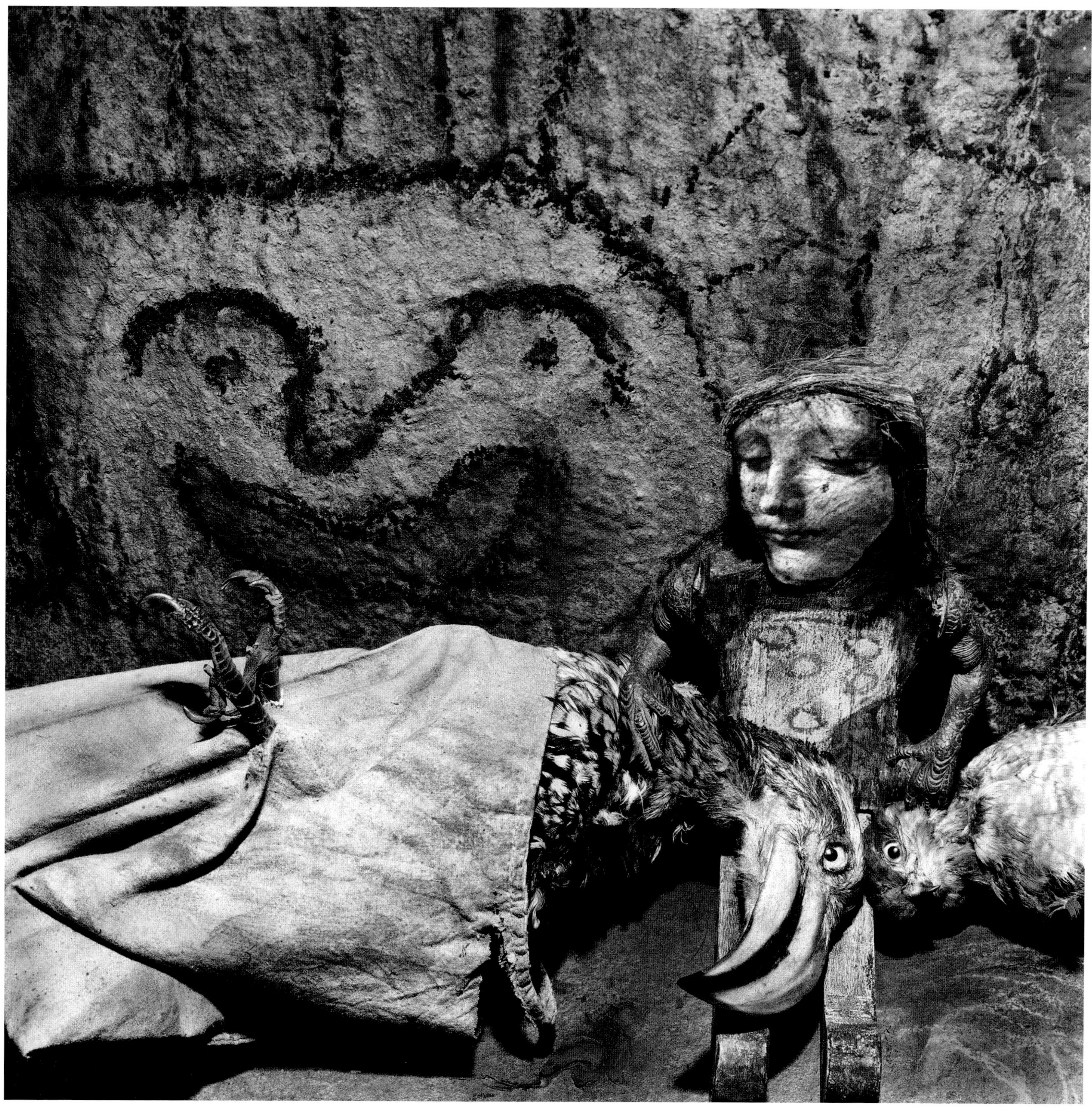

Wounded 2011

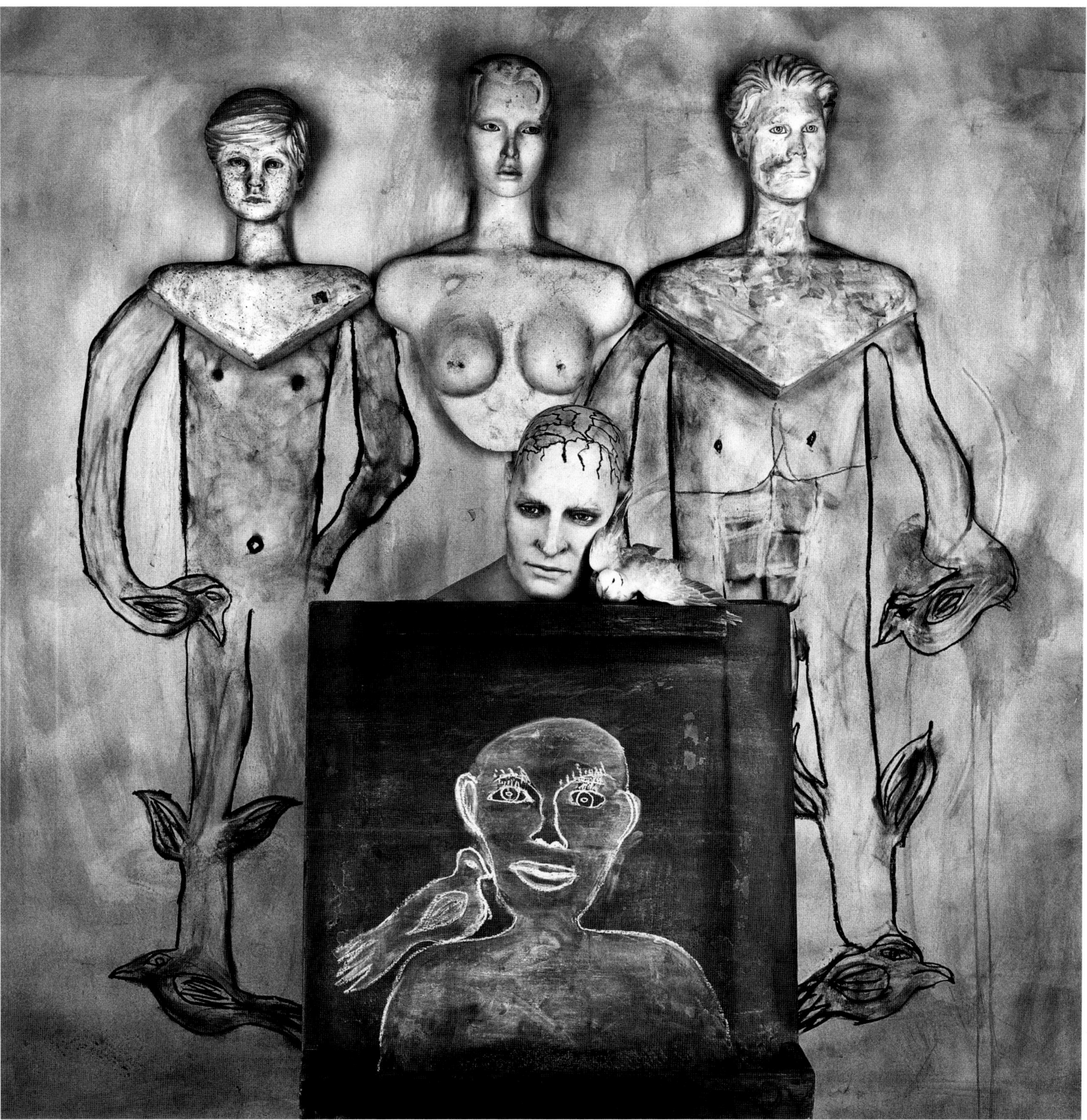

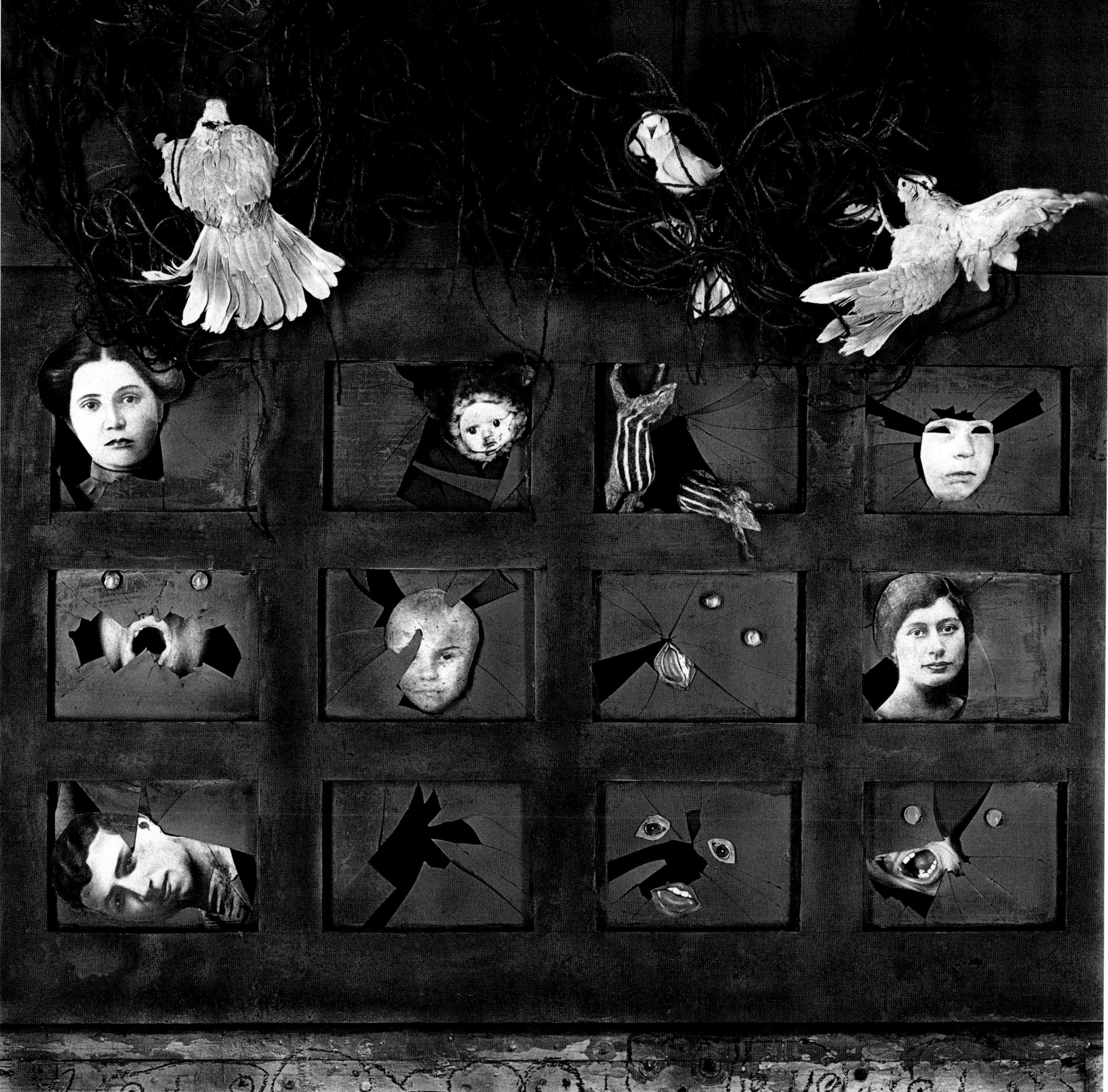

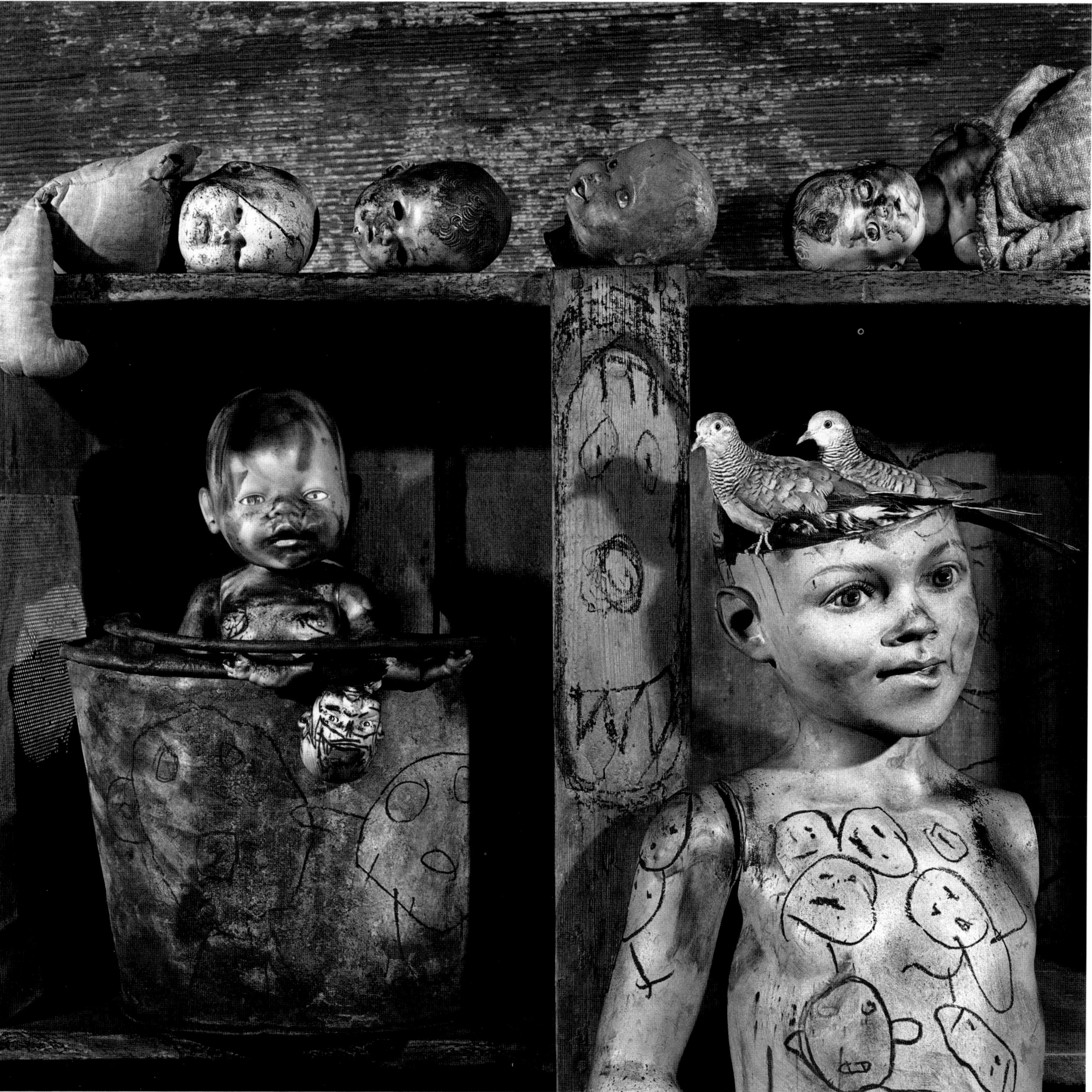

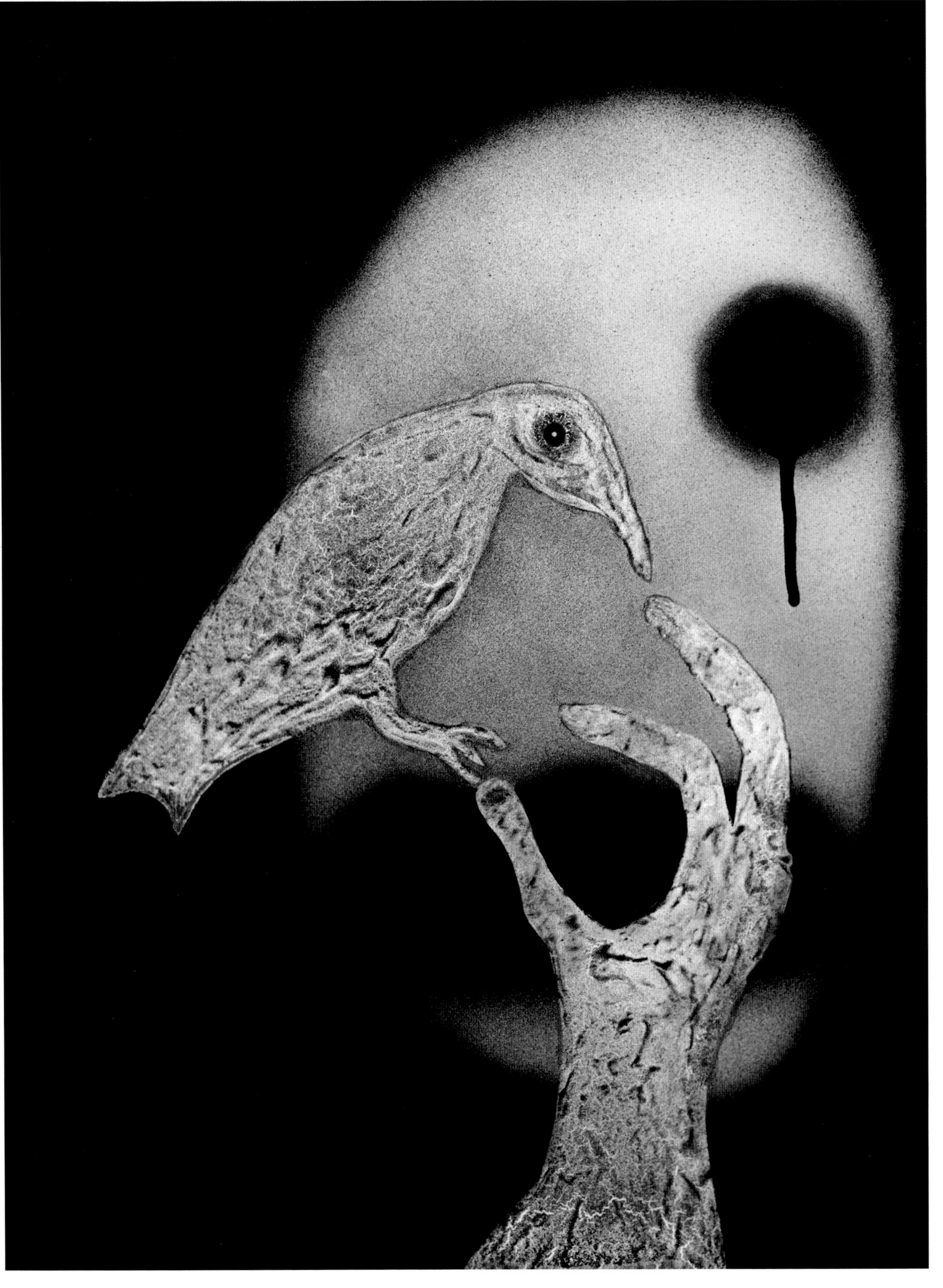

You Can't Come Back 2011

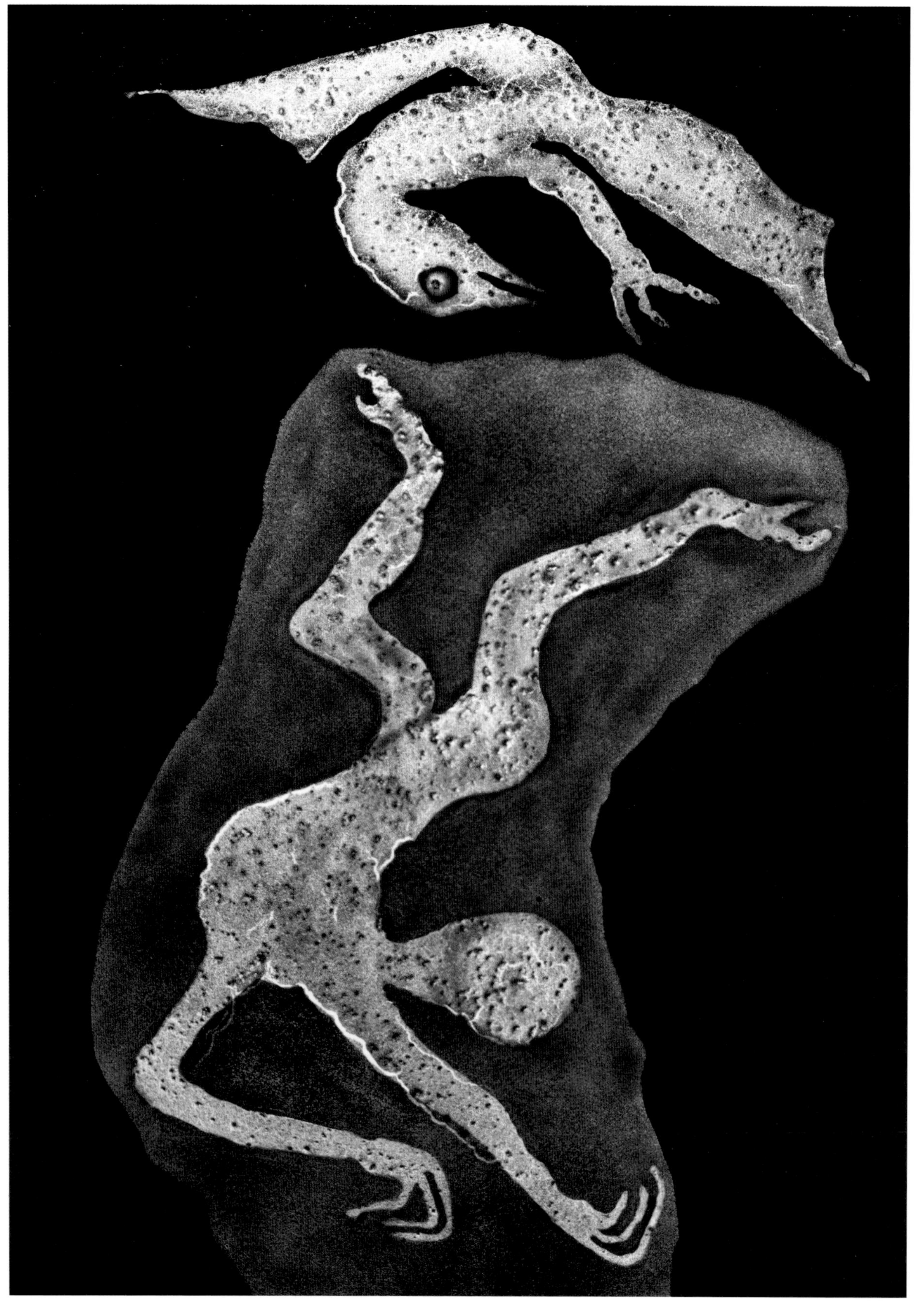

Free Fall 2011

156

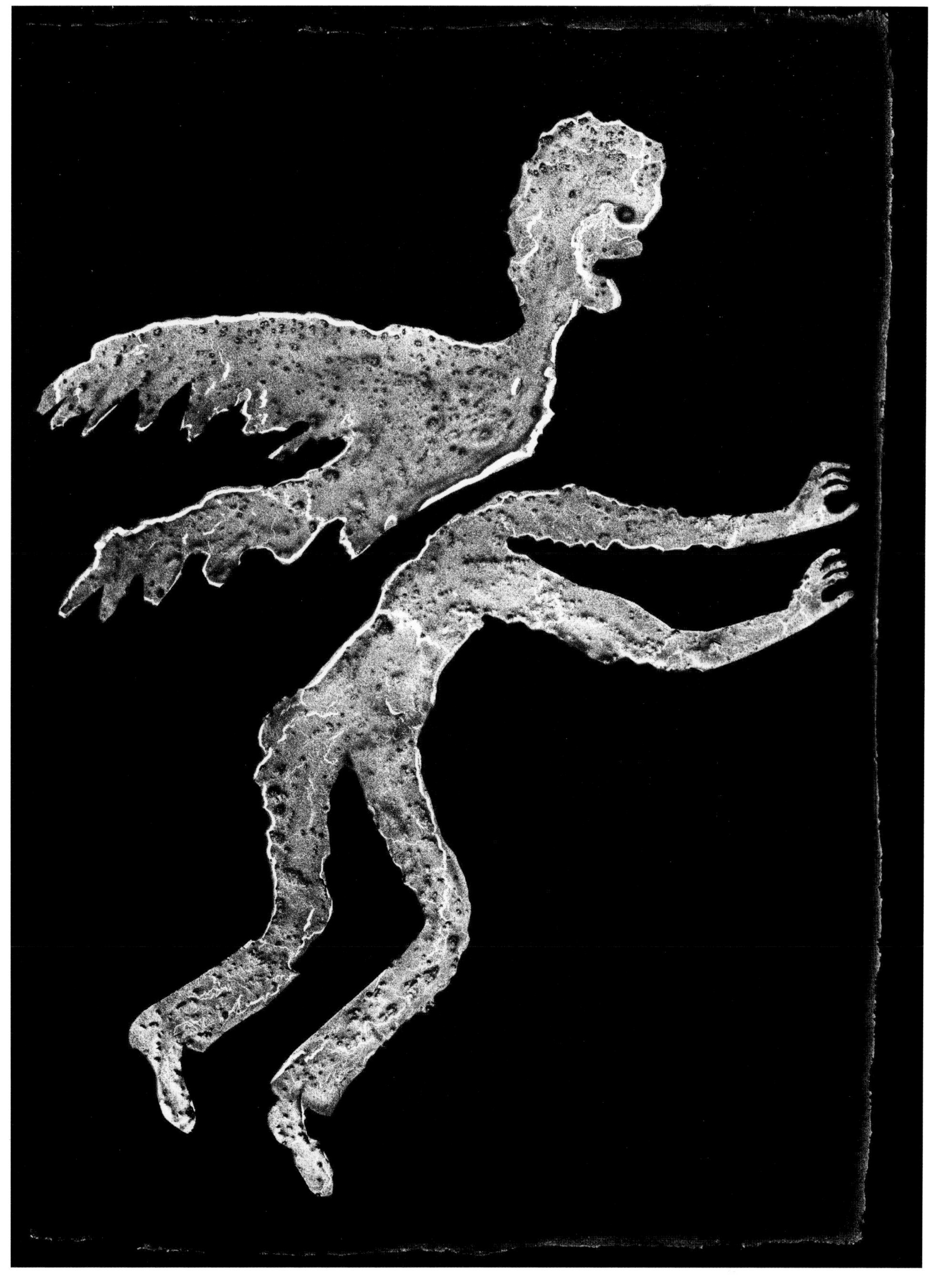

ASYLUM OF THE BIRDS

In *Asylum of the Birds* I have photographed birds interacting in a space characterized by discarded objects, other animals, smudged and ghost-like drawings that could have originated in a cave or been part of a funeral ceremony. Unlike my earlier images, human identities have been reduced to body parts; there is hardly a face to be seen in this book. Meaning and metaphor in these images come into being as a result of the interaction of the birds habituating this haunting, complex space. The physical space that I commonly refer to as the asylum is contrastingly a place of refuge and at the same time a place of insanity.

I often comment that a photograph began before I began creating it. So, a photograph starts deep down in some part of my mind, formed before consciousness was formed. And I'm part of all sorts of other consciousness that have existed throughout time. So, on a metaphoric level it's very difficult to know when the photograph actually began. On a more practical level, it usually begins with an object sitting there, a bird flying by, or a person, connecting one thing to the next. I'm basically an organizer – organizing visual chaos into coherency.

Birds are difficult to photograph: they move incessantly; get nervous at the click of the camera; fly away through open windows. One cannot fathom what goes through their minds, give them instructions, or expect them to be interested in being photographed.

There's movement all the time: things and drawings are being put up and down; people are coming in and out; birds are flying and bobbing their heads… At a precise point, unity, life, intensity and poetry come about, and it's my job to know that point.

These photographs comment on various aspects of the human condition…my condition. I am not able to be precise about the meaning of any of the photographs in this book. In most cases, the photographs often express opposite visual sensibilities. As much as I often try, I cannot find appropriate words. My best photographs are the ones I do not understand.

I believe that the relationship between animals and humans is essentially adversarial and exploitative. Most societies try to deny this fact, but it is clear that the destruction of the natural world continues at an unabated rate. In the years that I spent photographing this book I became more and more convinced that human nature is the ultimate culprit responsible for the worst of all holocausts. The links that bind us to the planet are tangled and broken. The birds' view downward from the sky is ominous, it is becoming difficult for them to find nests to return to.

Where did this obsession with birds begin? Perhaps it was chirping that I heard in 1950 as I lay in my mother's womb. As a child, I was baffled by the fact that birds could fly and I was stuck on the ground. I thought of them exclusively as creatures habituating the heavens.

During the summer of 1969, I worked as a construction worker in Brooklyn, New York. On my way home every afternoon I would scout the sidewalks for possible subjects to photograph. I located an old man and his pet parrot one day. This was my first bird shot. The next day, I photographed my TV set as men went far into the skies beyond birds to land on the moon.

In 1973, following my mother's death, I painted passionately for a period of six months. Then that side of me went dormant. I did not think I would ever be involved with this art form again. The concept of using drawing in my photographs evolved initially as a result of photographing subjects against walls in homes saturated with their lines, marks and drawings. As time progressed, I began to interact with my subjects and sometimes asked them to draw. So drawing in my imagery evolved from street photography – from 'real life'. In 2003, thirty years after I stopped painting, this passion reappeared with a vengeance and has dominated my work ever since.

My aesthetic evolved as a result of endless small steps adding up to bigger steps. Since 2000, my images have been increasingly dominated by drawings, paintings and graffiti, sometimes created by one or more inhabitants, by myself, or by unknown passersby. It is quite ironic that many of the people that I have worked with on this project have the same style of drawing as me.

The image of a disorientated dove against a wall (*Five Hands*, 2006) was taken in a Johannesburg room in which a number of people were lying together in the same bed with their charred hands raised. Looking back, it was the starting point for this project. From this time on, birds were no longer confined to the heavens, but to a space dominated by chaos, ambiguity, violence and death.

I am the last generation to have grown up in a black-and-white photographic film world. Like the horse of a hundred years ago, this world is gradually disappearing from sight. You cannot separate the meaning of my photographs from the fact that they exemplify this medium. I am drawn to it by its minimalism, abstraction and subtlety. Only recently, after nearly fifty years of hard work, do I feel that I have come close to mastering this medium.

I never plan my photographs…depending on dreams and one's imagination alone will not guarantee a successful image. My images come about as a result of thousands and thousands of little decisions, just like the innumerable brushstrokes in a painting. There are infinite possibilities to follow: that is what makes photography so difficult, there is no limit to the possibilities.

I am inspired by blank white walls. They symbolize the challenge
that I regularly face: to find a way of transforming vast nothingness,
to give birth to imagery that has a life beyond my own. My
creative processes evolve from silence: they are filtered through
consciousness and hopefully end with the inexplicable.

Archetypal symbols from the deeper levels of the human
subconscious pervade my photographs. This place is untamable;
it has its own rules and functions according to its own laws.
As a geologist, I frequently go down mine shafts heading to the
core of the earth. As I spiral downward in the elevator, I pass
through different layers of the earth's history. Arriving at the
bottom of the shaft, I commonly reflect on my creative process.
When creating photographs, I often travel into my mind through
the layers to locate this spot, the black core, a place where
dreams and many of my images originate.

It is one thing to find yourself in this deeper subconscious, but it is
another to bring the buried fragments out so that they can manifest
themselves. That is the crucial step: bringing the pieces to the
surface and linking them with the exterior world that one is trying
to transform through the camera.

I do not work out of a sense of inspiration but rather out of a deep
existential need to define my own enigmatic identity. I am also not
concerned about what is real or not; the term defies definition.
Nevertheless, my images are meant to straddle the strange vague
line where illusion becomes delusion, fact is fiction and the
conscious merges with the unconscious. My photographs attempt
to break down the boundaries of logic and language and in so
doing, they shatter the enclosing walls of habit and fear.

My intention is to create photographs that challenge the mind…
to assist with the process of liberating the interior from itself.
I see my photographs as mirrors, reflectors, connectors.

I see myself as a formalist. Like in nature – there is harmony
between one aspect and the other. If one part works against the
other you end up with a cancer. So, form is crucial to what I do,
and I believe that the form is the basis of the content. If you don't
bring the forms together, you don't get the content. Of course,
a picture doesn't stand alone by its form. You can have forms that
relate, but there's no meaning. So, ultimately, a picture is judged
by its meaning, but dependent on its form…and I think that's what
a lot of people lose sight of.

I am hopeful that after you have looked through this book,
immersed yourself in its images, turned your eyeballs around
and peered inward, allowed yourself to be transformed by the
pages that you have viewed, you will have entered as one person…
but left as another.

Roger Ballen